To Gord

... keep the spirit ...

GUT INSTINCT

GUT INSTINCT

The Making of an Investigative Journalist

VICTOR MALAREK

MACMILLAN CANADA

TORONTO

Canadian Cataloguing in Publication Data

Malarek, Victor, 1948-
    Gut instinct : the making of an investigative journalist

Includes index.
ISBN 0-7715-7383-9

1. Malarek, Victor, 1948-   . 2. Journalists -
Canada - Biography. I. Title.

PN4913.M3A3 1996   070.92   C96-930957-0

Macmillan Canada wishes to thank the Canada Council, the Ontario Arts Council and the Ontario Ministry of Culture and Communications for supporting its publishing program.

Cover and interior design: Kevin Connolly
Cover photograph: CBC Photo/Andrew MacNaughtan
Typesetting: Archetype

Macmillan Canada
A Division of Canada Publishing Corporation
Toronto, Canada

1 2 3 4 5   FP   00 99 98 97 96

Printed in Canada

For Anna, my love

ACKNOWLEDGEMENTS

I would like to thank my wife and friend, Anna, for her patience and support in the writing of this book; my daughter, Larissa, for making my world a wonderful place to live in; and my mother, Jennie, and sister-in-law, Angela Boyce, for all their encouragement.

I am especially grateful to my patient and good-natured editor, Loral Dean, for keeping me on track and rescuing me from myself; to my friend, Andrea Mozarowski, for her perceptive comments, insight and advice; and to Amanda Valpy, the *Globe and Mail*'s omniscient librarian.

I would also like to thank Denise Schon, who pushed, prodded and bugged me to write this book, as well as the outstanding team at Macmillan—in particular Karen O'Reilly and Nicole de Montbrun.

A special thanks goes out to the CBC and *the fifth estate* and to the *Globe and Mail* where I spent fourteen incredible years.

Lastly...throughout my years in the world of newspapers, I've met a number of incredible people who've had a marked effect on my career. They are Wayne Clark, Frank Lowe, Paul Rush, Don Foley, Donna Logan, Duncan Haimerl, Clark Davey, Dic Doyle, Warren Barton, Paul Palango, Shirley Sharzer, Jerry Kinoshita, and my late friend, Don Rennie. I thank them.

FOREWORD

I had put myself into extreme jeopardy—and for what? A story! An adventure! A chance to dance on the edge of a cliff. "I am a goddamned idiot," I shouted.

That is what it comes to for Victor Malarek: black rage against himself.

For what?

For "wanting to dig for stories that make a difference; that affect the lives of people in a profound way, particularly the lives of children."

It is a hunger that springs from nearly four childhood years in a Montreal home for delinquents and boys whose parents were unable to care for them. In his book *Hey Malarek!*, Victor told how a compassionate judge gave him his chance when he was seventeen.

In *Gut Instinct: The Making of an Investigative Journalist*, we are caught up in an acutely personal chronicle of what happened in the next twenty years.

Without much in the way of a formal education, Malarek bull-dozed and charmed his way through two of the country's largest news-rooms and on to a co-host's roving commission on *the fifth estate*.

For some of those years, I worked with Malarek at the *Globe and Mail*. I was always in awe of his hard edge as a hunter, and his soft side as a reporter. Later, his prize-winning probes were combined with foreign-corresponding and we witness him handing out garish T-shirts to emaciated teenaged boys in an Ethiopian refugee camp. He writes: "I lost it. I started weeping uncontrollably."

When Teddy Roosevelt attacked muckrakers in 1906, he was targeting newspapermen who made unjust charges of corruptions against public men. As the century ebbs, there are news-writers who take pride in the muck they rake. They attack the office holder and the corporate chief with innuendo and accusations. They leave it to their readers to judge the fairness of what they have done.

Not so Malarek. He boasts in this book's title his gut instinct to question much that he sees in politics, commerce and institutional practice. The gut triggers the investigative journalist's painstaking search for truth.

Ahead are the hours in libraries, the days in courtrooms and archives, the journeys to far places. At the gates are the bureaucrats to give him a hard time.

The one thing you can be sure of finding beyond the documentation in any story Malarek writes is a beneficiary—someone who, without Victor, would be remembered only as a victim.

Senator Richard J. Doyle

CONTENTS

PROLOGUE

This is not a memoir or an autobiography. It's a book about the life of an investigative reporter. More to the point, it traces my journey from a street-smart coffee boy at *Weekend* magazine, who dreamed of becoming a police detective, to a know-nothing police reporter (with an attitude) at the *Montreal Star*, to the personal job description I carry around inside my head today — investigative reporter.

In 1970, after a rough childhood on the wrong side of Montreal and a dangerous flirtation with juvenile delinquency, I got a break. Thanks to a couple of veteran newspapermen who believed in my potential and went to bat for me, I managed to elbow my way into the newsroom of the biggest newspaper in my hometown. Once I got there, I went from the police beat to my first bumbling attempt at an investigative story. It was a story about three kids nobody cared about who had hanged themselves in a juvenile detention centre. When I found myself back in the world I knew so well — this time looking in from the other side of the barbed wire and barred windows — I knew at last what I really wanted to do. I wanted to tell the public about these kids and get people to understand how they got there: how they started off as innocent children in need of society's protection; and how they eventually emerged bruised and battered on the other side with the roles reversed — with society in need of protection from them.

This book is about the stories *behind* investigative stories I wrote during my days as a newspaper reporter. Right from my quixotic start in this business, I've operated on gut instinct. When I was a lowly police reporter at the *Montreal Star*, I received a mysterious phone call. I agreed to a meeting with an anonymous caller, beside the monument of Admiral Lord Nelson in Old Montreal, because I had a feeling he had something important to tell me. He did.

What may look from the outside like an irrational response has got me through a lot of tough situations. I've learned never to ignore my gut feeling.

Investigative reporting is what gets the blood pumping in my veins.

Here's my definition: the ability of a reporter to uncover something important that someone wants to keep suppressed and, at the end of a long, winding trail, hold that person accountable for what has happened.

Obviously, I'm not the only one out there making life miserable for the bullies and the bad guys. There is an impressive collection of praiseworthy investigative journalists in Canada, each one of them trying to make a difference. During my two decades in newsprint, I had the opportunity to work alongside some of the best. They include Zuhair Kashmeri, Linda McQuaig, Jock Ferguson, Stevie Cameron, Michael Harris, Kirk Makin, Stan Oziewicz, Jeff Sallot and Andrew McIntosh.

Most investigative reporters I've met over the years have common traits; the most outstanding is a deep and committed passion for change. They feel a responsibility to get involved in issues...to push forward and not sit back in the stands, reporting the blatherings of elected officials and their spokespeople. Some have paid a heavy price for what they do and many are constantly under enormous pressures. I've found myself up against skittish publishers, nervous editors, envious colleagues and overly-cautious libel lawyers. My most trying legal experience happened when I took on the Toronto establishment law firm of Lang Michener and, later, the august Law Society of Upper Canada (chapter nine). The *Globe*'s lawyers were antsy for months as they labored under an ever-present threat of libel.

Death threats also come with the territory of an investigative reporter. I've learned to shrug off anonymous phone calls announcing my imminent demise, one of which occurred while I was investigating the case of convicted Palestinian terrorist Mahmoud Mohammed Issa Mohammed (chapter eight).

Despite all these pressures and frustrations, I remain convinced I've got one of the best jobs in the world. In my first twenty-five years as a reporter, I've had a front-row seat on some major historical events — the Quebec FLQ crisis, the patriation of Canada's constitution, the American hostage-taking in Iran, the Soviet invasion of Afghanistan, the famine in Ethiopia, the civil war in Somalia. I've experienced wars and droughts, deserts and jungles, isolated villages and crowded ghettos. I've interviewed prime ministers and crooks, CEOs and drug dealers, intellectuals and street people, refugees and torturers, victims of child abuse and murderers. I've been punched, kicked and spat at. I've had guns pointed at me and I very nearly died in a battle zone. I've slept in five-star hotels and on dirt floors crawling with bugs. I've dined in the best restaurants and in smoke-filled hovels in oppressive refugee camps. I've eaten filet mignon, snake, sheeps' eye in boiled milk, stewed camel, roasted monkey and honey-glazed grasshoppers. And I'd do all of it all over again.

CHAPTER 1

WEEKEND BLUES

*Two regular, one black two sugars, two double cream, double sugar and
one tea, double cream, double sugar.*

That was my lot in life when I joined *Weekend* magazine in 1968 in
Montreal as a lowly, underpaid, unappreciated copyboy. At 10:00 a.m.
and again at 2:30 p.m., I trotted around the editorial department taking
orders from the writers and editors on their choice of beverage. The
rest of the time, I was a gofer, delivering envelopes from one department to another, sorting mail and running errands.

I hated the job and wondered what I was doing there for a lousy
forty dollars a week. I figured it was something my mother said: "An
office job can lead to better things than a dead-end factory job." And I
had certainly had my fill of moving bales of cloth and packing boxes of
"mode" fashions in sweatshops in Montreal's north end during two
summer breaks from high school.

Weekend was my first full-time job since leaving high school a year
earlier. I didn't see it as a stepping-stone to a career as a journalist. A
life as a reporter had never entered my mind. What I really wanted to
be was a police detective. I remember the first time it occurred to me. I
was slouching at my desk in my last year of high school trying to figure
out what to write in the Montreal High year book under "Future
Prospects." I leaned back in my chair and drifted into another dimension. Through the haze, I saw myself solving mysteries. When I returned
to reality, I wrote down "Detective."

I figured I had some pretty solid credentials to make a good cop:
a high school diploma, a motorcycle driver's license and fluency in
French. And I'd been on the other side of the law enough times. I got
my early training in Weredale House — an abusive, mismanaged institution for boys from broken homes in Montreal. Those four and a half
years turned me into a street-smart "hard rock." I spent a lot of time

warming a wooden bench outside the judge's chamber in juvenile court or dodging a foul-mouthed probation officer I detested. I'd also been worked over a few times by Montreal's finest when they tried to make me rat on a couple of pals who'd been involved in brawls or petty theft. I finally hit rock-bottom when I was dragged into a barbaric juvenile detention center, charged with assault and robbery. I was four months short of my eighteenth birthday—the magic number that raised my status to the level of adult court and penitentiary. But thanks to an intuitive, gutsy judge who was willing to give a street kid a last chance, I'd narrowly escaped a stiff sentence that would have sent me to a rough-and-tumble training school deep in Quebec's Laurentian Mountains.

Yeah, I knew how the police worked, all right, and I understood how the bad guys worked, as well. Plus, I was one curious, inquisitive kid. I never accepted anything at face value. I'd picked that up in the boys' home. Whenever some crime was committed there—like a locker being broken into or a nighttime beating of a brown-nosing stool pigeon—I'd quietly dig around trying to figure out who was behind it. Most of the time I solved the case because I learned a very important lesson early on—criminals love to brag about what they get away with. They just have to tell someone about their "perfect" crime. It was second nature to them. If no one knew about it, what was the point of the perfect score? It was so easy to get them to boast. But I also learned never to brag about my little investigations—for reasons of personal safety and health. To be suspected of being a rat was damned dangerous.

So I saw *Weekend* magazine as a temporary pit stop while I waited for my application with the Montreal police force to be processed. Why, with my curiosity and nose for sniffing out evidence, I thought modestly, I just know I'll make a great detective! I figured the Montreal police force would snap me up in an instant.

After three months at *Weekend*, I got the call I'd been waiting for. With twinges of anticipation, I joined four hundred prospective police recruits in a cavernous high school gymnasium in the city's east end to write the police exam. I glanced around nervously and noticed that I stood out in the crowd. Everyone around me had a bean shave. My hair bounced around my shoulders. All the other applicants wore dress pants, white shirts and ties. I was wearing a black T-shirt, burgundy vest with a paisley design, black jeans and black suede boots with silver buckles. Well, *I* look cool, I thought—a perfect candidate for any undercover police operation.

On the test we were shown ten pictures and were given a minute or so to scrutinize each one. Then we were given a series of questions on what was happening in the photos. I have an almost photographic memory, so I had no trouble recalling even the most minute details. For example, the design of a tie that a man sitting cross-legged on a park bench was wearing, or the fact that a car's front left light was burned out, or that the traffic lights in the eastbound lanes were green and a clock inside a pharmacy window indicated it was 2:05 p.m.

I figured I'd aced the exam. A month later, I got the results in the mail. I'd ranked second in the written exam, third in the physical — and first overall. Out of four hundred candidates! I was ecstatic.

There was just one hoop left to jump through — the personal interview. I drew a stern-faced cop with an attitude. His first question gave me a major clue about where the interview was headed.

"What's with the hair?" He sneered.

"I'm thinking undercover work," I said, doggedly attempting a smile. Truth was, I was partial to my long locks. In the boys' home we'd been forced to wear a bean shave that made us stand out on the streets of Montreal like geeks with Dumbo ears. When I left the place, I swore I'd never look like that again. My hair became my signature.

"Do you do drugs?"

"No," I replied, looking him squarely in the eye. Like, even if I did, you think I'd admit it?

"Ever get in trouble with the law?"

"Nope," I said calmly. I knew that my juvenile record was sealed and could never be held against me.

"Why do you want to be a police officer?"

I'd practiced my response to this question in front of a mirror the night before. "I want to solve crimes and make the streets a safer place," I replied primly.

Constable Ramrod did not look impressed. He threw a hypothetical scenario at me. "Your partner chases a suspect for some distance and when he finally catches him, he gives him a few hits with his nightstick. The suspect is hurt, and your partner tells you to stick to a story that the suspect jumped him and attacked him like a wild animal. Your partner was just defending himself! What do you say to the investigators from Internal Affairs when they ask you what happened?"

A trick question. I thought for a moment.

"I'd tell the truth." The moment the words escaped my lips I heard the beeper blast in my ears. Wrong answer! My chances of becoming a cop were fizzling fast.

"Why do you want to be a police officer in Montreal? You're not French-Canadian. Why not go to Toronto?"

"I was born in Quebec and I speak French," I said evenly. I figured he was trying to get a rise out of me.

"But you are not a true Quebecer. What is the origin of your name?"

"I am a Quebecer. My name is Ukrainian but I was born in Lachine, Quebec."

"Okay. Interview's over. We'll be in touch," he said with a look of intense disdain. He got up and left me alone in the cubicle.

"Fat chance," I muttered. I knew I'd blown it. I'd plummeted from the top-scoring candidate to the bottom of the heap thanks to one anal-retentive jerk with a nasty streak. And there was nothing I could do about it.

A month later, I got a tersely worded form letter informing me that I did not make the cut. There was no appeal, no offer to try again at a later date. I tried to quell the disappointment by convincing myself that I wouldn't have been able to fit in with the rigid, militaristic mind-set of the Blue Machine. It didn't work. I was devastated. I slunk back to my job at *Weekend* with a major preoccupation consuming me — my future prospects.

I was living at home with my parents and two brothers, Fred and Peter, in a blue-collar, ethnic district in the north end of the city. Although we were a bare half-step above welfare, we were proud of our humble lodgings. We lived on a classic Montreal street of attached, three-story, low-rent tenements. Most of the houses emitted the aromas, sounds and sights of other nations. My friends were Jews, Greeks, Armenians, Ukrainians and Italians.

But life at home was hell. My father was driving me crazy. He was unemployed, sick and given to erratic, violent mood swings, fuelled by a steady diet of powerful painkillers, antidepressants and beer chasers. Our relationship was volatile, more so because we were very close. Of the three boys, I was his favourite. My parents had broken up for several years when I was ten years old, and it split our family right down the middle. When my brothers and I were put into a home for boys from broken families during their separation, my two brothers sided with my mother. I didn't take sides, but I chose not to desert my father. I just couldn't see him living alone in some run-down rooming house. So whenever we got a free Saturday or Sunday afternoon, my brothers would go one way and I'd try to find my father at some local bar. My mother understood. She was a gentle, kind soul, and it broke her heart to see the family torn apart. But she could no longer take the violent drunken outbursts, the verbal rants and the physical abuse. She was afraid for her own safety.

My dad was a powerful, handsome man with smouldering, dark brown eyes. He was a World War II veteran and had served five gruelling years in Europe as an infantryman in the Canadian Army. His brothers and friends often pointed out that he did not return as the proud patriot who went overseas to fight for his country. Toward the end of the war, he was wounded and sent home. He came back angry. He drank heavily and was prone to violent drunken rages, throwing bottles across rooms, upending tables and smashing his fists into walls.

He saved the worst for my mother — verbal tirades and beatings. It still hurts to remember. My mother worked hard as a waitress in a downtown greasy spoon, only to see her tips wasted on booze and my father's disgusting drinking buddies at the Royal Canadian Legion Hall.

Despite the pain I felt for my mother, deep in my soul I felt my father's pain, too. I saw it in his eyes. But I endured years of his outbursts and fits of rage, many directed at me. One day he would call me his favourite, tell me he'd die for me. The next he'd lash out at me. Then, when I was thirteen, the man I believed to be invincible was diagnosed with cancer. After his first operation, he shrivelled to skin and bone. A second operation almost killed him. But my father was tough. He hung on. I visited him every day when he was in the veteran's hospital, terrified every time I went that he would die and leave me.

Now, six years later, I could see his days were numbered. There was only so much a body could take before it crashed, and Dad's abuse of booze and pills was reaching epic proportions. Seeing him in such a weak and broken state ripped every fibre of my soul. I couldn't do a thing for him. I couldn't reach him. And I was fed up and pissed off with my own life. I was worried I was heading for an emotional explosion and I was afraid where it might lead.

On April 23, 1968, shortly after ten in the morning, I was doing the coffee run at *Weekend* when an icy chill shot through my body. I stopped in my tracks in the office hall, balancing two double sugars, three regulars and a black coffee.

"What the hell is wrong with you?" one of the secretaries asked, looking with shock at my white face.

"I've got to go home," I said quietly, placing the coffee tray on her desk. "My father just died."

I ran to the bus stop and jumped on the 80 heading up Park Avenue. A few blocks from home I jumped off, figuring I could outrun the traffic. I bolted onto the front porch and froze as my hand clasped the latch. I couldn't go in. I knew what I would find. Somewhere inside, Dad was lying dead. I was scared. My knees buckled. I settled down on the front steps and sat there staring blindly into space.

It was eleven o'clock. My mother finished her shift at the restaurant at three. I waited for her to come home.

At three-thirty, I saw her coming down the street.

"What are you doing out here in the cold, Victor?" she asked, perplexed. "Why aren't you at work?"

"Mom." My voice broke. "Mom, Dad's dead."

My mother glanced at the locked door. Then she looked at me questioningly.

"I didn't go in. I *can't* go in!"

"You stay out here," my mother said as she unlocked the door.

Seconds later she returned. In a flat, tight voice she said, "He's on the kitchen floor. Yes, he's dead. I'm going to call the police."

I went for a long walk. At first, I was numb. But slowly, as I walked, I got really pissed off at him for dying. He was only forty-eight and he didn't have to die. It was those fuckin' pills and the booze. I thought about the years of hell he'd put our family through. What had turned him into a mean and miserable drunk? As I wrestled with my anger and grief, I tried to make excuses for him. The war. His rough and violent childhood in a home with a boozing and abusive father. But the excuses had worn thin over the years. My father's face kept appearing before me, etched with a profound sorrow. There was a deep sadness in his dark, brooding Cossack eyes. He was wracked by an inner torment, which he could never bring himself to speak about. And I could never find the words or the courage to talk to him about it. Now he was dead, and I would never know the cause of his pain. I was sad and I was angry.

I drifted for hours. Eventually, I ended up on Mount Royal. As I gazed down at the city, I tried to force myself to think of the good times. It was important to me to remember that there had been good times. But every time a happy memory came to mind — Christmas, a birthday, an anniversary—it would be overshadowed by another memory of Dad's drunken outbursts. Beer bottles would smash against the walls and vile epithets would echo through the house. He scared me. He scared Freddie and Peter. Worst of all, he terrified my mother. Yet despite all the bad stuff, despite the terror and the beatings, I loved him. I didn't know why. And now he was gone.

My father didn't have many friends left. His drinking pals had deserted him when he got sick. His funeral was a small affair, an interminable Ukrainian-Orthodox mass with an open casket and plumes of blue-white incense smoking up the tiny church. As I stared at the icons hanging over the altar, I thought of my parents being married here twenty-two years earlier. I looked at my mother, standing stoically in front of his coffin, and wondered what she was thinking. My brothers stood on either side of her, expressionless.

As we followed the hearse to the cemetery, I held the silver mouthpiece of my trumpet in my glove to keep it warm from the damp chill. Before his first cancer operation, my father made me make a solemn vow that I would play "Taps" and "The Last Post" at his funeral. Over the years, he never let me forget that promise. As the priest threw dirt on the coffin, I put my trumpet to my lips and began to play. The crisp morning air carried the veteran's lament over the graveyard. When I finished, I looked down one last time and saluted.

★ ★ ★

Making the coffee rounds my first Monday morning back at work was hard. In addition to my grief, which had left me feeling drained, I could no longer avoid the fact that I was going nowhere at the magazine. A couple of arrogant staff writers had made the job close to impossible. They were phony, rude and malicious, and delighted in ordering me about like their personal valet. But I'd made one good friend among the writers, a staffer named Wayne Clark.

Wayne was into jazz, psychoanalysis and Johnny Walker Red. He was something of a superannuated hippie, with long hair and a wispy beard that served as a web for food chunks. He loved music and tooted on a tenor sax and a silver flute. I got him into a part-time band I had joined called Bizarre—nine eclectic musicians who played blues, rock, jazz and an entire set dedicated to the music of Frank Zappa and the Mothers of Invention.

Over beer one evening after work, Wayne suggested I give some thought to reporting. "You've got an inquisitive mind and you come from a different side of the street," he said. "You'd certainly bring a different point of view to the stories you would work on."

I was flattered. The connection between my dream of becoming a detective and the curiosity it takes to be a good reporter hadn't occurred to me. When I really thought about it, nailing criminals holding the smoking gun wasn't what interested me. What turned me on was the idea of solving challenging puzzles and figuring out what made people tick, particularly the nasty ones.

Of course, I'd never written anything beyond high school compositions and I quaked at the thought of writing stuff *strangers* would read. But Wayne gave me one of his Johnny Walker smiles and said, "Don't worry! Just come up with a story idea. I'll help you with the writing."

It didn't take me long to find a story. I zeroed in on the growing phenomenon of telephone crisis hot-line centres. A teenager I knew needed some help, desperately. She phoned and I jotted down what would become the lead three paragraphs of my first feature story. It was far from deathless prose, but it looked and sounded damned good to me.

I hadn't anticipated the rush I'd feel when I saw my name in print for the first time. *By Victor Malarek.* I grinned proudly to myself. I was hooked. My life as a reporter had begun.

★ ★ ★

In the summer of 1970, at the age of twenty-two, I married my high school sweetheart. Anna Cipriani and I had met in 1964, not long after I got out of the boys' home. I first saw her at a community dance and instantly fell in love. I told her that evening that I was going to marry her one day. She laughed and told me I was nuts. Anna was Italian with long, brown flowing hair and the face of an angel. She came from a loving, close-knit family. It took me years to get used to all the hugging, kissing and pasta. During our honeymoon in Italy, we talked about the future. Anna thought I should pursue writing. But I knew that I'd never make it as a writer at *Weekend:* I was typecast there as a gofer.

When I got back, *Weekend*'s editor, Frank Lowe, called me into his office. *Weekend* magazine is not the place for you, he told me calmly. I felt myself sinking. Shit, the bastard's firing me, I thought.

But Lowe wasn't finished. "I've spoken to Don Foley about you," he continued. "He's city editor at the *Montreal Star*. He's willing to give you a chance on the police desk as a junior reporter. He'll see you at four-thirty to talk about it."

I was stunned. To this day, I remain immeasurably indebted to Frank.

CHAPTER TWO

STAR DAYS

The police scanners were crackling with an earsplitting, urgent static. An armed robbery was in progress at a north end branch of the Bank of Montreal. Four cruisers, sirens screaming and red lights flashing, were charging to the scene. On the fire department scanner, a gravel-voiced dispatcher was getting an update on a stubborn five-alarm blaze in the city's run-down east end. And in the downtown core a rowdy demonstration of ten thousand Common Front union workers was rising to a boil. Every available police reporter at the *Montreal Star* was out, except me. I was stuck minding the police desk, trying to decipher the irritating static emanating from the cheap radios. I was pissed off and bored.

It was early January, 1972. I'd been on the police desk at the *Montreal Star* for a year and a half and I was still chasing cop cars, ambulances and red trucks.

When Foley had offered me the job, I figured it was my chance to uncover crime and expose the bad guys. But all I got were mundane corner-store robberies, bank heists and gangland slayings. No follow-up digging or sleuthing. I did get one major break during my first few months on the police desk, however: I lucked into the biggest, hottest political-crime story in Canadian history, the October Crisis. The kidnapping of British diplomat James Richard Cross and the abduction and eventual murder of Quebec Labour Minister Pierre Laporte by the Front de Libération du Québec (FLQ) made headlines every day for an entire month. For the hungry, ego-driven young reporters on the crime beat, it meant front-page bylines.

But then, with the discovery of Laporte's body in the trunk of a car, the arrest of his killers, the discovery of Cross in a north end duplex and the hasty deal to free the diplomat by guaranteeing his kidnappers safe passage to Cuba, the story was suddenly over. Eight weeks of running on adrenaline and we were back to the same monotonous routine — robberies, fires, traffic jams and endless obituaries.

I desperately wanted a change. I wanted to be a real reporter writing stories that mattered and made a difference. But I'd been pigeonholed on the cop beat. I was really ticked off, because I just couldn't seem to convince the senior editors I could do much better. They were narrow minded. They saw police reporters as a notch above lowly copyboys — probably because most of us sprang from that gene pool! We were good enough to monitor police scanners, chase fire engines and write about dead people, but in the eyes of the editors we didn't have the right stuff to make the grade as serious journalists.

All this became very clear to me when the newsroom staff voted en masse in 1972 for the right to be represented by a union. One of the first bargaining ploys by management was not to include the police desk in the reporter class. They wanted us designated in a clerk category. The union stuck to its position: we were reporters. Eventually, management caved in. But the insult was not lost on the eight guys manning the radios.

I knew I could do better, that I had the stuff to make a good, solid journalist. I was a young, cocky, arrogant s.o.b. with an edge. I felt I brought something to the newsroom that few reporters had — an inside knowledge of the seedier side of the street. *I* knew the suffering, the anguish, the anger and the pain. *I* knew what was behind it.

While I realized my attitude grated on a lot of people in the newsroom, I *knew* all I needed was an opportunity to prove myself. And to do that, I had to get off the police beat. I wanted to speak to Don Foley about this. Foley was the city editor who had rescued me from my dead-end copyboy job at *Weekend* magazine.

After the final-edition deadline, I figured I'd approach him and plead my case. What I wanted, specifically, was to be elevated to general reporter.

I watched him, trying to gauge his mood as he buzzed around the newsroom. He seemed upbeat but I knew in this business that could change in a heartbeat. Foley was essentially an easygoing editor. He was a short guy, about five foot six, with a heavily cratered face and a beer gut. He grimaced a lot when people spoke to him, like he was suffering from a painful case of hemorrhoids. When he smiled it was more a conniving, adolescent grin, as if he was contemplating something sneaky or perverse. That look kept most of his staff off balance. Foley had a wry sense of humour, a sharp wit and a good deal of patience for young reporters, except at this particular time of the day.

Deadline! That was when he became a hard-nosed, insufferable jerk. The paper had to get out, and a huge, important section of it rested on Foley's shoulders. He did his job like a pro and he expected no less from his editors and reporters.

The four o'clock final deadline was ticking down, and the vast editorial expanse was once again taking on the fervour of an assembly line. Nimble-fingered copy editors batted out stories filed over the phone by reporters at the scene of fast-breaking news events; editors yelled for more copy to decimate with their trusty HB-4 pencils; reporters stumbled over stubborn typewriter keys in an all-out dash to meet the deadline; haggard copyboys raced around the newsroom delivering copious amounts of paper to various news desks. Anyone who walked in off the street would see chaos. To us, it was just the normal insanity of life on a daily newspaper.

I watched the clock tick down, wondering what kind of mood I'd find Foley in when the deadline was over.

Then, at 4:01 p.m., as if by the wave of an invisible wand, the pandemonium abruptly ceased. The final deadline had come and gone. Any story that hadn't made it was spiked—slammed onto a six-inch spike on the city desk and later, if it couldn't be salvaged for the paper the following day, it was thrown into the circular file, never to make it as news in the *Star*.

The ultimate crime for any reporter was to blow a deadline. Deadlines were sacrosanct. Miss one and you got skewered. Like every junior reporter before me, I learned the hard way.

In my first week on the job, I was dispatched to cover a simple, three-alarm fire that should easily have made the second-edition deadline at noon. I called in five minutes late and got a blast by Foley. I then filed my copy for the final.

When I got back to the office, Foley was lying in wait.

"Malarek! Just what the fuck do you call this?" he shouted for the benefit of the entire newsroom.

I blanched. "It's my story on the fire," I ventured hoarsely.

Foley stared at the sheet of paper and read the first paragraph out loud. He was going to let the entire newsroom witness and savour my humiliation.

"'Great billowy clouds of thick black smoke oozed into the blue morning sky as a woman ran out of her burning house shouting: Fire, fire!'"

Several editors and reporters began to giggle. Foley glowered. My face turned crimson.

"Just what the fuck is this? A pathetic attempt at Creative Writing 101? This is a newspaper, not some dumb composition class. I don't give a shit about smoky labyrinths. Now sit down with the copy editor over there and he'll help you rewrite this worthless piece of shit, and just maybe it'll make it into *today's* paper!"

The grinning copy editor spun a sheet of paper into his typewriter and tapped out the following paragraph: "A three-alarm fire gutted a two-story home in the city's north end yesterday morning. No one was injured."

That was it. My eleven-paragraph opus of twisted hoses, stubborn flames and sweaty smoke-eaters was reduced to this. My hope for my first byline on the *Star* was gone. From my perch at the police desk, I looked over at Foley. I quickly realized this was not a good time. He was red-faced and screaming into the telephone.

"The final fuckin' deadline is 4:00 p.m. Are you wearing a watch? ... Then tell me, what time is it? ... That's right, it's 4:05. And what does that mean? It means you missed the deadline and the story didn't make it! That means the *Gazette* beat our butts. Get your ass in here now! I want you in my office in fifteen minutes, and if you blow this deadline, don't bother coming in!" Foley slammed the receiver and caught me looking at him. "What the hell are you gawking at? You've got another two hours on your shift. Do something useful. Find an ambulance and chase it."

"Up yours," I muttered to myself.

At that moment, my phone rang. The voice at the other end was hesitant.

"I was told to call you," the caller began.

"So now you've got me. What do you want?" I asked impatiently.

"I need to talk to you."

"About what?" I forced myself to decelerate.

"I want to talk to you in person."

"About what?" I repeated calmly.

"I'll tell you when I see you."

I hated meeting people on spec. Most of the time what they thought was a news story turned out to be a petty, personal beef with a nasty landlord or some sleazy car salesman. I was on the hunt for a big story, and instead I was being fed a steady diet of mindless complaints.

"Look, I need to know something about what you want to see me about," I said.

"It starts with the letter S," he said sarcastically.

"Don't screw around."

The caller hesitated. "A week ago I broke out of Berthelet."

"Berthelet Detention Centre?"

"Yeah."

I was impressed. I'd never known of a kid who had escaped from that place. It was a tough maximum-security institution in the far-flung northeast end of the island. It was built to hold hardened delinquent teenaged boys.

"What were you in for?" I asked.

"That's not important. I have something incredible to tell you about what's been happening in there."

"What?"

"When I see you I'll tell you."

"Where do you want to meet?"

"At Place Jacques Cartier in Old Montreal at five."

"I finish at six."

"Look, this isn't a fucking joke. If you don't want to meet me when I say, you're gonna miss a big story."

"I'll be there," I said wearily. "How will I find you?"

"I'll find *you*. Just bring your notebook and a pen."

I hung up, wondering what this kid had to tell me that was so important.

I gazed around the newsroom. The place was gearing down. Veteran reporters were sucking back black coffee. The corps of crusty copy editors relaxed in their stiff wooden chairs, smoking cigarettes or puffing on pipes. The door to Foley's office was shut. I knew he was in there. Everyone on the entire floor could hear him chewing out a hapless news hound about the peril of missing deadlines. I looked at my watch. It was almost five. I had to get going for my appointment.

Steve Kowch, one of the police-beat reporters, swaggered in through the double doors of the newsroom. He was beaming. His story on the bank heist was on the front page above the fold, and he had a byline. He always grinned when he got a front-page byline. Kowch was an ace crime reporter and excelled on the cop beat. He had a knack for cultivating solid contacts in the cop shop, particularly with detectives in the holdup and homicide squads. Within minutes of an arrest, he could call the Quebec Provincial Police or the Montreal dicks and get the full lowdown.

I usually elicited the opposite response. Most of the boys in blue disliked me. Not for anything I did. It was my appearance that pissed them off. They equated my shoulder-length hair and droopy Cossack mustache with the perceived depravity and immorality of hippie culture. The fact that I wore a peace button on the lapel of my vest confirmed their belief that I must be a weed puffer.

One time, for a joke, the dicks in the holdup squad grabbed me and handcuffed me to a chair. I stayed there the whole day — alone in an interrogation room knowing that the cops on the other side of a two-way mirror were pissing themselves with laughter over my predicament. I was worried Foley would blast me over my disappearance. Little did I know that he and a few of the guys on the cop beat were in on my "arrest."

"Kowch, I need a favour," I said. "I've got to meet someone. It's really urgent. Can you sit in and listen to the radios until Norm Provencher or Vic Riding comes in?"

"Sure. It'll give me time to read my story," he said, holding up the final edition. "Well, look here. Front page above the fold."

"Yeah. Great going. Tell Foley I went to check out a tip."

As I was heading out the door, Foley's voice ricocheted off the walls.

"Malarek! Your shift ends in an hour."

I froze.

"Where do you think you're going?" he asked, approaching me.

"I got a tip. I'm going to check it out."

"You got a tip. What tip?" he said with a tinge of sarcasm.

"This kid called. He broke out of Centre Berthelet and says he's got something urgent to tell me."

"What is Centre Berthelet?"

"A juvenile detention centre," I replied. I was surprised he didn't know the place. I figured Foley knew everything about the city.

"So he's a juvenile delinquent," he said.

"Yeah. I told him I'd meet him at five in Old Montreal. If I'm not there he might take off."

"He'll wait a minute or two if it's important. What's the tip?"

I felt really foolish. "I don't know. But I think what this kid has to tell me is important," I said lamely.

"You do. Why?"

"I just feel it," I said.

Foley looked at me and grinned. "You've got a feeling. Well, I certainly don't want to stand in the way of a feeling. Who knows what it may bring up. You'd better get going."

I looked at him, wondering if he was being sarcastic or supportive. I couldn't tell. I turned and left.

Place Jacques Cartier is a wide, cobblestone boulevard that stretches from the docks on the St. Lawrence River to the stately City Hall mansion in Old Montreal. Restaurants, noisy bars and cluttered souvenir shops line both sides of the square. In its heart is a sprawling plaza where street musicians, mimes and jugglers entertain throngs of tourists.

I leaned against the base of the towering statue of Admiral Lord Horatio Nelson and waited. I looked over every teenaged kid who passed by, hoping to make the connection. All I got back were contemptuous stares and one inviting smile. After a half hour, I figured the kid was a no-show and started to head out.

As I rounded the statue, I heard a voice: "Are you Malarek?"

"Yeah. How long have you been here?"

"About forty minutes," the voice replied.

I felt like swatting him.

The kid had an attitude. He was lean and scrappy, and his dark brown hair dangled limply to his shoulders. He wore a black sports jacket, a black T-shirt, black jeans and black boots. He reminded me of myself at seventeen. I didn't like him.

"Why the game?" I asked. "Why didn't you come over when you first saw me?"

"I was checking you out."

"And did I check out?"

"I guess. I was trying to place you in Weredale. You don't look like a Weredale boy."

My blood started to boil. I didn't want anyone knowing I'd been in the boys' home. It had taken me years to shake the torment of that dump out of my brain, and I didn't need any reminders about the place from some smart-ass punk.

"Who told you I was in Weredale?" I asked angrily.

"I also heard you did time in St. Vallier," he taunted. "And that you were some mean street kid. Liked to get into fights."

"I thought *I* was here to interview *you*. What's your point?"

The kid clearly revelled in riling me. "What's the matter?" he smirked. "Ashamed of your past?"

"I *said* what's your point?"

"No point. Pilon told me to call you and I did," the kid said flatly.

"Pilon!" Now there was a name from my not-too-distant past. Pilon and I had met in the boys' home in 1960. He became a good friend of my younger brother, Peter, and was forever getting himself into jackpots. He was a petty thief. If it wasn't nailed down and could fit in his pocket, he swiped it. He was an adept shoplifter. When he left the home, he moved on to break and enters.

"Pilon told me he was in the home with you and your two brothers. He also told me he was in St. Vallier when you were in detention for a major-league scrap with a gang of frogs."

"Look, I don't need an unsolicited biographical sketch of my life. I'm going to ask you one more time, what's your point?"

"Boy, touchy, aren't you?" he sneered.

"I don't discuss my past with anyone. Now, if you've got something to talk about other than me, spill it or I'm out of here," I said.

"Okay. Relax, man!" The kid quickly scanned the square for heat. I was nearing the end of my goodwill.

"What if I told you that boys were being taken out of Berthelet dead?" the kid said.

Now he had my undivided attention. "What do you mean, dead?" I asked.

"Dead. As in, they're pushing up daisies. The ashes-to-ashes kind of dead. They breathe no longer. They —"

"I get it. I mean, what do you mean taken out dead?"

"I know that at least five guys left their cells on stretchers and three of them had sheets covering their heads."

I looked into the kid's eyes for a long moment and knew he was telling the truth. He didn't flinch.

"When was this?" I asked.

"Over the Christmas period."

"How did they die?"

"Suicide. I saw one of them do it. A real fruit cake. Don't know what the fuck he was doing in Berthelet. The guy was a certifiable lunatic. He

17

belonged in an insane asylum. He kept yelling at invisible people. Screaming at them to shut up and leave him alone. The guys really bugged
him. They kept running up to him pretending to be crazy. Yelling 'ooga
booga!' The guards were pricks to him. They treated him like crap,
leaving him locked up in his cell for most of the day. That kid should
never have been in the joint. He should have been in a nuthouse."

The kid rubbed his hands together to warm them up and again
scanned the square. "Then, early one morning, the nut case starts his rant.
Screaming at invisible people. A jerk guard yells at him to shut the fuck
up but he doesn't, so the prick leaves the unit. Not much else he could
do except maybe slap the kid around a little or throw him into solitary
confinement. Then the nut case pulls a skate lace out of his pocket, ties
it to the bars of his cell, slips the cord around his neck and drops.

"I flipped out and started shouting for the guards. They took their
sweet fucking time coming into the unit. I guess they were on their coffee break. Finally this pig pops his head in and yells at me to shut up. I
called him a dumb fucking frog. That got his attention! He charged into
the unit. I figured he was going to hammer me out. Then he sees the nut
case hanging. The jerk turns sheet-white and almost passes out. Can
you believe it? This big tough bastard almost faints."

"What happened then?" I asked.

"Instead of cutting the kid down, he runs and hits the panic button.
Then all hell breaks loose. Me and the other guys are taken out of the unit
and sent to the gym where we waited for about three hours. When I got
back, the boy's cell was empty. After that, no one ever said a thing about it."

I was stunned. In all my years in the child welfare system—in foster care, the boys' home and detention centres—I had never heard of
anyone committing suicide.

"Pretty fuckin' incredible story, eh?" the kid said, breaking the
uneasy silence.

"Yeah. Pretty fuckin' incredible."

"You believe me, don't you?" the kid asked.

"Yeah. I believe you."

"Then what are you going to do about it?"

"Check into it. If it's true—"

"You just said you believed me. It's true. So write it," the kid shouted
angrily.

For the first time, I saw real torment in the kid's eyes. He was
haunted by what he had witnessed.

"It's not that easy. I've got to confirm it. My editor is not going to take your word for it, and I wouldn't expect him to. I'll check it out, and if what you say did happen, I'll make sure it gets in the paper."

The kid stared at me a moment, shrugged his shoulders and headed off down the street. Half a block away, he turned around and shouted sarcastically: "Yeah, sure you will."

I winced.

That night I hardly slept. I thought about the time I was entombed in a dark, windowless, cinder-block cell in St. Vallier, the most notorious juvenile detention centre in the city.

The three weeks I suffered in that hole were my worst hell. During my first twenty-four hours in solitary, I smashed the walls with my fists, splitting open the skin on my knuckles. I punched, kicked, screamed and ranted. And I punched again. Then finally, I crumbled to the floor exhausted, and wept.

On day three, I was completely spent. My rage had subsided. The jumble inside my brain slowly began to sort itself out. I felt a calm settle over me. In my miserable seventeen years, this was the first time I had ever had to confront my demons and figure out what was happening to my pathetic life.

I experienced something very strange and very spiritual in that solitary-confinement cell. I had gone in an emotional wreck. My spirit was numb. My mind was in a fog, and I was angry. But in that time alone in the blackness, I saw a path before me. I was going to dump the baggage and split from the guys on the street. And I would leave home. Living at home was tearing me apart. I was going to take control of the rest of my life and make something out of myself.

My only hurdle was to get the judge to believe in me and give me one last chance. That would be no small feat. My probation officer was definitely not on my side. But a shrink who assessed me while I was in detention *was* pulling for me. It was a flip of the coin. I wasn't optimistic. But my pessimism proved wrong.

Judge Gammell, who had a reputation for being tough on young hooligans, gave me a break when I really needed it. I walked out of the detention centre ready to get on with the rest of my life. I was scared but determined not to fail.

The newsroom was beginning to rustle after a quiet, uneventful night. General reporters were getting their assignments and beat reporters were updating various editors on possible stories. I sat at the police desk staring blankly at the radio scanners, wondering how I would tackle the suicide story. Foley was just about finished his city-desk briefing. I needed him to spring me for a few days to flush out the facts. But I was worried about his reaction to my one and only source — a smart-mouthed, juvenile-delinquent detention-centre escapee who hadn't even bothered to give me his name. As a source for any story, the kid was about as credible as a backwoods hunter claiming to have been abducted by aliens from the planet Zordon. The only thing the kid had going for him was that I believed him.

"You look like hell," Foley said as he approached the police desk. "Try sleeping at night. It usually works wonders on the appearance."

"I had a bad night thinking about this story I'm working on," I said.

"Oh, yeah. The tip. So what's it about?"

I recounted the conversation with the kid. Foley sat on the corner of my desk listening. When I finished, he said sarcastically, "Your source is a juvenile delinquent. A punk. An escapee. That doesn't cut it around here, Malarek. But more to the point, the policy of this paper is we don't cover suicides." He hopped off the desk.

"That's it?" I said, my heart sinking.

"Yup, unless you've got at least one hard fact to add to that mish-mash of claptrap you just shoveled in my general direction."

"Yeah. I do," I shot back. The trouble was, I didn't.

"Well?" Foley said, arching his eyebrows in mock expectation. "I do have a paper to get out and I've got an obituary that cries out for your skillful writing talents."

"The point here is not the suicides," I began. I was groping, and I hoped Foley wouldn't realize it. "It's what led the boys to kill themselves. That's the story." I was on to something solid now. My voice took on new resonance. "These boys, from what I'm told, should never have been in detention in the first place!"

"Really?" Foley's tone was skeptical.

"Yeah, really." I stood my ground.

"And how do you know that?" Foley said, not skipping a beat.

"The kid told me — "

"The kid is a juvenile delinquent, and you don't even know his name!"

"But I *know* he was telling me the truth," I said stubbornly.

"How?"

"I don't know. I just know it. You know, you just get this feeling in your gut. That's how I know." The desperation was showing on my face. I felt the walls crumbling around me.

Foley looked at me, shook his head and grinned. "Good. Then prove it and we'll print it. But I'm not going to give you a long time on this, Malarek. You've got till the end of the week, and that's it."

Foley was heading to his office when Kowch strolled in. "Good story yesterday on the bank heist. Now let's see if you could do as good a job on this obituary."

Kowch grimaced.

I felt like puking. Foley had thrown the ball squarely into my court, and I could feel he was just waiting for me to foul out. I was on my first investigative assignment, and I had no idea where to start.

My initial move was one of the dumbest a cub reporter could ever make. I phoned the director of Centre Berthelet.

His voice was hard and detached. He was a man of few words and little patience. As I sputtered, he asked me point-blank what I wanted.

"I'd like an appointment to see you for an interview," I said.

"About what?"

My heart began to pound. My palms were sweaty. I took a deep breath. "I've been informed that some boys committed suicide in—"

"There have been no suicides," he interjected.

"Yes, but I was told—"

"By who?"

"A source told me that—"

"Who is this source?"

I was getting rattled. "I can't identify him but he told me—"

"What are the names of these boys you say committed suicide?"

"I don't know the names, that's why—"

"Then I cannot help you."

"Did three boys hang themselves in your detention centre?" I asked, trying to sound forceful.

"*If* such an event did occur, I would not discuss the matter with the news media. The law clearly states we cannot divulge any information about a juvenile in our facility. The law requires that a child's anonymity be protected."

"What good is anonymity if the kid is dead?" My confidence was returning.

"Your point is what?"

21

"My point is, the only people being protected by not discussing these suicides is you people."

"I have nothing more to say." With that, the director hung up.

I'd blown it, and I knew it. But I didn't know enough not to dig an even deeper hole for myself. Without missing a beat, I committed my second major journalistic blunder. I called the media relations department for the Quebec Ministry of Social Affairs. The response from the disembodied voice of the public relations man was a curt, unequivocal denial that the "events" I was alleging had occurred.

So much for my first day in the trenches. A total write-off. I was beginning to doubt the kid. Worse, I was beginning to doubt my instincts.

That evening, the kid phoned me at home. My phone number was unlisted.

"How did you get my number?" I asked angrily.

"Trade secret. How's it going?" he chirped.

"It isn't. My editor doesn't believe you."

"Do you?" he asked coyly.

"Just what the fuck is so amusing?"

"What's with you?"

"Your attitude. That's what's with me. You're pissing me off!"

"And I asked if you still believe me."

"And I bloody well told you I did. But I'm not getting very far on this. The jerk who runs Berthelet said the suicides never happened."

"Oh, they happened, all right. That you can bet on. Those kids killed themselves just like I said. All around the Christmas holidays. I don't know anything about the other two guys who tried to kill themselves. But I know the first names of two of the nut cases who succeeded. One kid was Richard and the other was Wayne. Richard was the nut cake I saw hang himself. That was a few days before Christmas. It was on the twenty-second, around seven o'clock."

"You're sure about this?"

"I saw it, okay? The other kid, Wayne. He pulled the plug just before New Year's. A friend of mine in another unit told me about it. Same way. Hockey laces around the cell bars and lights out. The guards went nuts. Then it was like nothing ever happened. The joint just continued like every other boring day in detention. *You* know what it's like," the kid said like some long-lost confidant.

"Yeah. I know."

"You sound like you're . . . I can't find the word."

"Perplexed," I said. "I don't know how to go about proving this. That's what I've got to figure out. Maybe you could give me your name, for starters."

"Sure thing. Listen very closely." The kid hung up.

I was chewing off my last fingernail and sucking up the blood from a torn cuticle when Foley came over to my desk.

"How's your big investigation going?" he asked.

"Rotten. I called the director of the detention centre. He said the suicides didn't happen. Then I called the social affairs ministry and the PR guy also said they didn't happen. Then last night, the kid calls me at home and gives me the first names of two of the dead kids. Now I'm lost."

Foley grinned. For once, it wasn't a malicious "I told you so" kind of grin. It was a "what kind of idiot are you?" grin. Time for a short, intensive crash course in investigative journalism.

"First thing in a story like this is you don't jump out of the blocks and approach your key players without hard facts. Most times they can smell a fishing expedition, and they're not going to give you a rod to reel them in. They're not going to make your job easy. You've got to go out and find sources — real, reputable sources that don't have numbers attached to glossy black-and-white photographs of themselves — and then get them to substantiate the allegation."

"Yeah, but I don't have much to go on. I've got two first names."

"And what else?"

"An approximate period of time in which the suicides occurred."

"That's a lot to go on. Did you bother to check the coroner's office to see about bodies coming in from this detention centre? The coroner has to do an autopsy on all suspicious deaths, especially those that occur in government-run institutions. It's the law. And what about the cops? They're first to respond to an emergency call. Go down to the cop shop and look at the occurrence sheets. Do you know anyone at the juvenile court?"

I winced. I knew a platoon of people at the court.

"Maybe someone there has heard something. You see, there are a lot of roads you've got to travel before you rush off for the major confrontation. You should be ready to go with the story even if it's hotly denied. You should have all the facts in place first before you go in for your final accountability. You should never rush out asking questions based on what could well be the fantasy world of some wacky, spaced-out kid."

Foley's advice was sound and logical. And it stung. I felt like a dolt. I just hoped I hadn't blown it entirely. I grabbed my notepad and headed for the coroner's office.

An officious bureaucrat drummed his fingers incessantly on the counter as I explained what I wanted. He was not about to offer me any assistance.

"I need full names and the date of the death," he said. "Without that, it's impossible. Do you have any idea how many people die in this city in one month?"

"No, and I just bet you're not going to tell me, either."

My next stop was the police station that normally would respond to an emergency call from Centre Berthelet. The sergeant handed me all the major-occurrence sheets for every day of December and January. There was not one reference to a suicide or emergency at the detention centre. My spirits were sinking fast. I was beginning to seriously wonder whether the kid was pulling my strings.

On the way back to the *Star,* I decided to take a drive over to the detention centre. Berthelet sat in a frozen field in bleak Riviere-des-Prairies, on the northeast side of the island. It looked as if someone had plucked it from the farthest reaches of Siberia. The sprawling institution, which housed 240 boys, was surrounded by a fifteen-foot-high chain-link fence topped with barbed wire. In a corner yard, a dozen boys in navy blue parkas were playing a game of pickup hockey under the watchful eyes of three guards. I looked at their skates and wondered if the guards were now checking for laces when the equipment was returned.

The centre was run by Quebec's Ministry of Social Affairs. Officially, it was a detention and re-education institution. In plainer language, it was nothing more than a jail for boys aged fourteen to seventeen. From what I knew about Berthelet, it was no better or worse than any other detention centre, except that it was more modern, having been built in 1968. Most of the guards were poorly educated, underpaid and indifferent. They did the bare minimum expected of them, which was to keep the misfits in line. As for re-education, forget it. Berthelet was a huge holding tank that took every kid dumped on its doorstep, delinquents and psychiatric cases alike. During the day, the boys hung around, passing endless hours in the gym, watching TV or playing cards. At night, they were locked in their cells.

The juvenile prison was divided into eighteen units with thirteen cells to a unit. They surrounded a sparsely furnished common room shared by the boys. There was a television, a couple of couches and little else to suggest how the inmates spent their time. Each Spartan, cinder-block cell contained a bed, a desk and a chair.

The boys were sent there on three-month renewable sentences for offenses ranging from running away from home to break and enter, car theft and drug abuse. The place also housed psychiatric patients who were rejected by hospitals and treatment centres because they were simply too difficult to handle or didn't fit into the treatment model.

I walked up to the main entrance and was buzzed in. At the reception area, I asked to speak to the director, Jean Leblanc. The secretary asked if I had an appointment. I told her Leblanc might be expecting me. As I sat in the waiting room, I was struck by the silence. On the other side of the cinder-block wall, there were more than two hundred hard-ass delinquents, and I didn't hear a peep. It was like being in a mortuary. Ten minutes passed before I heard heavy, purposeful footsteps approaching. I knew it wasn't Leblanc. It was the pounding boots of a guard. His instructions were clear, and he was only too obliging to carry them out. In the voice of a drill sergeant, he commanded me to vacate the premises. With his next breath, he warned me the police would be called if I didn't move my butt, and I would be charged with trespass.

As I stared into the guard's eyes, I knew the kid was telling the truth. I was determined more than ever to blow it wide open.

An hour later, I stood outside the juvenile and family court building dreading my next move. I had no contacts or sources inside the building, but I knew an awful lot of people in the place: my former probation officer, a few judges and a whole raft of do-gooder social workers. As I squeezed my way past a crowd of distraught mothers and their troubled offspring jamming the narrow corridors, I ran into Lionel Kaufman.

For four miserable years, this probation officer had been the bane of my existence. Kaufman was a small man, bald and pale with a surly look. He bellowed and barked to his charges. He hollered so loud that everyone on the second floor, where the probation cubicles were housed, heard him. Kaufman had probably the best education among the motley pool of probation officers — a BA in literature — and he never let anyone forget it. He bragged incessantly of being able to land a much better job with better pay. I wondered why he didn't. I figured his immensely negative outlook on life had something to do with it. The man saw crud under every Persian rug, no matter how bedazzling the craftsmanship. I assumed that was probably caused by his physical disability. As a child, he had contracted polio, and his right arm was virtually useless and his leg was in a brace, which he dragged when he walked.

Kaufman never had a kind word for me. His preferred method of dealing with me was to issue threats and ultimatums. If I was hauled before him for fighting—the cause for most of my court appearances— I would be assailed with grating yarns about his days as a youth when "I would beat the crap out of punks like you with one hand tied behind my back."

I hadn't seen him in four years. Now we were standing in a hallway, and I couldn't think of a single polite thing to say to him. While I struggled to find the words, Kaufman upstaged me.

"Well, well, well. Look who the cat dragged in," he said with a wry smile. He shot out his left hand and we shook hands. "Come, let's go up to my office. You're not in any trouble, are you?" He laughed.

His office was a tiny cubicle made even smaller by two metal filing cabinets jam-packed with files of his "active" cases of about 140 boys. A foot-high stack of file folders circled a black manual Royal typewriter on his wooden desk. As I looked at the files, I wondered how anyone, given such an absurd caseload, could deal effectively and honestly with any one boy.

"As you can see, I'm still a very busy man. But I've always got time for one of my star pupils. Get it?" he cackled.

"Yeah, I got it," I said, forcing a smile.

"I see you decided to make something of your life, Mr. Malarek," Kaufman said in a sermonlike tone. "We're all very proud here that you've made it. I'd like to think I had something to do with that. It goes to show you that my toughness paid off. Every time a story of yours hits the *Star* I brag about you to all my colleagues. So what brings you down here, Mr. Malarek?"

I took a deep breath to calm my nerves. I couldn't believe this idiot was discussing my past with other people. I was sure it was against the law. But this was no time to blow my cool.

"I'm working on a story about Centre Berthelet, about three boys committing suicide there."

"Yes, that's a sad, sad story. Those boys were so young. They had their lives ahead of them."

"So it did happen!" The words were out of my mouth before I realized I'd put my foot in it yet again.

The surprise in my voice startled Kaufman. "This is strictly off the record. You understand that. You cannot use anything I just said to you because we can't discuss any cases with anyone."

"We never agreed to anything being off the record," I said.

"You said nothing about your visit being business."

"Like I would come here on a social call," I said acidly. "I'm a reporter."

"You have to understand that I cannot discuss any case with anyone."

"Well, you seem to relish discussing my case. I'm sure you know that's illegal. And I strongly suggest you knock it off. I'm not part of your dog-and-pony show."

Kaufman exploded. "You get the hell out of my office and don't ever set foot in this building again!"

"Mr. Kaufman, you don't own the courthouse. It's a public institution. And for your information, I am not taking your comments as off the record. And lastly, I want to remind you as firmly as I can that if I hear you've discussed my past with anyone ever again, I'll make sure I get you fired. And I'll sue you!"

"Get out!" Kaufman boomed, his face purple with rage.

Outside his office, a school of social workers had gathered to eavesdrop on their colleague's latest rant. They scattered when I suddenly appeared. I left the court through a side entrance and found myself standing in front of St. Vallier detention centre.

From the outside, the seven-story, red brick building looked like a dilapidated factory. Inside, it forcibly held almost five hundred adolescent boys for crimes from shoplifting to murder. They were kept for a day to six months before being released outright or transferred to training schools or treatment centres. Two stories underground, in a dark, windowless basement, was its notorious chamber: the solitary-confinement unit where I had been locked up when I was seventeen. Images of the night I had been dragged into the basement, stripped naked, sprayed with DDT, then shoved and swatted on the backside by guards intent on provoking me to retaliate flashed through my mind. Four of them had sat on a bench and watched me shower. Then they'd kicked me in the ass as they marched me into solitary.

The next morning I got a phone call at the *Star*. The woman caller sounded frightened and very nervous.

"I heard what happened yesterday in Mr. Kaufman's office. I have some information that can help you."

"About the suicides?"

"Yes. I know about one of them. But you have to promise me that you won't tell anyone I spoke to you."

"I promise. But for my own protection I need to know who you are and what you do. I swear I'll never, ever name you."

I was learning.

The phone line sounded for a moment as if it had gone dead. I wondered if I'd flubbed it again. Then she gave her name and added, "I'm a social worker at the court."

"What do you know about the suicides?" I asked.

"The boy I know about should never have been sent to Berthelet. He was being seen at the psychiatric clinic here. He had a lot of serious problems. He should have been in a treatment setting, but no one would take him. They all said he was too much trouble for them to handle. The boy had no one. He was an orphan. He entered the custody of the state when he was just a child."

"Why was he sent to Berthelet?" I asked.

"He had nowhere else to go. It was Christmas. No treatment centre wanted him. Centre Berthelet was the only place with a bed."

"You mean a jail cell."

"If you like. But the places that should have taken him rejected him. What were we supposed to do? We can't force the treatment centres to take the kids they don't want, and the boy was in the care of the state."

"You call it care?"

"Listen, I'm trying to help and you keep shooting barbs at me," the woman said.

I sucked in my breath and told myself to pull back.

"I'm sorry. It's just the words you chose. Bed and care. This kid was dumped in a jail cell because no one cared. And now he's dead."

"I know he's dead and I feel absolutely sick about it—and about the other two boys, too. But there's no reason to take it out on me."

"I'm sorry if I upset you," I said, trying to calm her down. "What was the boy's name?"

The woman hesitated. "I don't think it would be proper to give you that information."

"He's dead. What difference will it make?"

"I'll give you his first name only. It's Richard. He was seventeen. He died at seven-thirty in the morning on December twenty-second. It was his third time being committed to Centre Berthelet. He was sent there on the sixteenth. He suffered from hallucinations and he'd tried to commit suicide before. We had recommended strongly that he be placed in a specialized institution equipped to handle his case. The place we had in mind was filled to capacity, so in the interim he was sent to detention — over the strenuous objections of his psychiatrist at the clinic here."

My heart was pounding as I scribbled down what she was saying.

"Do you know anything about the other two kids?" I asked.

"I heard that one was an orphan, as well. His name was Wayne. He was sixteen. The guards found him hanging in his cell by the laces from his hockey pads. The police came and administered oxygen but it was too late."

"Do you have a date when this happened?"

"December 29, at 3:30 p.m."

"You don't know anything about the third boy?" I asked.

"No, but I could try and find out. It's just that I have to be extremely careful."

"How can I get in touch with you?"

"You don't ever get in touch with me. Do you understand that? I'll call you."

"When?"

"In two days, at noon, when I take my lunch break."

"I was also told that at least two other boys tried to kill themselves in Berthelet but weren't successful."

"I didn't hear that but I'll see what I can find out."

Finally, the break I needed! The knot in my stomach eased ever so slightly. The kid wasn't lying after all, and I had an official source with a name and a credible title. I raced over to Foley's office with the news. He smiled and reminded me there was a lot more work to do before the story got in the paper.

"You need another solid source to corroborate what this social worker just told you. Go out and find it," he said.

That evening, I parked myself in front of the police station in Rivieres-des-Prairies and buttonholed every cop going into or out of the building. I asked each one if he had responded to a call from Berthelet regarding a suicide. On my third try, I struck pay dirt.

29

"Yeah, my partner and I got one in December," a bulky officer said. "It was the afternoon of the twenty-ninth. The boy hanged himself with laces. It was the second in two weeks. My friend, he got the call for the other one. I'll get my book from upstairs and see what I wrote."

A few minutes later he was back outside, flipping through a black notebook. "Here it is. December 29 at 3:30 p.m. A sixteen-year-old male. He was hanging from a hook in front of his window. He used the laces from his hockey pads. We administered oxygen but it was no use. He was pronounced dead on the scene by a doctor. The boy was transported to the morgue. That's it."

"Did you get the boy's name?"

"It was Roger. He had no family. He was a ward of the province of Quebec."

"Can I ask you why this wasn't included on the daily major-occurrence sheets?"

"We don't put suicides down as a major occurrence," the officer said matter-of-factly.

"Suicide is not a major occurrence?" I asked.

"No. It's not a crime. There's no criminal. It's an open-and-shut case."

"What about your friend? The police officer who handled the first suicide. Is he around?"

"He's on the road but he should be back in an hour for his dinner break. He's in car seventeen."

At precisely ten o'clock, car seventeen rolled into the parking lot. A porky police officer jiggled out of the driver's seat. He looked at me suspiciously as I identified myself.

"I talked to your buddy earlier. He told me about the suicide he responded to at Centre Berthelet on the twenty-ninth. He said you handled one a week earlier."

"Yeah, and I also responded to one about ten days ago. It's all very, very bizarre," he said. "Three young boys to die like that. Putting laces around their necks."

"Can I get the names and dates from you?"

"I would have to check with the sergeant about that," the cop said.

"It's not all that complicated. Your buddy gave me the information. All I need is the dates and names."

The police officer looked me over skeptically. I was certain my long hair was giving him a problem.

"You wait here." He disappeared into the station. Ten long minutes passed before he reappeared carrying two black notebooks.

The story was starting to fall into place. I'd finally caught the lying bastards, and they were going to fry.

"The first death was on Wednesday, December 22, at 7:30 a.m. The boy was seventeen. His name was Richard. When I got there, a guard was giving him artificial respiration but it was too late."

The officer flipped open the second notebook. "Friday, January 14, a seventeen-year-old boy, Roger, was found hanging in his cell at 10:30 p.m. He was hanging from the cell bars. He used laces from a pair of ski boots. That's all I can tell you."

"You've been a real help." I flashed the most charming smile I could muster. "Thanks a lot. I really mean it."

It was the confirmation I so desperately needed, and it was official. But why were the deaths such a secret? I wondered. And why had the head of Berthelet and the PR man at the social affairs ministry lied?

The next morning I called Leblanc for an official comment. The receptionist curtly informed me that he had nothing more to say. I called the Ministry of Social Affairs and got a fifteen-minute bureaucratic shuffle before the line went dead. I then phoned Claude Castonguay, Quebec's highly respected minister of social affairs. One of his political aides adamantly denied there had been any suicides or attempted suicides at any of the province's juvenile institutions.

"I'd like to speak to Mr. Castonguay directly," I said.

"The minister is very busy, and I have already told you the facts. The story you tell me is simply not true. We categorically deny it. You have your facts wrong," the political aide insisted.

"I don't have my facts wrong and I would like Mr. Castonguay to tell me on the record that the deaths did not occur. I don't want to hear from one of his flunkies." My charm-school background had bubbled to the surface again.

The aide slammed down the phone.

Foley waved me into his office and told me to shut the door. "How's your little investigation going?"

"I've got it all confirmed. I found the cops who responded to the calls, and then there's the social worker I told you about."

"What does the detention centre have to say?" Foley asked.

"The director won't respond to my calls. They're sticking by their story. No suicides."

"Did you call Castonguay's office?"

"Yeah. His political aide denied any suicides. The guy's a jerk."

"Then that's their problem. When can you have the story ready?" Foley asked, rubbing his hands together.

"Later today. I'm expecting a call from the social worker. She might be able to give me a little more information. I'd also like to get into what led these boys to kill themselves. Why they were in detention in the first place. This social worker said two of the boys should never have been in there."

"Let's just get the story done. Don't try to take on too much," Foley said.

"I want to get at the truth. It's important!"

Foley stared at me for a moment. "You get out there. I want the story on my desk after today's final deadline. It goes in the paper tomorrow. Got it?"

At noon on the dot, the social worker called as promised.

"I couldn't find out anything more on Wayne without creating suspicion. All I know is that he was an orphan. The third boy, Roger, is a sad story. His father is dead, and his mother simply took off to Europe with her boyfriend for the Christmas holidays. The boy was picked up on the street one night, and when the police found out he was living all alone, they transferred him to Berthelet for his own safety."

"Jesus! This caring thing never stops, does it?" I interjected bitterly.

"I also found out that the same day Roger hanged himself, another seventeen-year-old slashed himself with a jagged piece of glass. The other attempt happened on the same day as the first suicide. An eighteen-year-old slashed his wrists with a razor blade. Both were found in time and taken to the hospital. That's all I can tell you."

"I want to thank you for this. I know what it took for you to come forward," I said. I did have some manners.

"I have something else to tell you. Kaufman is on the warpath. He's really upset over the way you talked to him. He's bad-mouthing you all over the place and threatening to get you fired."

"The man is a fool. Anyway, I'm not worried about him," I said confidently.

"When do you expect this will appear in the paper?" she asked.

"Tomorrow."

I sat down at a desk in a corner of the newsroom and nervously began typing out the first paragraph of my first investigative story.

Alone in their cells, frightened and in despair, five
youths over the past month decided to put an end to
their agony and kill themselves at the Centre Berthelet
detention and re-education institution for boys in
Rivieres-des-Prairies. Three succeeded.

Before I handed my copy over to Foley, I phoned Castonguay's
office one more time. His political handlers were in no mood to listen
to what I had to say.

"You're fabricating this incident. There have been no suicides at
that institution," an aide insisted. "You will be in big trouble if you
print these lies."

"I live for trouble. And don't forget to read the *Star* tomorrow."

I paced around the newsroom for most of the evening in a state of
severe agitation. I had a feeling that something was going to go wrong.
And sure enough, shortly after nine o'clock Foley burst out of his office
holding a telex.

"Malarek! Get over here!" he shouted.

I raced to his side.

"The *Gazette* has this. Castonguay's office has issued a press release
announcing a full-scale inquiry into Centre Berthelet!"

"Holy shit! I've been scooped by the *Gazette*!"

"No. Not necessarily. This is a carefully worded release. There's no
mention of any suicides at all in it. It just says the inquiry will 'examine
conditions at Centre Berthelet.' Maybe the *Gazette* won't twig onto it."

The first edition of the *Gazette* usually arrived in the newsroom at
eleven. When the copyboy barrelled through the doors, Foley yanked a
paper out of his hand. I watched tensely as he scanned the front page
and ripped through the inside pages. Then he grinned. I knew everything was all right. I quickly inserted a few paragraphs about the government inquiry, adding that the minister refused to elaborate on why
he had initiated it.

On Thursday, January 27, 1972, the *Star*'s banner headline read:
THREE DETAINED YOUTHS HANG SELVES. Above it was a sub-headline
that read: Castonguay orders full-scale inquiry.

When I walked in the next morning, the newsroom was buzzing.
Kowch and Provencher slapped me on the back and congratulated
me. Several editors smiled and shouted: "Great story, Malarek! Good
work!"

I was on top of the world. I even got a call from CBC radio. Tony Burman, who hosted an afternoon information show, wanted to interview me. It seemed no one from the Quebec government or Berthelet was willing to talk about the story, let alone confirm it. It was my first radio interview. I called my mother and told her to tune in.

Burman could tell I was tense. "Look, just relax and don't worry about freezing up," he said.

But that wasn't what I was worried about. I was tense because I knew myself too well. I wanted to keep the conversation civilized. I knew that when I got a head of steam blowing, I had a tendency to slip into street language generously laced with four-letter words.

The interview went off without a single profanity. I was riding a cloud. When I got back to the newsroom, there were more kudos and an important phone call. It was the kid.

"See, I told you it was all true," he said smugly.

"I never doubted you. I want you to know that. And I want to thank you for telling me about this," I said.

"No. I want to thank you."

"Look, let's meet. I'll buy you dinner," I suggested.

"Can't. I got caught. I'm back in detention. Gotta go."

I was rereading the paper for the umpteenth time when I felt a pair of eyes locked onto me. I looked up and saw Foley staring at me. He looked tense. He waved at me to come into his office.

"Close the door," he said as I entered. His tone was ominous.

"Castonguay's office just called."

I took a breath, fearing the worst.

"Needless to say, they're upset with the story, but they've now confirmed the suicides did occur."

"Well, it's about time."

But something else was troubling him.

"Is there anything else?" I asked hesitantly.

"Yeah, there is." He pulled a letter out of his drawer and placed it in front of me. It was typed and not signed.

"It seems you've had a very interesting past, and I gather from this letter you've seen the inside of a few detention centres."

"The prick!" I said.

"Who?" Foley asked.

"The bastard who sent you that letter. I was a juvenile when these things happened. I'm twenty-three now. Are you going to hold that against me?" I shouted.

I stared at the letter on his desk. Reading upside down, I could make out the words "Weredale," "assault," "probation" and "St. Vallier detention centre." I closed my eyes and bit my lip.

"It appears I am now pinned on the horns of a dilemma," Foley began, breaking the uncomfortable silence. "Do I fire you or do I give you a raise?" He paused for maximum pain and effect. Then he grinned. "I think I'll go with the latter. Starting next week you'll go from seventy-five dollars a week to a hundred. You did a great job."

He burst out laughing. Foley reveled in mind games. This was one I didn't appreciate, but I wasn't about to make an issue out of it.

He picked up the letter, ripped it up and handed me the pieces.

"Thanks," I said shakily. My legs were like rubber. I wasn't ready for what came next.

"Tomorrow you're back on the police desk," Foley said.

"What?" I was devastated. "But I want to follow this story!"

"There's nothing to follow. The story's done. There's a full-scale provincial inquiry. It's over," he said firmly.

"But it's not over! There's more to this story than just the suicides. I want to get at what led these boys to kill themselves! These kids were dumped by the very system that was supposed to protect them. I want to get at that! All this government inquiry is going to do is bury the real issues and make some dumb recommendation about keeping skate laces out of kids' hands. These kids should never have been in that detention centre in the first place. A lot of people in positions of authority knew that. A lot of social workers, psychologists, probation officers knew that. But no one did a thing about it. You've got to understand — the story isn't over!"

I was in a panic.

"It *is* over. The government has launched an investigation, and we'll wait for the report. You broke the story, Malarek. You should be proud of that. End of topic. Tomorrow. Ten o'clock, police desk." Foley picked up a galley sheet and began reading.

I stood up and walked out of his office feeling like a jilted lover. I was back to chasing cop cars.

CHAPTER THREE

1001 DAYS AS A BUREAUCRAT

It took me all of one day as a civil servant to realize that I had made a big mistake taking a job in the federal bureaucracy. It was the spring of 1973, and the living suddenly became real easy. In one quick scrawl of my signature on a government employment form, my salary more than doubled, from $6,000 a year at the *Star* to $12,500 in the department of the Secretary of State. And it came with an impressive title: press attaché.

On my first day, "news" was in the making. I was put right to work. My task: compose a press release on increased funding for French-language training in post-secondary education across Canada, beginning with the all-important phrase, "Secretary of State Hugh Faulkner today announced..." No, I wasn't announcing World War III. Nor did the writing require the IQ of a rocket scientist. But it was what happened *after* I drafted the press release that really put me to the test. Before it went out the brass doors, it had to be approved. And so my single page of placid prose embarked on a journey of Homeric scope. Everyone with a job title longer than his or her name had the right to read, review, revise and edit the document. This sheet of paper, stamped "secret" *(secret!)*, careened through a maze of offices in the heart of the nation's capital. Why, Canada's future appeared to be at stake if I inadvertently split an infinitive or left a participle dangling! No fewer than twenty-two bureaucrats and political aides checked, edited, rechecked, re-edited and initialed my paltry offering before routing it onward and ever upward in the chain of command.

Ironically, the only signature that mattered was the minister's. What he approved went out the door. Nothing more, nothing less.

Peter Cowan, the former Paris correspondent for the *Montreal Star*, lured me across the line. Cowan had left the paper a few months earlier for a job as news media chief with the Secretary of State. He was tall, heavyset and appreciated the better things in life. He loved haute cuisine, good French wines and sleek, beautiful women. With his boyish charm, he adapted quickly to the Ottawa scene. He walked the walk and talked the civil service bafflegab. He was the bureaucratic version of a used-car salesman.

Need I say I lacked Cowan's gift? Nor did I have any desire to cultivate it. But I admit I admired his unerring ability to flatter and praise mediocrity.

Cowan got wind that I was miserable at the *Star*. There'd been a management shift, and the momentum of the newsroom was flagging. Don Foley, lured by big bucks and smoky back-room politics, had left a year earlier to become an aide to federal Solicitor General Jean-Pierre Goyer. Before he departed, he'd elevated me to general assignment reporter. After two years on the police beat, no more cops, ambulances or fire trucks. Or so I thought.

My new boss didn't like me. Maybe it was my old bugbear, my hair. I never really found out. But the feeling was mutual. When David MacDonald and I talked, which was rarely, MacDonald focused on the wall or the floor, anywhere except me. In a few short weeks, he succeeded in quashing any affection I felt for the newspaper. And he had shoved me back onto the cop beat. When I asked him why, he looked at the wall.

One afternoon as I started my shift, I noticed some of the copy editors snickering as I plunked myself down at the police desk. A moment later, I found out what they were so amused about. A buzzer sounded. By now the copy editors were choking back howls of laughter. I looked around, trying to figure out what was happening. Then the buzzer sounded again. I sat frozen to my chair, fixing my eyes on the police-radio scanners.

The supercilious editor rose from his roost on the copy rim, and marched to the police desk.

"Did you hear the buzzer?" he demanded.

"Yeah. So?"

"When I buzz, it means you or whoever is manning the police desk is wanted at the city desk."

"Shit, David. If you want me, all you have to do is call or wave. You're less than fifteen feet away, for Christ's sake!"

MacDonald responded with an icy stare and returned to his perch. Norman Provencher, who was also on the evening cop watch, walked into the newsroom.

"You won't believe what that asshole has done," I said as he sat down.

"What now?" Provencher asked.

"He's installed a freakin' buzzer, and when the big jerk buzzes, we're supposed to jump, roll over and fetch him a bone."

Not a heartbeat later, the buzzer sounded. I refused to budge. Provencher winced. Two long blasts followed. Slowly, Provencher rose from his chair, smirked at MacDonald, saluted and sat down. I broke out laughing.

After a stern lecture inside his office on employee discipline, MacDonald dismissed us. Ten minutes later, he lumbered over to his perch on the copy rim. The moment he sat down, he buzzed. But this time, there was no beep, no buzz. Just dead air. He pressed the button a few more times. Still no sound. His face was red as he steamed over to investigate. Then he exploded. The wires to his seventy-five-cent Command Central One had been snipped, and his beloved buzzer had been mangled by a grinding heel. I was immediately summoned to the managing editor's office where, with the expression of an injured angel, I denied any and all allegations of sabotaging company property. Sabotage was a firing offense.

The buzzer was never reconnected. But by this time, I had had it. It was time to look for another job.

The thing that bothered me most about becoming a civil servant was the cold shoulder I got from many of my former reporter colleagues. My fellow journalists felt I had committed the cardinal sin: I had become a public relations man. I was now regarded as a turncoat. I had crossed over to the other side. In their eyes I was a prostitute who had sold himself for the money. Well, they were partly right.

Loathing PR people is a long-standing tradition among reporters. It comes with the press pass. Reporters see PR flaks as roadblocks, constantly running interference for their political and bureaucratic masters. For the PR lackey, the spin was more important than the facts. And journalists hated anyone who dickered with what they perceived as truth and the public's right to know. But there was also another, unspoken side to this intense dislike. A lot of reporters suffered from PR envy.

What really bugged them was the fact that PR people got paid more. Much more.

Once ensconced in the enemy camp, I got a rude wake-up call about my former profession. The civil service granted me a vantage point on a side of the reporting world I certainly hadn't experienced on the frenzied police beat. I got to see how incredibly lazy most reporters were, and how ignorant many were of the issues they were covering. Ottawa was filled with self-important babblers who could not handle a simple interview, carry out a basic investigation or bring themselves to ask a tough question at a press conference. Even when information was spoon-fed to them, which was most of the time, they managed to mangle the facts. And more often than not, the wool was pulled over their eyes by crafty politicians and their media-savvy spin doctors. The Hill scribes seemed content to accept the catchall, "We're looking into it." They would ooze with syrupy self-satisfaction when a politician began a response with: "That's a very good question." The bottom line was there just wasn't much serious digging by the platoons of political pundits covering Parliament. Just a lot of "background" sifting in a shallow sandbox. About the only person doing any serious investigating on the bureaucracy in Ottawa was the auditor general. But that made front-page news only once a year.

As I left my spacious office overlooking the Rideau Canal after my first day on the job, I swore to myself that the civil service would be a blip on my curriculum vitae. I resolved to regard it as a sort of training ground before I re-entered the world of reporting. I would get to know the maze, decipher the code and find where the skeletons were routinely hidden. And then, one day, I would return to the world of newspapers and reporting, armed with inside information on the bureaucracy.

For the moment, however, I was trapped. I decided to make the best of an untenable situation. And, I thought, I can use some of the free time suddenly available to me to free-lance stories to *Weekend* and its competition, the *Canadian Magazine*. The seeds for one of the first feature stories I free-lanced (to the *Canadian*) had been planted way back in 1959.

When George Brugman walked into the games room or, for that matter, when he walked into any room in Weredale boys' home—the dormitories, the gymnasium, the dining room, the locker rooms, the auditorium—all activity abruptly ceased. Which was rather amazing when you consider the brouhaha of 170 boisterous boys between the ages of ten and seventeen hushed to a quiet hum of uneven breathing.

Brugman ran the boys' home like a Marine drill sergeant—nasty and tough. He was an imposing figure, standing taller than six feet in his institutional uniform, a bland grey suit, starched white shirt, tie and spit-and-polished black Oxford shoes. When Brugman barked an order, you never dragged your butt. Disobey a command and he made you pay: he grabbed your ear and hauled you up to within inches of his scowling face; he rapped you on the back of the head with his knuckles or he gave you "the biffs," six strokes of a leather strap across your bare backside as you knelt on the footrest of an antique dentist's chair in the clinic. He was a master at instilling terror and meting out punishment. Everyone feared him.

Beside Brugman stood a new boy who looked like a frightened puppy. He was frail and very thin. His skin was yellow, and he was dressed like a beggar. But it was his eyes that drew my attention. He appeared tormented.

As Brugman scanned his tattered domain, the boys stared nervously in his direction, avoiding eye contact. We learned fast that it was better to fade into the background than stand out and fall under his scrutiny.

Just six months earlier, my two brothers and I had been hustled into this room by Brugman. We were scared, not knowing what lay before us. We were the new boys that day, about to be initiated into the punishing rites of Weredale House. Like this kid, our hearts were pounding. Weredale was a legend in the schoolyards of Montreal. We had heard harrowing tales of life behind the vine-covered, brown brick walls of the massive, four-story institution. Despite the fact that the institution was a way station for kids from broken homes, public perception was that Weredale was a reform school for juvenile delinquents.

Today's new boy picked nervously at his fingernails. Glancing at him, I wondered what he must have gone through to look like that. I could almost feel the abuse he had gone through.

It was June 26, 1959. I remember the date clearly because it was my eleventh birthday. The first of four I would spend in the home.

Brugman's eyes suddenly landed on me and a wide grin spread across his face. "Malarek! Get up here."

I ran up and nervously stood in front him. "Yes, sir?"

"You're the birthday boy today. Think you're mature enough to take care of the new boy?"

"Yes, sir."

"Good. I want you to meet Phillip Gillis. Gillis, this is Malarek. He'll be taking you around, showing you the routine. Any questions, ask him. Everyone else, get ready for lunch! I don't want to see one dirty hand in the lineup. Now move it!"

With that, Brugman left. The games room emptied as boys scrambled down the stairwell to the locker room to wash before lining up for hand inspection in front of the dining room.

Gillis didn't move. He was glued to his spot. He still hadn't looked at me.

"I'm Victor Malarek. The guys call everybody by their last name but I've got two brothers in here. Fred and Peter. So don't get mixed up if you hear someone calling Malarek and another guy answers."

He didn't respond.

"I'll show you your locker so you could put away your stuff. Okay?"

Still no response. I was getting a little peeved at his stony silence. I gazed to the ceiling and wondered, why me?

"Are you deaf?" I asked.

"No," he replied in a hoarse whisper.

That was about it for our conversation. Gillis was locked inside his solitary, macabre world, and I wasn't interested in drawing him out. I was preoccupied with going home after lunch to visit my mother to celebrate my birthday. And just maybe, if I was lucky, I'd get to see my father if he bothered to show up at his apartment.

When I left, the new boy was sitting alone on a dirt slope in the yard behind the home. I told him I'd see him when I got back for curfew at eight. He just stared at the ground.

My birthday was a bust. I didn't get to see my father. He couldn't tear himself away from the Legion Hall and his boozing buddies. My mother announced that she was not going to go back to him. She refused to suffer any more of his drunken rages, she said. In my mind, that meant only one thing — Weredale was going to be home, my prison, for a long time to come. The welfare worker gave my mother no way out. She was refused welfare, and told if she worked we wouldn't be allowed to stay home alone. She was given two choices: return to my father and she would get us back, or stay separated and we would remain in the boys' home.

When I returned that evening, Gillis was missing. He wasn't in the dormitory, and no one had seen him for hours. I raced through the building searching for him. I was getting pretty ticked off because I was cutting it close for check-off. Being marked late meant a detention and no day leave the following weekend. I finally found him cowering in a dark corner in the basement. He was sobbing. Some of the smaller guys had thought the time was right to show Gillis where he stood in the pecking order: at the absolute rock bottom. And a few of the nastier older boys muscled his locker combination out of him and swiped his few possessions.

"You should have taken leave," I said.

"I don't have anywhere to go," Gillis mumbled as I helped him up from the floor.

"Go visit your mother or father. That's what leave is for."

"They're both dead. I'm an orphan."

Perfect! On top of being depressed and pissed off, I now had the added burden of guilt to deal with. I didn't know what to say. I stared at this pathetic-looking kid, feeling rotten inside. My family life might be lousy, I thought, but at least I had one. And even though my mother and father lived apart, I knew I could still count on them.

At that moment, I decided that Gillis was my unofficial foster brother and part of my family. I didn't care what he felt about that. *I* had made up my mind. And, as it turned out, my decision suited him fine. He accompanied me on leave for family visits. He spent Christmases with my mother and soon started calling her Mom. On the odd Saturday afternoon, we hung out with my father. But Gillis was deathly afraid of him, especially when he was loaded. He often made excuses not to come with me. And he never called him Dad, just Mr. Malarek.

Fred and Peter readily accepted Gillis as one of us, and everyone in the boys' home soon saw him as an extension of the Malarek clan. They learned quickly that if they beat up on him, they had to deal with his three brothers. So it was better just to leave him alone.

Four long years passed before my brothers and I were sprung from Weredale, in late June, 1962. My mother had grudgingly volunteered to go back to my father when he got cancer. She desperately wanted the family to be together, and because of my father's immensely weakened condition, she no longer feared his violent physical outbursts.

Gillis remained behind, but visited on weekends. Then in 1964, when he turned sixteen, his life took an unexpected and unjust turn. For a Weredale kid, he was doing fairly well in school. He was in grade nine, and averaging about seventy percent, when Brugman suddenly yanked him out of class and put him to work as a gofer in the office at the home. He got paid a Dickensian six dollars a week plus room, board and clothing. Gillis was shattered. He didn't want to drop out of high school, and any notions he had harboured about going to college were gone forever. His problem was he had no one to fight for him, no one to turn to for help. He didn't know who his social worker was or how to get in touch with her. After he was dumped in the home, all contact with the child welfare agency had ceased. He was abandoned. They never checked up on him. They never visited. He became a name on a file in a steel cabinet, gathering dust in some agency's basement like so many of the other boys who were warehoused in Weredale.

When my mother tried to question Brugman's decision, he curtly told her to mind her business and reminded her that she had three onerous brats at home to handle.

Gillis's life became a mind-numbing routine of running errands in the home and around the city. On weekends, when he visited, he usually spent the first hour ranting about Weredale and his deep hate for Brugman. He desperately wanted to escape from his indentured labour.

After a year, I convinced Gillis to run away and come live with us. He blanched. He was scared Brugman would call the police and he'd be hauled off to a training school.

"You won't be sent to training school. They won't even care that you're gone. Brugman will replace you in one day. He's got 170 guys to choose from!"

I was right. Gillis bolted, and no one searched for him. No one asked about him. No one cared, and after just a few days, his locker was emptied out and a new boy was assigned to his bed and laundry number. Gillis was history.

One Friday evening in early June, 1973, I jumped into my brand-new Toyota Celica (courtesy of my fat salary with the federal bureaucracy) and barrelled east along Highway 17 — my escape route from Ottawa. I was going home to Montreal for the weekend. The following day, I dropped in on Gillis at his one-bedroom basement hovel. He was now twenty-four. He'd inched his way to a spindly five foot seven. He had a ratty mustache and longish brown wavy hair. His eyes still bore the haunted look I remembered from Weredale. He was electrically charged and acted like a nervous wreck. He never sat still for more than a minute. He was constantly in motion, always twitching and talking. If I hadn't known him, I would have sworn he was on amphetamines.

Whenever we got together, we would reminisce about Weredale. Funny thing: we hated the place but we could always pull out memories of a lot of good times. Gillis never spoke about the painful stuff buried deep inside. Our conversations were very superficial.

Even now, after we'd known each other for fourteen years, Gillis rarely spoke about his pre-Weredale past. If I asked, he'd shrug off the question or reply with a mumbled, "I don't know." For him, the past was a haze of pain-filled memories and a parade of blank faces with no names, locked away securely in his memory vaults. He saw no reason to cart them out for show-and-tell.

But through the bits of information I managed to pry out of him, I learned that both his parents had died within months of each other in the early 1950s, and that before being trotted off to Weredale, he had lived in a string of foster homes and orphanages. Each placement had left a mark. He had been beaten and discarded. As a result, Gillis had built a thick, protective wall around himself. No one was allowed in.

It was the first time Gillis and I had seen each other in a few months. I felt claustrophobic in his cramped apartment. We went for a walk. Outside, we puffed coolly on wine-tipped Old Port cigarillos. The journalist in me waded in.

"Do you ever wonder where your parents are buried?" I asked.

Gillis looked up at me with a bewildered expression. "I don't know," he said. "I've thought about it a lot but I never knew how to go about it. But I sometimes wonder, you know, who I am, who my parents were. Stuff like that," he said, drifting off into his private thoughts for a moment.

"Well, I was a reporter, you know," I said. "It shouldn't be too hard for me to find a grave."

Gillis was taken aback. "And then what?" he said.

"Maybe we might turn up a relative. Wouldn't it be incredible if we found a brother or a sister?"

"I don't think so. I don't remember any kids in my family. Just me."

My motives were not entirely altruistic. In fact, I had three precise reasons for my interest in Gillis's past. The first related to my years in Weredale and the resentment I felt about the whole "child welfare" system. The second was my eternal quest for a good story. In this case, I smelled an explosive tearjerker. The third reason was purely selfish. I needed a story. I was desperate to keep my fingers in ink and I saw this project as a quick, short-term fix.

Gillis wasn't too keen at first. He was a very private person. But I finally got him to sign on. I think he just hated seeing a grown man beg.

The first place I phoned was the Ville Marie Social Service Centre, the agency whose battalion of social workers kept Weredale well stocked with their clients. A week later, Maria Wicher, head of the agency's foster care section, phoned back and said she knew about Gillis's case history. I made an appointment for Gillis arfd me on Friday, July 20, at six-thirty.

Gillis was a tightly wound spool by the time we arrived at the centre. You could practically see his nerves popping along his wiry arms.

"Calm down," I said.

"Yeah, I'm calm. I'm calm," he rattled.

Miss Wicher met us at the door and led us into a lounge furnished with chrome and simulated walnut, leatherette chairs and matching Arborite-topped tables.

"I guess you know what I'm here for," Gillis began hesitantly.

Miss Wicher stared at him for a moment and then opened a file folder resting in her lap. She cleared her throat.

"Well, Phillip, we first had contact with you in 1956 when you were eight years old. You came to us through the adoption section and, although I didn't have anything to do with you directly, I was quite aware of your case. Before that, we had no responsibility for you. You were brought in by a social worker from Rouyn, Quebec," she said.

Reading from the files, she explained that he was placed in Alancroft, a home for younger children awaiting placement with adoptive or foster families. Phillip had come in from a failed foster placement with a farm couple.

Gillis looked up and laughed. A locked door suddenly burst open. "Yeah, I remember that foster home. It was on a farm and that big fat foster mother, all she wanted was a slave to feed the chickens and clean the barn. She kept whacking me with the broom so one day I just grabbed it and hit her over the head. The next day I was out of there."

"Good going," I said, giving him a high five.

Miss Wicher shifted uncomfortably in her chair. She was not amused.

"We were exploring another foster home in the meantime," she continued, turning to me. "But Phillip wasn't ready to trust people at that time. He sort of held himself aloof. Phillip seemed to have become self-sufficient after being knocked about so much."

"I wonder why," I shot back sarcastically.

From the files, Miss Wicher noted that Gillis remained at Alancroft for three years before being transferred to Weredale in 1959, because of his age. At ten, he was deemed too old to be placed with a family.

Now came the first explosive piece of information. Miss Wicher focused on Gillis's face, took a breath and began in a calm, measured tone, "You were adopted by the Gillises in 1950."

Phillip was stunned. His jaw dropped, and his eyes almost bulged out of their sockets. "You mean my mother and father weren't my real mother and father?"

"No," Miss Wicher answered softly. "I was under the impression you knew that."

"Ah, no ... no, I didn't," he said, slipping into a deep retreat.

"Your father, Mr. Gillis, that is, died in 1953, and two years later, Mrs. Gillis, your mother, died," she explained.

Gillis didn't respond. He was drifting in another world.

I jumped in: "If Phillip was adopted in 1950, then where was he for the first two years of his life?"

"With his own mother and father until the adoption," she said.

Gillis snapped out of his daze. "Do you know who they are? Do you know their names?" he asked, his voice shaking.

Miss Wicher said she didn't know anything about his father, but she did have some information about his mother.

Gillis was on the edge of his seat. "Who is she?"

"That I can't give you, by law. Certainly not without her permission," Miss Wicher said. "But I could tell you a little about her if you'd like."

"Sure I'd like!"

The social worker said his mother had moved from British Columbia to Rouyn with her husband. Their marriage failed and she eventually returned to British Columbia. But before heading back, she placed a little boy and a baby girl into adoption.

A second startling piece of information.

"You mean I have a sister?" Gillis asked.

"Yes, but we can't help you there. We weren't involved in her adoption."

"Did you—the agency—ever hear from his real mother?" I asked.

"Yes, in 1956 when she called the agency from British Columbia. She was worried about Phillip because she had heard the Gillises had died. She was told not to worry, that her son had been placed into a good home at the time."

"*A good home?*" I exploded. "He was dumped in a rotten foster home! And then he got stuck in Alancroft for a bunch of years, and then that torture chamber across the street called Weredale House!"

Miss Wicher bristled. She didn't respond. She sat quietly for a moment, observing Gillis. Social workers were good at that. Then she asked: "Would you like me to try and locate your mother?"

"Do you know where she is?" Gillis asked.

"No. We don't even know if she's still alive. But if you want, we can try to find her. Would you like us to try?"

"Yes...yes, I'd like that very much," he said.

"I feel it would be the right thing to do," Miss Wicher said, turning to me.

"No kidding!" I said caustically. I no longer cared about maintaining any appearance of objectivity or distance.

Miss Wicher turned to Gillis. "From what I recall, the circumstances regarding your adoption were exceptional. Your mother cared about you, but she wasn't in a position to do much. She might be very happy to hear you landed on your feet. In a lot of cases when parents give up a child, it's out of disgrace, and if the child starts tracing, it could do a lot of harm. But in this case, the circumstances were different. Your mother was a very honest and straightforward person. From the information we have here, your father deserted her and disappeared. She was stranded, with nothing and no one to help her."

Gillis stared at the social worker. Nothing seemed to be sinking in. It was too much to take in all at once.

"You have to realize that the last we heard from her was in 1956. A lot may have happened to her since then. She could be dead. And I must warn you that if we do find her, she may not want to see you. She may have a new life and be too embarrassed about seeing you after all this time."

"I'll take the chance," Gillis said. "When can you get started?"

"Tomorrow morning, first thing," Miss Wicher promised.

Outside, Gillis and I jumped into my car. Gillis sat bolt upright. He was tense, staring straight ahead and picking nervously at his fingernails. Then he started to laugh uncontrollably. He laughed for almost five minutes before stopping.

"It's incredible," he said, drying his eyes. "I never thought I had a mother...I mean I know I had a mother, but I thought she was dead. It's all really weird."

I began to feel a little uneasy. This journalistic foray had taken a very bizarre turn and could easily end up imploding. What if his real mother was dead? Or worse, what if she was still alive and refused to have anything to do with Gillis? How would he handle that? Maybe I should have left well enough alone.

The next three weeks were tough for Gillis. He had difficulty sleeping and keeping his mind on his job. He was a shipper in a large electronics plant, and one screw-up could prove very costly in terms of lost production time. He had to be on the ball or he'd be out the door.

Every time the phone rang he jumped, thinking that maybe this was the call. Then finally, a letter arrived. It was from Miss Wicher. Bad news. It said the agency that last handled his mother's file in British Columbia lost track of her. The workers hadn't heard from her in ten years and had no idea where she might have gone.

Gillis was inconsolable. After a long pep talk, I persuaded him to call Miss Wicher to ask where we could go from here. She assured Gillis that she was not going to give up. She had made his case a priority, she said.

Miss Wicher then tried a classic million-to-one shot. She placed an ad in the Vancouver newspapers. It began: "Would Mrs. Joan Currie or anyone knowing her whereabouts please contact..." That was the name of Gillis's mother.

An acquaintance spotted it and phoned Joan Currie. She was living in Kelowna, in the interior of British Columbia. Mrs. Currie immediately sent a telegram to the box number in the Vancouver newspaper asking for more information.

On September 24, Gillis and I arrived at the Ville Marie centre. Miss Wicher met us in the reception area. She was smiling.

"We heard from your mother. She wants to contact you. I have a letter from her to give you."

Gillis ripped open the envelope and began to read.

Dearest Son,

I just don't know where to begin except to tell you that I love you and thank God that He has answered my prayers after all these years...

Gillis read the letter over and over. His eyes were tear-filled, and he was beaming. "She says it's her birthday on the twenty-fourth, and hearing from me has got to be the best present a mother ever had. Today's her birthday!"

At midnight, he placed a long-distance call to Kelowna and talked to his mother for almost an hour. A few seconds after they said goodbye, my phone rang.

"Boy, was she ever happy to hear from me! I didn't know I could talk so much. She was laughing and crying. Hey, you'll never guess this ...I have a brother—a real brother. He's older than me but only by eleven months. His name is Jerry. Man, am I ever happy! Did I wake you up?"

His mother explained that when the family broke up, she had managed to keep Jerry, but was forced to give up her two youngest, Gillis and his baby sister. She promised to tell him as much as she could at their planned reunion.

In the span of three weeks, Gillis and Mrs. Currie exchanged a dozen letters. His mother mostly wrote about how happy she was and what she was doing in Kelowna. She carefully avoided questions about the past. She would discuss them when they met face-to-face, she said.

"Please don't form any special opinion of me until I've explained the things that puzzle you," she pleaded to her son in one letter.

In the meantime, I was growing impatient. I wanted to see the story in black and white, and so far, it was stuck in the mail. There were a lot of things that puzzled me about Mrs. Currie, and I didn't want to wait for an anticipated reunion sometime in the future to get the answers. I was in my reporter mode and I was annoyed that my investigation was being stalled by other people's schedules.

Gillis planned to go to Kelowna in late October, he told me. I was annoyed. October was too far off for my liking, and besides, I now had a deadline to meet. The *Canadian Magazine* wanted the story.

I phoned Mrs. Currie to get some background. She was hesitant about talking to me but I promised her I wouldn't discuss our conversation with her son until after his visit.

"Well, I answered the ad in the paper with a telegram because I wanted to hear as fast as possible what it was all about," she said. "The welfare agency in Montreal sent back a special-delivery letter. I read the first paragraph...I had to read it over several times...I couldn't make sense of it. My emotions got the best of me and I just...well, I just couldn't believe it all!"

Mrs. Currie's voice was cracking. She began to cry. "They were telling me about him looking for me, and wondering if I wanted to write him, or whether I didn't want him to know anything about me, or whether I'd be embarrassed, and all those kind of questions."

She was shocked to discover that her son had never been readopted after the Gillises died. In late 1955, she had received a letter from a friend in Rouyn who informed her that Phillip was in an orphanage. She said she fought a short, desperate battle by phone and mail with the social welfare agency to get her boy back, but was defeated when she received a terse notification saying, "Phillip has been adopted into a very good family."

"I wanted him back and then they told me he was readopted into this wonderful family, that he would probably have a better chance there than I could give him here. The one thing I could have given him was a mother's love. And now, after all these years, to find out that he was never with any such family." She began to weep.

"Well, I can tell you that my brothers and I made sure he was treated okay in the boys' home, and when he came to live with us for a couple of years, my mother and father treated him like one of us," I said, trying to console her.

Mrs. Currie regained her composure and continued with her story. When she began writing to her son, she tore up the first four letters, she said. She didn't trust the agency and was afraid they might open the envelope and read the contents. She didn't want to say anything that might destroy her chances of seeing her boy.

I was tense after our conversation. During all those years Gillis was bounced from one foster home to another, then penned up for a dozen years in uncaring, brutal institutions, his real mother had been led to believe he was safe and loved. For some reason, the child welfare system had decided it was in the boy's best interest to remain in the care of the state. I knew from experience that once the system had you, it just hated to let go. And I also knew from firsthand experience that the state was a lousy parent.

On October 20, 1973, Gillis boarded an Air Canada flight to

Kelowna. He was a bundle of nerves. Several hours later, he was reunited with his mother after twenty-three years.

When he got back to Montreal, Gillis told me the story of his reunion. "As I was nearing the airport, I was kind of nervous and tense," he said. "I didn't know what I'd feel when I got off the plane—how I'd react. It was raining when I walked down the plane's steps to the tarmac, so I ran toward the terminal building. I didn't see my mother. Then suddenly, she grabbed me. It's hard to say how I felt. I was kind of nervous and shocked. I was happy. She was crying. Then I saw my brother and grabbed him, and oh, I don't know. I was really happy. It's kind of hard to put these feelings into words."

That night, in a long, emotion-filled conversation that went on into the early-morning hours, Gillis's mother filled in the details of the missing early years of her son's life. She told him the story about their family's breakdown. It was a gut-wrenching story any way you interpreted it, but when Gillis recounted it to me later, it sounded to me as if his mother had softened some of the harsh truths for her son's ears.

She told him his father was a poor, misbegotten soul. "We didn't have any money," she recalled. "We had to beg for food. We had just sort of come to the end of the line. And I had to think seriously about who was more important in the world. Your father was a wonderful man in many ways, but he didn't realize his responsibilities toward us, especially you and your brother. He just didn't know any better. Then, when he was hospitalized for a while in Montreal, I couldn't cope with the situation any longer. I was working nights to try to support him and you children and trying to stay awake all day and look after things."

The family situation went from bad to dangerous when her husband was discharged from the psychiatric hospital. Afraid and concerned for her family's safety, Mrs. Currie decided to put up Phillip and his sister, Peggy, for adoption.

This was the one piece of information that deeply troubled Gillis. Somewhere out there was a young woman he hadn't known existed. He wanted to know more.

His mother was circumspect. Peggy had been adopted by a very good family, she said. She had met the family. But when she agreed to let them adopt Peggy, she had also agreed to remove herself from the girl's life forever.

As for his brother, Jerry, Mrs. Currie explained, when the family broke down, he was taken in for a time by his paternal grandmother.

And the Gillis family eventually took Phillip, she continued. They were an elderly couple who had looked after him while she was trying to sort out her family problems.

"Mr. and Mrs. Gillis fell in love with you and begged me to let them have you. We talked about it, and I felt they truly loved you as much as I did. Mrs. Gillis promised she'd bring you up a real good boy, and I was convinced that the Gillis family would look after you the way I would have done myself."

So Phillip's mother made a solemn vow to Mrs. Gillis that she would never come back and take her boy away. She made the same promise to the family that adopted Peggy. Then she left Rouyn and went to Ontario.

"But every day my heart broke more and more when I thought about what I had done. Although I did it for the children, I wanted them back with me. But I realized I couldn't go back on the promises I'd made. There was one child I'd made no promise about, though — Jerry. If there was any chance whatsoever, I wanted him back. I don't know to this day what happened but I received a phone call from Rouyn and was told that he was on his way to me in a bus."

Shortly thereafter, Mrs. Currie returned to British Columbia. She remarried. Her second marriage was breaking up when she received a letter from a friend informing her that the Gillises had died and that her son was in an orphanage.

Mrs. Currie took her case to the Children's Service Centre in Montreal. But she got no help. She hit brick wall after brick wall, and finally gave up. And now, in her tiny living room, she desperately wanted her son to understand. "I was told you were adopted into this grand family," she said sadly.

Gillis had listened to his mother's story in numbed silence. He was sad for her and all she had gone through in life. And he was not about to add to her misery by recounting his painful trek through the child welfare jungle. For the moment, he was happy. "What did I look like when I was born?" he finally asked, to break the silence. "Was I ugly?" He and his mother laughed and hugged each other.

They spent the next two weeks together. They were the happiest two weeks Gillis had spent in all his twenty-five years.

When I picked him up at the Montreal airport, Gillis looked at me and shook his head.

"I don't believe it. You won't believe it, either."

"What?" I asked.

"It's something about my past."

"What? What is it now?"

"My real name is Paul Bouchard. I'm a Quebecois!"

★ ★ ★

Gillis's story appeared in *Canadian Magazine* on February 23, 1974, under a bold, black banner that read: I'm Not An Orphan After All!

It began: *Phillip's search sounded simple enough: to find his parents' graves and maybe learn a little about his early childhood. He'd wanted to do it for most of his 25 years, but for some reason he'd never got around to it. Until last summer.*

★ ★ ★

It was a morale boost I desperately needed. I'd gone more than a year without a byline. Trouble was, the story didn't send editors scrambling to their phones with offers to join their news staff. I sat back in my well-appointed office and vegetated. The money was great, the work was light and the benefits were abundant. All I had to do was stick around for a quarter century and I was guaranteed a healthy retirement package for serving my country.

Within a year, I was promoted—a double-step leap to media relations coordinator for National Welfare. My salary jumped to $22,000 a year. My star was rising. I was bilingual and I was an ethnic. I filled the federal government's all-important Ukrainian quota! And I excelled at my job. But inside I was miserable. There's something insidious about the bureaucracy that atrophies the brain and lulls you into a coma. And I'd gained twenty-five pounds from "doing lunch" with fellow bureaucrats. I looked like a beleaguered cherub in a suit. The civil service was winning. I was quickly losing control of my life. In the end, the job almost buried me.

At the start of 1976, I was offered another tempting promotion, this time with the solicitor general at a salary of $28,000 a year. Not bad for a twenty-eight-year-old. Yet I knew that if I took the job, the monolith would own me, body and mind, for the rest of my pathetic working life. I gagged. I had done a thousand and one days in this purgatory. It was time to get out.

On my third anniversary with the feds — having read (during work-ing hours) every book written by Fyodor Dostoyevsky, Mikhail Sholok-hov and Mikhail Bulgakov, as well as a good cross-section of Leo Tolstoy, Alexandre Dumas, George Orwell and John Steinbeck — I quit.

Anna supported my decision completely, and I'll thank her forever for that. She knew I wasn't cut out to be a bureaucrat and that I was truly miserable. I put together a résumé, grudgingly including my years in Ottawa as a PR man. It was either that or tell everyone I had been in prison for the past three years. My salvation would have to come in a face-to-face interview. And I was ready to grovel.

CHAPTER FOUR

I DON'T DO PRESS RELEASES

Like most reporters in Canada, I aspired to landing a job one day at the *Globe and Mail*. I was conditioned to believe that the *Globe* set the standard in Canadian journalism. The rest were all humdrum and local. Don't get me wrong! I would have jumped at a job at the *Toronto Star*, the *Vancouver Sun* or the *Ottawa Citizen*. I had applied to every one of them. But it was the good, grey *Globe* that beckoned from the news-stands.

Before sending off my résumé, I read the *Globe* religiously from front to back for a month. Just in case I lucked into an interview, I figured I'd better be well-prepped. I got to know the various reporters from their bylines and quickly concluded that, in general, they wrote concisely and informatively but without any passion. Most seemed content to hitch their notebooks to press releases and news conferences, dutifully jotting down whatever politicians said, no matter how mindless. All of which convinced me the paper could use a guy like me, a brash young scrapper who wanted to take on the world. And after three years on the sidelines, I was itching for a fight. My only worry was whether my reflexes had dulled. I had the desire and the passion. But I wondered if I could still burn.

On New Year's Day, 1976, I wrote the *Globe*'s managing editor, Clark Davey, and politely suggested that with my experience at the *Star*, in addition to my thorough understanding of the bureaucratic maze, I would be an asset to his paper. To my absolute surprise, he replied with an invitation to an interview.

A few weeks later, I was sitting nervously outside Davey's office listening to my stomach gurgle. I stared intently at the newsroom. My immediate line of vision was the *Report on Business* section. Everyone was dressed in basic business drab: jackets and white shirts held in place by uninspired ties. The haircuts were barbershop specials. I was worried. If this was the *Globe*, I would never fit in. I still wore my hair long and I was downright vain about my Cossack mustache. My standard work uniform was tan leather jacket, burgundy knit tie hanging loosely from a dusty blue, open-necked shirt and navy blue gabardine pants.

The managing editor's secretary, a stiff-upper-lip Englishwoman, sat in front of an electric IBM typewriter, her fingers playing across the keys like buzzing bees. After several very long minutes there was a beep. The queen waved me into her boss's office.

As I entered the chamber, Davey leaned back in his chair. Clearly, he was sizing me up. As I walked toward his massive oak desk, I did the same of him. He was rotund, a man who obviously loved food and drink. He wore tortoiseshell glasses and a dark, baggy suit, and his tie was askew. He looked every inch *my* idea of a newspaper man. Davey got straight to the point: "What can you bring to the *Globe* that we don't already have?"

"A desire to dig up stories that mean something to people."

"Are you saying we don't do that now?"

A trick question, I thought. If I say no, then why would the paper need me? If I say yes, then I've insulted the *Globe*. Better to charge up the middle, I decided.

"It's just that I don't see anyone out there fighting for the little guy. I really think someone should be out there digging up stories about the day-to-day crap that people have to face."

"Are you still an angry young man?" Davey interjected.

That *definitely* threw me! Davey knew more about me than I'd anticipated.

After I broke the story on the three teenage suicides at Centre Berthelet for the *Montreal Star*, Don Foley cut me off the cop beat and sent me over to Donna Logan, the features editor. She let me loose. I started hammering away at stories involving the abuse of children in government-run institutions and wrote a five-part series lambasting Quebec's system for dealing with juvenile delinquents, which created a furor among child-care professionals.

As the editor responsible for my stories, Logan had her hands full. A lot of my copy had to be edited for tone and editorial comment. More than once, Logan asked me why I was so angry.

"I just don't like the way these kids have been dealt with," I would reply curtly. I didn't tell her about my past.

When I wrote about the barbaric induction ritual at Saint Vallier Centre, the hellhole where I at last made up my mind to clean up my act, Logan wondered how I could describe it in such detail, since journalists were barred from these places.

"I just know," I mumbled, staring at my typewriter.

Almost every time I wrote about yet another young victim of the child welfare system, I'd blow my cool. I'd storm around the newsroom ranting and raving. And one day, a *Star* colleague joked, "What's the angry young man up to today?"

Davey stared directly into my eyes waiting for an answer to his question. I scratched my head and said, "I'm more pissed off than ever."

Davey replied with a phrase I'll never forget. "The light in my belly button just turned on," he said intently. "You've got the job!"

I took a deep breath and exhaled very slowly. I had finally extricated myself from the land of nod.

On March 5, 1976, I began my job as a senior reporter. Gone forever were the vestiges of the former copyboy. There were no coffee or ink stains on my shirt. This was a new start. From now on, I would be taken seriously. Let anyone even think about minimizing or trivializing my position, and he or she will be in for a blast!

My introduction to the newsroom was short and sweet. The city editor, a stocky, easygoing New Zealander named Murray Burt, was my immediate boss. My other boss, Warren Barton, was his aide de camp. Barton was a big kid, who had short blonde hair with a cowlick and a hint of playful malice in his eyes. The guy loved to tease, taunt and devour reporters for sport. Most times I got along with him but he could be a colossal pain in the butt. At times I felt like smashing his head in. But a sense of self-preservation kept me in check. Barton pumped iron, and I knew if I hit him, he'd shake me off like sawdust and hammer me good in return.

My first week was spent learning the rumble of the newsroom, a massive expanse that stretched the length and breadth of a football field. I got a desk in a quad facing Jeff Sallot, a general reporter with a keen interest in the nefarious deeds of the Royal Canadian Mounted Police, and John Beaufoy, the paper's legal beagle who, in his drab grey suit and white shirt, could have passed for a Bay Street lawyer. Beside me sat Vianney Carriere, whom everyone called Sam. A wonderful writer, Sam covered the courts. But I sensed a mysterious, foreboding side to him. I fantasized that he might be a defrocked Anglican minister with a scarlet past. Behind me sat Don Grant, a roly-poly police reporter whose shirt buttons popped from the stresses of his wife's Hungarian cooking. Peter Whelan perched beside him. He was supposed to be the environmental reporter but preferred crouching in a thicket in Point Pelee with binoculars spying on the sex lives of yellow-bellied sapsuckers. An avid ornithologist, he wrote far more copy on birds than he did on the dangers of acid rain or chemical garbage.

I revelled in getting to know the eclectic assortment of journalists who worked on the news side, especially the legends: Joan Hollobon, by far the best medical reporter in the country, who knew more about medicine than most general practitioners; Wilf List, the noble dean of labour reporters, who dutifully phoned his mother a dozen times a day; and Kay Rex, an affable and caring features writer who worked on what then was still called the Women's Page.

At the start of week two, Barton figured it was time to flex his biceps and cut the new kid down to size. He ambled over and handed me a press release.

"I need a story on this by five. Think you can handle the pressure of such a tight deadline?"

He grinned. The deadline wasn't for six more hours.

I stared at the two-page announcement and tossed it unceremoniously on the floor. "I don't do press releases." I said crisply. "I was hired as a senior reporter to do serious stories. Get some junior reporter to rewrite it."

Barton didn't even blink. He just kept smirking and walked away.

"You're in deep trouble," Grant warned. "I'd have fired you for that."

"I know what I'm doing," I said tersely.

I had set the tone. I wasn't going to do press releases and I wasn't going to be treated like a junior reporter.

Two weeks passed, and the ice had not melted. Barton was a master of cool detachment. He didn't give me a single assignment. I finally approached Murray Burt and asked him what was going on. He shrugged and shot a conspiratorial glance at Barton, who suddenly popped up by his side.

"You're the senior reporter," Barton said mockingly. "Find your own stories."

Burt was clearly in Barton's camp. "By the way," he said with studied casualness, "I'm sure Clark informed you that you're on a three-month probation period, and if you don't produce at the level of a... what's that level again?"

"A senior reporter," Barton taunted.

"Then I guess you're history, mate," the city editor pronounced.

Great, I thought. Here I am in a new city and a new province, working at a new newspaper, and already I've landed myself in trouble.

"How am I supposed to produce if you guys aren't going to assign me to a story?" I argued.

"Senior reporters are hired for their ability to ferret out stories on their own," Burt said. "That's why you were hired. That's what Clark told me," he added, his voice dripping with mock innocence.

"Yeah! You're the new hotshot. The lone gun. The angry young man," Barton added. "Clark is really high on you. He told me he expects big things from you."

I realized I had dug myself into a really big hole. Either I came up with a story that couldn't be ignored, or I was gone.

I needed a front-page story. But I was brand-new to Toronto and didn't know my way around. I had no contacts in the city and I was starting to doubt my ability to drum up any decent sources. I drifted around the city, my confidence flagging fast. The most I could shake from anyone was puff stuff: press releases or thick information packages chock-full of glossy brochures and annual reports. No one was willing to share anything meaningful with me.

The clock was ticking. March came and went like a kitten. Not so much as a cheap tip. The drought continued throughout April. I was in deep trouble. Everywhere I dug, I came up empty. I was sinking deeper, and Barton and Burt weren't about to throw me a rope. Desperately, I returned to familiar turf — my former stomping grounds, Montreal. I called some of my dormant *Star* contacts in the child welfare field and begged them to toss me a few names in Toronto. Someone, anyone who might lead me to a story, I pleaded.

Finally, a tiny break. A social worker at Montreal's Juvenile Court, whom I knew from former years as a conscientious and caring employee, gave me the name of a Toronto colleague.

"His name in Don Munro," the social worker told me. "He's a

little odd, comes across like a boring reverend, but he's a good guy."

Munro sounded cautious when I introduced myself. "I play by the rules," he began. "I'm bound by patient confidentiality."

I figured I'd snagged a dud. Then he added in a cynical whisper, "But there isn't much I can do if you somehow manage to sneak a peek at my cards when I'm not looking!"

I relaxed. Maybe, just maybe, something would come of this.

Munro worked at the child and adolescent unit of Toronto's Lakeshore Psychiatric Hospital. His boss, Milton Marcilio, was a psychiatrist with a reputation for not suffering fools gladly — an attitude that repeatedly got him into trouble with the anal-retentive bunch who ran the nest. Dr. Marcilio was anathema to mental health bureaucrats. He challenged every move, every diagnosis and every inane label attached to a kid's file. He preferred grating to being ingratiating. He called it the way he saw it.

The children in Dr. Marcilio's care were his first concern. Everything else came a distant second. This included the mindless memos, endless forms, sophomoric studies and self-serving reports that emanated from the cubbyholes at the Ontario Ministry of Health. Dr. Marcilio had made a lot of enemies. He was my kind of guy.

Munro suggested I give his boss a call. The psychiatrist was upset about how a particular case was handled by the hospital, Munro confided. He might talk to me about it.

Fortunately, I caught the good psychiatrist in a miserable state of mind. He was primed and set to blow. With a little prodding, Dr. Marcilio confided that he had received a phone call from Family Court judge James Fuller on December 18 asking him to assess a fourteen-year-old Portuguese-speaking boy. However, the patient never showed up. Thirty days later, the kid was found wandering in a drug-induced haze in the hospital's geriatric wing.

Dr. Marcilio was fit to be tied. This was not a simple case of bureaucratic bungling, he learned. The lad's side trip had been engineered by an officious hospital director who wanted to show the doctor he held the power.

Dr. Marcilio suggested I call Judge Fuller to get details on the story.

The mere mention of the case sent Judge Fuller into a rage. "I was shocked when I heard what had happened to the boy," he said. "The boy is a tiny lad. He looks ten years old rather than fourteen. And no one found it strange that he was in an adult ward for thirty days when there's an adolescent unit on the hospital grounds! What upsets me even more is that he did not get the assessment I intended."

He had telephoned the adolescent unit at Lakeshore, Judge Fuller explained, to have the boy admitted for a thirty-day period. "I knew Dr. Marcilio spoke Portuguese and understood the cultural background of Portuguese-Canadian families," he explained. "That's the reason I wanted the boy placed there. But I was informed that the policy of the unit was that no child would be admitted to the ward before an assessment. I was a little annoyed with this policy, but the unit director, Dr. Marcilio, told me he would be happy to assess the boy the next day."

The judge said he felt the boy needed immediate temporary removal from his family, so he called the medical director at Lakeshore to have the boy committed to an adult ward "for no more than a day" while he was waiting for his assessment by Dr. Marcilio. However, the medical director was not available, so the judge was rerouted to the hospital administrator, a man named Wayne McKerrow.

"We discussed the case at some length, and Mr. McKerrow said he would admit the boy," the judge said. "There was absolutely no question in my mind that the boy would be assessed by Dr. Marcilio the following day and would be placed in the adolescent ward afterward."

But when he received the psychiatric assessment report from Lakeshore a month later, Judge Fuller smelled a rat. The report recommended that the boy be removed from his home for up to one year. This was not what the judge had expected.

"It was obvious that Dr. Marcilio did not assess the boy, because whoever did did not understand the boy's problem. As I understood it, his problem was basically cultural. And it was obvious from the assessment that there was a communication gap," the judge concluded.

The following morning, I called McKerrow. He was curt and wondered aloud whether he should even be talking to me about the case. He cited regulations on patient confidentiality.

"I'm not going to identify the kid," I said. "But I can tell you, Judge Fuller is really upset about this. He discussed the case with me and told me about what happened at Lakeshore."

This last comment loosened McKerrow's tongue. "I'm aware he's upset about the boy being on the adult ward for the month," he said. "But that sometimes happens in unusual circumstances."

I went for the jugular. "Was this an unusual circumstance?"

McKerrow hesitated. "No. It wasn't an unusual circumstance."

"Then how did the boy get dumped into the geriatric unit for a month?" I asked harshly.

McKerrow was too smart to get drawn into a debate in the pages of the *Globe and Mail*. "I have no comment on the case," he said curtly. "I won't go near it. You're looking at the tip of a very big iceberg."

On my second call to Dr. Marcilio, the psychiatrist expressed concern that by talking to me, he would be arming his detractors at the Ontario Ministry of Health with just cause to fire him. So he said, "I'll make my staff available. I'm sure they will speak to you."

An hour later, Peter Zitney, an affable child care worker in the unit, phoned. He recalled that on the afternoon the boy was to be admitted to Lakeshore, he received a call from the hospital administrator.

"Mr. McKerrow told me to tell Dr. Marcilio that he had made other arrangements for the boy and not to worry about it," Zitney said. "I thought it rather peculiar since the judge insisted in his call to us that morning that the boy be assessed by Dr. Marcilio because he speaks Portuguese and has an understanding of the culture." However, Zitney passed on McKerrow's message to Dr. Marcilio as requested, and the psychiatrist accepted it without question or suspicion.

Then Munro called me. A month after the boy had been admitted, Munro said, he received an inquiry from a colleague in another ward at the hospital.

"She asked if I knew of a placement home for a fourteen-year-old Portuguese boy. I asked her why, and she told me about the boy on her ward. I said I'd call back and went to discuss the matter with Dr. Marcilio. He was upset to learn the boy had ended up on the adult ward. We had him sent off to us immediately."

Margaret Craw, a gravel-voiced psychologist attached to Dr. Marcilio's unit, remembered the boy's arrival for the reassessment. "He was zonked out on drugs and scared out of his mind."

I closed my eyes and thought about this poor kid spaced out on powerful tranquillizers, floating around a geriatric ward. What a nightmare—and it went on for thirty torturous days! I wondered what kind of cruel game was being played out at the hospital and why this boy had become an expendable pawn.

Dr. Marcilio's team did the reassessment that same day and discharged the boy. He was sent home to his parents with a recommendation for outpatient therapy for him and counselling for his family.

I had my front-page story. My pulse was racing as I pounded out the copy on an uncooperative manual typewriter. I had two hours until deadline.

Barton passed by my desk. "Press release?"

"No. It's my own work from my own digging and it will be on the front page tomorrow!"

I handed him a carbon copy of the first page. He read it intently and headed for Burt's office. A few minutes later, the two editors were standing by my desk reading over my shoulder as I hammered away on the second page.

"Great stuff," Barton said, grinning.

"Good work, mate. Let's just hope it's true," Burt added.

I turned sharply and gave him a cold, challenging stare.

"Just joking, mate. Just joking."

Barton and Burt laughed.

The next day, the Ontario Legislature exploded. Aghast politicians waved the *Globe and Mail*, demanding answers. In response, Premier William Davis's Conservative government ordered a full-scale inquiry into Lakeshore Psychiatric Hospital. Shades of my first big story at the *Montreal Star*.

Clark Davey summoned me to his office. Without looking up from a letter he was reading, he curtly informed me that I had barely passed my probation. That was it. No congratulations, no kudos for a job well done. I left the building totally deflated.

★ ★ ★

In September, I got a call from Don Munro. He sounded agitated. "You should call Thistletown," he began.

"What's Thistletown?" I interjected.

"The Ontario Ministry of Health's crown jewel in the treatment of disturbed children," he said, his voice laced with sarcasm. "It's in the north end of Toronto."

"And why should I call them?" I asked.

"To ask for Norma Dean," Munro said.

"Who's Norma Dean?"

"A fourteen-year-old girl Thistletown somehow managed to dump off on a training school. She hanged herself in her closet two months ago."

I was stunned. Had I heard him correctly? "I haven't heard any-thing about a suicide in a training school," I said.

"That's because it's a well-guarded secret at the Ministry of Corrections and the Ministry of Health. They don't want any word of this to get out because, from what I've been told, what happened to that girl is a scandal."

"What do you mean, scandal?" I was pacing around my desk, the phone clenched in my fist.

"I was told she was admitted to Thistletown as a voluntary patient. She wasn't ordered there by the court or put there by the Children's Aid Society. When she went in as a patient, she had no juvenile record. Then somehow, the girl becomes a juvenile delinquent and ends up in Kawar-tha Lakes Training School in Lindsay, Ontario."

"How did you hear about the suicide?"

"Dr. Marcilio. He heard about it from a few of his colleagues in the field."

My phone call to the psychiatrist's office was returned within a matter of minutes. "How can I help you?" Dr. Marcilio asked.

"I was talking to Don Munro," I began. "He told me a disturbing story about a girl named Norma Dean."

"Yes. It's a very sad and tragic story. I knew the girl. She was a patient of Dr. Flora Danziger at the York Child Guidance Clinic. I am a consultant to the clinic."

"What can you tell me about her?"

Dr. Marcilio didn't want to discuss the matter over the phone. He suggested we meet at a diner off the grounds of the Lakeshore hospital. The place was virtually empty when I arrived. A lone figure sat in a booth at the back of the greasy spoon.

Dr. Marcilio looked every bit the shrink. He had intense eyes that bore right through me and long, wavy, salt-and-pepper hair that gave him a distinguished look. He was wearing a stylish, double-breasted suit and expensive Italian loafers. There was a hint of Latin arrogance to the man.

We shook hands firmly and ordered coffees. While we waited for the waitress to return, the doctor sat back and observed me.

"I don't want you to use my name in this," Dr. Marcilio began.

"I won't."

Another interminable pause as the psychiatrist studied my face. He cleared his throat.

"I saw Norma about three years ago," he started. "She had been in group therapy following the separation of her parents."

"What was she like?" I asked.

"She was a very anxious girl. She feared separation from her mother. She had a very strong, symbiotic relationship with her mother. And from what I recall, she responded well to the therapy and went back to school," Dr. Marcilio replied.

"Then what happened?"

"I understand that a year later, Norma Dean's father remarried and the girl's problems reappeared. She was referred by a school guidance counsellor to Thistletown. Dr. Danziger's clinic was not contacted by the school board."

"So she ended up in Thistletown," I said.

"Yes. But I never saw any need for hospitalization. There was no evidence that she was disturbed. She was a normal child who needed to work through her phobic symptoms. She had responded very well to Dr. Danziger and she should have been sent back to the Child Guidance Clinic."

"Do you know anything about why the girl was sent to training school?" I asked.

"I'm not clear on that. But I do know that Norma Dean should never have been put in training school."

"Do you think Dr. Danziger would speak to me about it?" I asked.

"She might. She is very upset about Norma's death."

Flora Danziger had a reputation as an exceptionally skilled child psychologist. She agreed to see me at her clinic.

I was mesmerized by her appearance. To call her striking would be an understatement: she had milk-white skin and long, flowing auburn hair. Her voice was soft and angelic.

At the mention of Norma's name, Dr. Danziger's face filled with sadness. She nodded. Yes, she remembered the girl vividly and with sincere affection.

"I was shattered by the news. I couldn't believe it," she said.

"What was she like?"

"Norma was a lovely child. She was tall for her age and thin. She had short blonde hair and freckles. She loved sports, stuffed animals and she was always anxious to please. But she was a desperately unhappy girl. She loved her mother deeply and she was always worried about her, especially her smoking. She also got quite sad when her behaviour was the cause of unhappiness at home.

"The thing I remember most about Norma was she had a core of decency and caring for others," she continued. "There was this one incident where she showed great courage and a strong sense of conscience. She was out with four girls. One of them cooked up a story accusing a truck driver of exposing himself to them. He was arrested and charged. Norma was deeply troubled by what had happened. She told me about it. She was upset that an innocent man had been falsely accused and decided to blow the whistle. She knew she would lose her popularity in the group but she felt she had no choice."

"She sounds like a wonderful person," I said.

"She was. But Norma was also capable of very real rages, especially when she was provoked or put down, and that's what got her into trouble."

"And into a training school," I noted.

"I was shocked that Norma was placed in training school. She didn't belong there. She was not the sort of child who should have been in detention or training school. She should have been dealt with sympathetically."

"What was at the root of her problems?" I asked.

"I don't want to discuss the details. I can't."

"Can you tell me if Thistletown consulted you about Norma Dean's case when she was admitted into their centre?"

"No. Had we been, I feel we could have helped. The fact that there were people who knew her well and were not consulted disturbs me greatly."

Dr. Danziger added sharply: "The health ministry is always sending us on seminars to Thistletown so we can learn how to gather information from other treatment facilities on clients. They show off Thistletown as a model we can all learn from."

My next call was to the director of Thistletown. Dr. Shamsie came on the line, his voice chipper. "How can I help you?" he asked.

I didn't waste any time. "You had a patient there. Norma Dean. I'm told she ended up in training school, where she committed suicide. Could you explain to me how a patient of Thistletown suddenly ends up dead in a juvenile jail?"

I figured the shrink would roll out the standard patient-confidentiality carpet and hang up. Instead, he floored me with his candor.

Without hesitation, Dr. Shamsie launched into an explanation. Norma Dean was first referred to Thistletown in February, 1976, he said. But after several months of intensive treatment, things just weren't working out. "What she needed was a closed setting, which we could not provide."

Closed setting! Now *there* was a euphemism I detested. It meant, plain and simple, a lockup, a jail. Treatment professionals hated to refer to things as they really were.

"So you got her locked up in a training school," I said.

"There is more to this case. She was constantly running away, which made it difficult for us to make progress with her. Although she did make some progress. However, we came to the conclusion that a closed setting was the only setting for Norma. But the only closed setting in Metro Toronto is Corrections. There are no closed settings to hold a kid who doesn't want to stay put in the Ministry of Health."

"What was her problem?"

The psychiatrist's view of Norma was vastly different from Dr. Danziger's. He described the girl as aggressive and destructive. "Norma's case was quite intriguing," Dr. Shamsie continued. "Our diagnosis was behaviour disorder."

What a meaningless label, I thought.

"We didn't get any idea that she was disposed to suicide. There was an occasional mention of her saying, 'I will kill myself,' but this is common among girls."

I could feel my blood starting to boil. Is this guy listening to himself? Norma *did* kill herself!

"Was Norma convicted of a criminal charge under the Juvenile Delinquency Act to get put in training school?" I asked.

"Yes, that is correct. We felt it was time to confront her with reality, show her that if she was going to break things, she would have to go to court and face a judge. Our plan was to expose her to the fact that there was a court and a law for destructive behaviour. We made the recommendation to Juvenile Court that she required more control than we could give her."

I was at a loss for words. Here was this so-called state-of-the-art treatment centre giving up on a difficult teenager.

"Your centre is trumpeted by the health ministry as 'the jewel in the crown' of children's mental health care," I noted. "If you won't keep her, then what other treatment centre will take her?"

"We could no longer help her here," the psychiatrist replied lamely.

"Did your staff try to obtain the files on Norma Dean from the York Child Guidance Clinic?" I asked.

"We usually get information from other places. But I don't know whether records or information was sought from York. However, it was mentioned on her file here that she had been treated there."

"I was told Thistletown never asked for those files. I was told that if your staff had gotten those files, they might have gained invaluable insight into Norma that probably would have helped in the kind of treatment approach they had decided on."

"I would have to check into that." With that, Dr. Shamsie drew the interview to an abrupt halt.

My next call was to Donald Kerr, head of information services for the Ontario Ministry of Corrections. He was about as much help as a transistor radio with a dead battery.

"I'm not at liberty to release any information until the coroner's inquest has been held," he said officiously.

"And when will that be?" I asked.

"I can't release that information because a date hasn't been set."
I suddenly realized I didn't have the exact date that Norma Dean died. "Then could you tell me when the suicide occurred?"

"I can't release that information."

"Boy, I gotta tell you, you're one fountain of information," I said derisively.

"It's not that we are trying to cover up anything, but we'd rather not see an inquest held in the newspaper."

"The way you're handling this, that's exactly what you're going to see."

A half hour later, I was skulking around the halls of the Ontario Legislature at Queen's Park looking for John Smith, the Honourable Minister of Corrections. I caught a glimpse of him scurrying out of the premier's second-floor corner office. But there were too many reporters lurking about. I raced across the third floor and intercepted him in a stairwell.

Smith was a little man with the appearance of a Bible thumper.

"I'm very glad to meet you, Victor. How may I help you?" Smith asked.

I instantly get my back up when politicians call me Victor, as if I was some long-lost high school buddy.

"I've been told that a girl by the name of Norma Lee Dean hanged herself in one of your training schools."

Smith was startled. The abruptness of my opening statement caught him completely off guard. Obviously, his PR flak hadn't warned him I was coming.

"Yes," he whispered with the voice of a bereaved parent. "It broke my heart when I learned of the girl's death." The expression on his face dissolved into pain and sadness.

"Could you tell me why she was sent to training school?"

"I don't know the details," the minister said. "But I'm told she had suicidal tendencies."

"Could you tell me when the inquest will be held?"

"I don't know. But I'm told that this is the first suicide in one of our training schools in twenty-two years."

I bit the inside of my cheek and mentally counted to ten in an effort to control my impulse to tell him what I really thought about him. "You say her death broke your heart. Yet you haven't even bothered to find out anything about the girl. Who was she? Why was she in one of your training schools?"

Sweat formed on Smith's upper lip. He glared at me and offered no comeback. A moment later he was steaming down the hallway.

My phone was ringing when I got back to the *Globe*. It was Don Munro with the information I needed. "Norma Dean died on August 20. She was found dead in the closet in her room. She tied a macramé cord around her neck."

Barton and Burt hovered near my desk as I typed out the story. My mind was focused on my notebook and on the clock. Barton yanked each page out of the typewriter after I'd completed three paragraphs and passed it on to Jerry Kinoshita on the copy rim. Kinoshita was probably the best copy editor in the place. Not only could he spot the most minute grammatical error, he could also help a blocked reporter with a nifty turn of phrase.

The story was slotted for the banner on the front page. I made the deadline with a half hour to spare and decided to head home. I was halfway out the door when the switchboard operator paged me. "You've got an urgent call," she said.

The caller identified himself as Family Court judge F. Stewart Fisher. He sounded troubled.

"I've been informed that you're doing a story on the death of Norma Dean," the judge said.

"Yes. It'll be in tomorrow's paper," I said, wondering if he was going to order an injunction and tell me the *Globe* couldn't print the story.

There was a long pause. It sounded as if he was trying to maintain his composure. "I sent Norma to training school," he said finally.

Whoa! I thought. This is too much.

"Why?" I asked.

Judge Fisher said he couldn't discuss the case. But he added that he was anxious to do so at the inquest. "It is imperative that a transcript of the case be obtained by the people who run the inquest. I'll do my best to see that they get it."

I got the message loud and clear. I had to get my hands on that transcript.

"No one person or one centre is responsible for Norma's death," the judge added. "It's a lack of resources. If someone is to be held accountable, we can say there was negligence on the part of the community. We don't have the facilities to handle children like her."

Then Judge Fisher stirred the murky waters further. "What appeared to be in the best interest of the child was quite different from what was done."

"What do you mean by that?" I asked.

"That's why it's important the inquest get a transcript of the case," he repeated.

After he hung up, I thought, Guilt is a mighty force!

With minutes to deadline, I raced back to my desk and hammered out a sidebar on Judge Fisher's pronouncements from the bench. That night, I kept wondering what he meant by *the best interest of the child was quite different from what was done*. I wasn't going to wait for some inquest to solve the riddle. I knew in my gut that Norma Dean's suicide had little to do with Kawartha Lakes Training School and everything to do with that sparkling gem called Thistletown.

The next morning, Barton sauntered over to my desk. His face was beaming with pride. "Great story!"

"I'm far from finished with it," I snapped. I thought back to the *Montreal Star* and Foley's decision to take me off the story I had uncovered about the three teenaged boys who hanged themselves at the Centre Berthelet in Montreal. He robbed me of the opportunity to chase down the real story behind those deaths. Foley and the paper were satisfied that the Quebec government had launched a full-scale inquiry. The outcome was exactly what I had expected. The government came down with a series of meaningless recommendations such as better communication and training, to avoid a similar tragedy in the future. But the most important questions were never posed and never dealt with. I felt it was vital to find out why those boys were behind bars in a maximum-security juvenile detention centre when they hadn't committed any crimes. In the end, the people — the treatment and child care agencies — who had put them there were never held accountable.

"I'm not letting go of this story," I said firmly.

"I don't expect you to. I want you to go after the training school and find out what went wrong," Barton said. "Get the place shut down!"

"It's not the training school," I countered. "This thing started way before Norma got to training school. It started at Thistletown. I got a feeling the child care professionals over there are circling the wagons."

"Then burn them," Barton said.

"Victor Malarek. Phone call," the switchboard operator announced over the P.A. system.

Another distraught voice. This time a woman.

"How could you? How could you do this to my little girl? Why couldn't you let her rest in peace?"

It was Norma Dean's mother.

"I'm really sorry about what happened to your daughter," I said.

"No, you're not. All this means to you is a story on the front page of your newspaper. I hope you're happy, because you broke my heart."

I felt like pond scum.

"I'm sorry about that. But you've got to understand that there is something very, very wrong here, and I'm trying to get to the root of it. I've got a feeling the circumstances around your daughter's suicide are being covered up because a lot is at stake here. I think it's important we talk about it."

"I have enough guilt over her death. I have to live with it every day of my life. I loved Norma! I lived for her ... and now she's gone." Mrs. Dean's voice broke. "I have to ask myself constantly why I didn't fight harder to keep them from sending Norma to training school. Should I have fought harder?"

"Given the way the system operates, you probably fought as hard as you could," I said. "You shouldn't blame yourself on that score."

She was weeping.

"Tell me about Norma," I said.

"No. I don't want this in the newspaper," she pleaded.

"It's important. I really believe her death was needless, and getting to the bottom of what really happened to her is important."

Mrs. Dean was quiet. Several minutes passed. I thought she was going to hang up. Then she broke the silence.

"I knew my little girl. She was not one for getting into trouble. It's just that at times things got so hectic at home that I couldn't cope with her. Norma's troubles began when my husband and I separated," Mrs. Dean explained. "But Norma always knew I loved her!"

"From what I can tell, a lot of child care professionals have been involved in Norma's life," I said.

"And they all knew what was best for Norma, and it didn't matter what I said because as far as they were concerned I didn't know what I was talking about! They were the experts in child care. Surely to God in the six years all these people who said they knew what was best for Norma, someone could have helped her." Mrs. Dean was weeping again.

"What happened when your daughter went to Thistletown?" I asked.

"Norma's trouble with the law started there. She was easily influenced by the others because she wanted so much to belong. The staff got her charged with breaking into her unit at Thistletown and she was sent to a detention centre. That was the middle of July. She got mixed up with all kinds of things she didn't need there ... drugs, delinquents ..."

While Norma was in detention, Mrs. Dean said, child care professionals at Thistletown promised to take her daughter back. They explained her incarceration was a temporary thing that had to do with understanding the consequences of her actions.

"Then they refused to take her back. They said they didn't have the controls to deal with her. But while she was at Thistletown, they did nothing for her except beat into her head how much they 'cared' for her. And then they threw her out!" Mrs. Dean's voice resonated with anger. "Norma was so confused when they said she couldn't come back. She said, 'Mom, nobody really cares about me at that place. They say they do but I know nobody cares.' She was really hurt by them."

"And your daughter, who never had a juvenile record until she was charged by Thistletown, gets sent to training school for this offense?" I asked.

"I was told by a staff member that Thistletown's recommendation was that Norma be sent to training school. I said it would finish her. But they wouldn't listen to me — again. I knew she didn't belong there.

I told the judge that. And I told her probation officer and her counsellors at Thistletown. But nobody would listen to what I had to say. You have to believe me. I fought hard. I was down on my knees pleading with Judge Fisher not to send her to training school." Mrs. Dean sobbed.

I waited a moment and asked in a gentle voice: "Was your daughter suicidal?"

Mrs. Dean regained her composure. "Yes. It was in her files at Thistletown. But they were never sent along to the training school. So they didn't know this, and when she did threaten to do something, they figured maybe it was an attention-getting thing."

"Did you visit your daughter at the training school?"

"Every weekend. I was devoted to her. Then the weekend before her death, they said I could only visit her once a month. They said Norma was unkind to me, but I said I don't mind. I think this is what did it to her, finally. She was really hurt by that. I could see she was hurting inside. She said, 'Mom, I really can't live without your visits. You're all I have.' I felt so weak. There was nothing I could do."

It was at that last visit that Norma scratched her mother's name into her arm with a safety pin. And it was the last time Shirley Dean saw her daughter alive.

The *Globe* story had triggered an emotionally charged debate during Question Period at the Ontario Legislature. In a subdued voice, Stephen Lewis, the eloquent leader of the Ontario New Democrats, asked John Smith about the suicide.

"Does the Honourable Minister of Corrections want to make, or does he feel he might make, a statement on the very sad story that appears in the *Globe and Mail* this morning about the suicide of the young, fourteen-year-old girl in a training school? Can he in the process of the reply talk about the bitter irony which had that young girl presumably referred to the training school by a government ministry institution?" Lewis asked.

Smith, sombre and studied, rose. "It is a most unfortunate and tragic incident and one such incident is too many. However, it might be pointed out that this was the first suicide of a child at a training school in the past twenty-two years."

The legislature dissolved into a dance of indignation, with members popping up in the hopes that someone in the press gallery would jot down their outrage and insert them into the next day's news offering.

Norma Dean's death gave them reason to pontificate about the short-comings of Ontario's child welfare system.

On this particular day, Norma Dean's suicide was the rallying cry. Tomorrow, it might be an oil spill or a botched government program, I thought cynically, as I observed the antics on the floor from my perch in the press gallery.

Dr. Stuart Smith, a psychiatrist and leader of the Ontario Liberals, directed his question at Margaret Birch, the prim Provincial Secretary for Social Development. Her job was to oversee the coordination of services between various ministries such as Health, Social Services and Corrections.

"Can she tell us...when the inquest was ordered into the tragic suicide? Was it ordered in August when the matter occurred or today, when the matter became public knowledge?" Dr. Smith asked.

Looking extremely agitated, Mrs. Birch replied: "As to the date of the inquest, I have no knowledge." And then, her voice quivering with emotion, she lowered the political boom. "I had no knowledge of the suicide that took place on August 20 until this morning."

The debate suddenly and sharply changed focus. The suicide now took a backseat to political skulduggery.

Up popped Liberal Robert Nixon. "I wonder, is the minister concerned, as I am, that she, who has not only the wide policy responsibility but obviously a great personal interest in this important matter, was not informed of the suicide until she saw it in the paper today? When it occurred two months ago?"

Mrs. Birch rose slowly and replied to a hushed house: "I feel betrayed."

Premier William Davis was visibly angered by the minister's choice of words. He turned and glared icily at her. The Tory leader demanded Cabinet solidarity in public from all his ministers.

Stephen Lewis pounced. "By whom was the minister betrayed?"

"By the officials and by the interministerial committee that I have reporting directly to me," she said.

"By the minister's colleague, who heard about it on the day it occurred?" Mr. Lewis asked.

"Yes," Mrs. Birch replied.

A steely look swept over the premier's face.

John Smith was shaken by the exchange. He could see his political future fizzling.

The legislature moved on to other business. But moments before Question Period adjourned, a page handed the corrections minister an envelope with a red *urgent* tag stapled to it. Smith scanned it quickly and motioned to the Speaker of the House for permission to rise.

"Mr. Speaker, in view of the seriousness of the incident that has been discussed here this morning, I feel it is incumbent upon me to report to the House the absolutely exact nature, as I now have it, of the circumstances surrounding this girl being admitted to the training school." It was Smith's moment to redeem himself.

An expectant hush fell over the cavernous room.

"She was at Thistletown until she appeared in Family Court on May 18 on a charge of break and enter and theft. On May 18, she was placed on probation and the case adjourned until September 14 on condition that her probation would be terminated if her behaviour was satisfactory. Unfortunately, her behaviour continued to deteriorate and she appeared in court six times between May 18 and July 7. On July 7, she was charged and appeared in court before a judge on a common assault charge, at which time she was committed to training school."

I shook my head in disgust. Here was a guy who a day earlier blubbered about how the news of Norma Dean's suicide broke his heart. Yet in the two months since her death, it was obvious he had never once bothered to look into it. Now the bumbling politician was scrambling with a hastily gathered bunch of so-called facts designed to cast Norma Dean as the victim of her own misfortune.

Late that afternoon, the Ontario coroner's office announced that an inquest into the death of Norma Dean would be held on November 24 in Lindsay, Ontario. The Kawartha Lakes Training School was on the outskirts of the town.

Early on Monday morning, the first of November, I buttonholed Frank Miller, minister of health, outside his office. Thistletown fell under his jurisdiction. The affable minister had managed to escape a barrage of questions and acrimony in the legislature on the previous Friday because he was away. I wanted to find out what he knew and if he'd tell me anything.

Miller was a rare breed of politician. When asked a question, he usually gave a straight and honest answer. He appeared troubled over Thistletown's handling of Norma Dean, particularly the centre's decision to lay criminal charges against her.

"I just find it difficult to understand why child care professionals at a centre treating disturbed children would lay criminal charges against a patient," he said.

"Did you ask Thistletown for an explanation?" I asked.

"I asked a couple of questions on that but I wasn't satisfied with the answers I got," he said.

I kept pushing. "So you got a report from Thistletown."

"Yes, I did and it left me stuck for a rationale as to what they had the girl charged with. I can assure you that this will be explained in detail. Whether they made the right decision in sending the girl to training school." Miller mulled that last comment over in his mind. "Obviously they didn't because the young girl killed herself," he added.

The next day, I was summoned to the office of Richard J. Doyle, the editor of the *Globe and Mail*. Doyle was the ultimate power in the newsroom, the man who presided over the editorial board. In my seven months at the paper, he had never spoken to me. Occasionally, I'd see him standing at one end of the newsroom, arms folded, observing his domain. A thin, gray-haired man with reading glasses dangling from a string around his neck, Doyle rarely cracked a smile.

As I walked into his office, my mouth was dry. I didn't sit down. Doyle didn't tell me I could. I stood in front of his antique oak desk and waited until he finished proofreading an editorial.

When Doyle finally looked up over his bifocals, I felt I was under a microscope. He cleared his throat. I swallowed hard.

"I am told that you're pretty upset about the death of Norma Dean."

"I'm upset," I said barely above a whisper. I wondered what he was driving at. Did someone lodge a complaint against me? Was he going to take me off the story?

"What upsets you about it?"

"The fact that she didn't belong in that training school. That's what upsets me." I could feel the blood rush to my face. "She was dumped there by the very people who were supposed to be treating her. She needed care and understanding, not punishment."

"And what of the training school?"

"The training school? The training school is simply the end of the line. The dumping ground. They *had* to take the girl. The real story here is how she ended up there! When she went into care, she had never been in trouble with the law. She had no juvenile record. She was a patient in a treatment centre for kids. Then out of the blue, these child care professionals at Thistletown suddenly pin on badges and become cops, and she becomes this little criminal monster. *I* know what's going on here."

"And what is going on here?" Doyle asked.

"They've circled the wagons. These so-called child care professionals at Thistletown have screwed up big time, but they're never going to admit it. They're never going to admit they're wrong, that they made a mistake. No way! They're going to blame the victim. You just watch. Norma Dean will be depicted as this vicious, despicable little monster. By the time they're through with her, everyone will be saying, 'Thank God she's dead.' It's already happening."

Arms folded, Doyle stared directly into my eyes. "Why the interest? It's one death."

"Yeah, it's only one death. What did that twerp corrections minister say? 'The first suicide in twenty-two years in an Ontario training school.' Norma Dean's death says everything about what's inherently wrong with the child welfare system. It's completely screwed up. You've got people making decisions about children's lives with absolutely no accountability. They play God, and thousands of kids are being hurt, and no one challenges these people. No one says, 'Hey, why did you dump the kid into that place? Why didn't you follow up on the case? What happened to the treatment you promised?' It's all done 'in the best interests of the child' and no one questions it. It just keeps on going and then one day, a kid decides enough is enough and commits suicide. I know what really happened here. *I* know why Norma Dean killed herself! They dumped her and made her feel like garbage, like she didn't matter, like..."

I was out of breath. I stopped talking and met the editor's stare. Doyle seemed taken aback. I figured he wasn't accustomed to passion and anger in the newsroom. He took a deep breath.

"I'm sure we'll be talking again about this," he said. With that, I was dismissed.

On Wednesday, November 3, the headline on the *Globe*'s lead editorial read: Secrecy, disorder, inertia. "Norma Dean's death raises questions — and these demand answers," it began.

The editorial listed a dozen questions and pointed out: "Many of them have been raised in recent debate in the Ontario Legislature, and four Government Ministers fumbled, shrugged, shook their heads. They do not have the answers; at best, they have only excuses."

The editorial concluded: "One child's death, it is true, is not an indictment of the entire system. That system — bulky, confused, unresponsive, secretive and stagnant — is its own indictment."

I had a powerful ally in my corner.

The next afternoon, with her 1950s beehive hairdo sprayed firmly in place, Margaret Birch rose "with reluctance" to deliver a chronology of Norma's trip through the child welfare jungle. The chamber, noted for its animal-house antics during Question Period, was attentive, respectful and silent.

"According to the records, Norma's behavioural problems first appeared in grade two," Birch read. "In the fourth grade, in 1972, she was referred by the school mental health services to a child guidance clinic. As a result of problems at home and at school, Norma was referred in 1973 to Dellcrest School for day classes. She was discharged in June of 1974 and returned to the regular school system. However, her behaviour subsequently deteriorated, and a referral was made to Thistletown Regional Centre, where she was admitted on February 10, 1976." Birch reached for a glass of water.

Then she went on. "Facts, culled from reports and records, have been stripped to provide a concise chronological summary of the events preceding Norma's death."

Right on, I thought. I tried to concentrate while she delivered an unenlightening list of dates and movements within the system by the hapless Norma Dean. For even the most attentive listener, it was impossible to read between the lines about what really was going on in Norma's unhappy life.

"On July 22, 1976, a case conference was held, attended by the Oakville multidisciplinary team and three representatives from Thistletown," Birch said. "It was decided that Norma should be placed in the prime worker program at Kawartha Lakes [Training] School, an institution stressing limited security and a normal lifestyle. The goal was to transfer Norma into a long-term rural placement for treatment as soon as possible."

Norma was interviewed by the chaplain and a social worker at the training school on at least a half dozen occasions, Birch said. "Norma was transferred to Kawartha Lakes School on July 29, 1976. At the time of transfer, a senior member of the Oakville staff discussed the case by telephone with a senior member of the Kawartha Lakes School. The clinical notes from Thistletown were forwarded to Kawartha Lakes but did not arrive until five days following Norma's death.

"Norma Dean was found dead in the closet of her room by two staff members on August 20, 1976."

Outside the Legislature, a hungry pack of reporters surrounded Birch. I led off, asking her whether Norma's treatment records indicated that she was suicidal.

"Yes, they did."

"Then why the delay in getting these records to the training school?" I asked.

Birch leered at me. She recognized me as the messenger of her misfortune and it was obvious she didn't like my presence in the legislature or my asking her questions outside the august chamber. "Maybe the mails are not as efficient as they might be these days," she said acidly.

"Do you know when the records were mailed?" I continued.

"No. I don't. But I do know there was oral communication between Oakville and Thistletown staff at the assessment conference on July 22 and by telephone between a senior member of the Oakville staff and a senior member of the Kawartha Lakes staff at the time of the transfer," Birch said.

I kept pressing. "Are you aware of what transpired in that phone call or if it was discussed that Norma was suicidal?"

"No, I don't know." She stormed off down the corridor with her aides bustling behind her.

The reporter pack moved on to their next prey: Stephen Lewis, for political reaction. He began by rapping Thistletown for laying criminal charges against Norma.

"I find it hard to believe in my heart that that was the right decision. To take a child and charge her with an offense she committed within the grounds of the institution where she was being treated is beyond me," Lewis said. "Whatever she did ... In my limited knowledge in working with disturbed children and treatment centres, I can recognize the symptoms. It was either a cry for help or it means that the institution has failed in its relationship with the child."

Lewis, the grand master of media impact, paused for maximum effect. "I worry about Thistletown — this very expensive treatment centre — laying charges against a child. I cannot bring myself to believe that bringing charges against a child is treatment."

Lewis was not telling all. I could sense he was holding something back. But he was shackled by his word. He had accepted the government's confidential report on Norma Dean on the proviso that it was for his eyes only. Birch had rooked him into the secrecy. Now he was co-opted and part of the conspiracy. He looked uncomfortable.

After the scrum, I walked with him toward his office, pushing him for more information.

"There's something very rotten in this, isn't there?" I asked.

Lewis nodded. "It will all come out."

"Yeah, sure. Just like today. The information is being vetted and sanitized, and you know it."

"I can't talk about it right now," Lewis said.

"You sort of went after Birch on Judge Fisher's decision in Norma's case, and Birch seemed to get a little unravelled. What was that all about?" I asked.

"You may find out tomorrow," Lewis replied.

The NDP leader was first on his feet for the Friday morning session of Question Period. He immediately went after Birch, telling her that he was confused by some of the information he had been given on the Norma Dean case. He ruefully pointed out that he had taken it upon himself to call Judge Fisher.

"I asked about the disposition which perplexed me yesterday. In the last part of the transcript of July 7...the following words appear from Judge Fisher: 'I would think probably in my view that Norma should not go to a training school. I think that would be a bad mistake. I am not an expert in this area, but my feeling is that it would not be my rec-ommendation that she should go to a training school at all.'"

The chamber was stone silent. Birch was glaring at Lewis, who con-tinued in a defiant tone.

"Can the minister explain to me why that terribly pertinent fact, involved in all the events preceding Norma's death, was not shared with the House yesterday?" Lewis demanded.

Birch lost her composure. "I think there are many events that have not been explicitly explained. That will all be dealt with at a public inquest, where people will be subpoenaed and asked to testify under oath. I feel very strongly about it and I am most disappointed by the Leader of the Opposition. I gave him information which he agreed to keep confidential. At this point, I'm going to advise the Opposition and everyone else that I am not going to answer any more questions that specifically deal with this case."

From that moment on, the doors to the Dean case were sealed. Any further comment would be reserved for the inquest.

The coroner's inquest was held in a government building in the sleepy, rural town of Lindsay, Ontario. The air in the makeshift courtroom was thick with anticipation as Dr. John MacKay, the regional coroner, swore in the jury of three women and two men. The room was packed with grim-faced psychiatrists, psychologists, social workers and child care workers. All of them, at one time or another, had been involved in Norma's short life. I found it bitterly ironic. There sat all the king's horses and all the king's men, and not one of them had helped Norma Dean when she needed it most. And now...

When Shirley Dean entered, the professionals drew a collective breath. No one spoke to her except Flora Danziger, who quietly offered her condolences. Mrs. Dean took her seat in the first row. She was tall and gaunt. Her thin face was shrouded by sorrow. I walked over and introduced myself. The move triggered a chorus of whispers and subtle finger pointing by a contingent of child care workers from Thistletown.

"I wanted to tell you personally how sorry I am about what happened to Norma," I said. "I just hope this inquest will do some good."

Mrs. Dean's hands were trembling. She was frightened. "I don't know. There's been so many rotten lies told about my daughter. I can't believe these people could say such things when they know it's not true."

"Well, maybe this inquest will get to the bottom of things and Norma's death will mean something."

"And if it doesn't?" she asked, her eyes filling with tears.

"If it doesn't, then I promise you I'll get to the bottom of it. This inquest better deal with the real issues, because I'm not going to let it go!"

As I headed to the table reserved for the press, a stout, matronly woman intercepted me. A social worker, for sure, I thought. The messianic look gave her away.

"I just want to tell you that you and your paper have done a major disservice to the dedicated people at Thistletown who are devoted to the children they treat," she said bitterly.

"Tell that to Norma Dean. Better still, her mother is sitting right there. Tell that to her," I said, nodding in Mrs. Dean's direction.

"I hate your newspaper! In fact, I don't read it anymore. I switched to the *Toronto Star*," the woman continued.

"Great! They've also got a reporter here who I'm sure will be doing a bang-up job in reporting Thistletown's dirty little role in all this," I said coldly.

"I think you are a despicable and dangerous human being."

"Well, at least I didn't send anyone to their grave."

The woman's face went red. "Drop dead!" She stormed to her seat alongside the Thistletown cohorts.

Crown Attorney Chris Meinhardt called the first witness: psychologist Flora Danziger. As she took the stand, there was a hiss from the back of the room. I knew exactly what it meant. For having the courage and compassion to speak out, she had become the target of sneers, snubs and vicious rumours and innuendo from her peers.

For more than two hours, Dr. Danziger responded to questions about Norma's first years in the child care system. Meinhardt appeared to be setting the stage for a long and arduous inquest through his tough and meticulous interrogation of the psychologist.

Dr. Danziger said Norma had attended a psychotherapy group at the York Child Guidance Clinic for about a year before being referred to the Dellcrest Children's Centre in 1973, where she attended special classes.

"At that time, the prognosis had been hopeful as far as I was concerned," she said. "Norma was a school phobic, a child in a panic about having to go to school. Both the mother and daughter had a great attachment to each other."

The psychologist explained that school phobia was more than a normal reluctance to go to school. She described it as an intense, irrational fear of leaving a parent with whom the child has a deeply dependent attachment. Unable to make the normal moves toward separation and autonomy, the child ends up resenting this dependence, and that, in turn, leads to feelings of anger, anxiety and depression.

In Norma's case, Dr. Danziger noted, the problem was complicated by the absence of her father, who left their home when she was four. "Norma only acted out or lost control on very rare occasions when she was very tense. Generally she was keen to please, willing and prepared to talk about her difficulties and problems, and prepared to do something about them," the psychologist said, adding that the girl's first experience with treatment, which lasted about a school year, held promise of a healthy future.

But Norma did not return to the public school system right away. Because of lost time, she was referred to a school at Dellcrest, a treatment centre where she continued to do well. After a year, she went back to regular public school.

I looked over at the Thistletown crowd. They were whispering to each other and casting glares at Dr. Danziger. While admitting she knew nothing about Norma's behaviour in the intervening years, the psychologist was unequivocal in the course of action she would have recommended.

"Norma was not a child who should have been sent to training school. She did not have to be resocialized in terms of normal behaviour. She had a strong feeling of what was right and wrong, and what was the truth," Dr. Danziger said.

Sidney Klotz, a lawyer representing the family's interests, asked Dr. Danziger if there was any contact by Thistletown "with you or your agency prior to sending Norma to training school?"

"None. I was not even aware that Norma had been at Thistletown, either," she replied. "It seems ironic to me that I did not know anything about it when I had just been to a workshop at Thistletown on good record-keeping and contact between agencies. This is not what happened with respect to Norma Dean."

That comment sent the Thistletown pack into a chattering frenzy. Then Meinhardt asked Dr. Danziger what she would like to see done to ensure that the maximum information be made available to agencies involved with children. That was my first clue about where this inquest was heading: right down the road to inconsequence. I knew at that moment that this hearing was not going to get at the truth.

The psychologist looked inquisitively at the Crown as she gathered her thoughts. She pointed out that records exist in all agencies that have had previous dealings with a child and suggested a procedure be instituted whereby these agencies are called when a major decision is to be made about that youngster.

Day two was Thistletown's turn at spin control. Their cheerleaders came out in force. A dozen smug child care professionals took up two rows of seats at the front of the spectators' gallery. It got me wondering. With all these professionals attending the inquest, who was left behind to mind the kids at the treatment centre?

Ann Kulik, a treatment program coordinator, was the first witness. Her testimony set the tone. She described Norma as a serious trouble-maker — running away, sniffing glue, breaking into Thistletown facilities, assaulting other adolescents and destroying property. When Norma was admitted to the centre, she was firmly told that violence or criminal behaviour would bring a warning the first time, but would lead to charges before the courts for repeated offenses, Kulik said. Then fifteen days later, Norma "retaliated" when a boy threw a Bible at her. She belted the kid, and she got her one and only warning, Kulik testified. Two weeks later, the same boy called her "brain dead," and Norma "hit him across the back fairly hard." So on May 5, 1976, Norma was trundled off to court for her first-ever appearance before a judge. Judge Fisher gave her a warning.

One after another, the parade of Thistletown child care givers hustled onto the stand and painted a portrait of a vicious child out of control.

During one employee's disparaging testimony, a reporter turned to me and said: "What a nasty little bitch!"

I knew what was happening. They were attacking the victim to protect their asses. It was just as I had predicted during my rant in Richard Doyle's office.

The star witness for Thistletown was Cynthia Gertzman, a staff psychiatrist. She described Norma as a girl with "tremendous aggression and destruction who demanded a lot of attention from the staff. Most of the cause for her behaviour appeared to centre around her home situation."

Dr. Gertzman said she saw Norma's problem as twofold: "truancy and a tremendous destructive behaviour at home toward her mother." On a positive note, she added she was quite impressed with Norma's ability to express herself, and conceded that the teenager had potential and was willing to accept help.

As the day wore on, I began to notice a distinct change in the Crown's attack — or lack thereof. For some reason, Meinhardt had traded in his hammer for a feather duster. Thistletown witnesses were making astounding observations, accusations and revelations that begged tough follow-up questions. But Meinhardt simply let them zip by unchallenged.

In one instance, Dr. Gertzman admitted that Thistletown was responsible for bringing Norma before a judge to face charges for offenses committed at the centre. She said the action was taken after a "group decision" in January, in which *patients* participated.

Now there was a stellar treatment approach, I thought. Giving seriously disturbed and troubled kids, kids who are having tremendous difficulty dealing with their own screwed-up lives, the opportunity to decide on the fate of one of their peers. Anyone with any experience dealing with kids like this should know that they are routinely very punitive in their decisions — inappropriately punitive.

Dr. Gertzman reiterated that the group decision was that any child who committed an offense would be allowed *one aggression.* After that, the child would face a judge. She explained the decision to bring Norma before the judge was because child care workers and patients felt she might benefit from the court experience. Norma's first appearance before a judge was on the assault charge over the Bible-throwing incident.

"Did she benefit?" Meinhardt asked.

"The overall effect was not successful in helping Norma," Dr. Gertzman said.

That was a telling comment, I thought. I sat on the edge of my seat and waited for the obvious follow-up. But instead of pursuing the matter, the Crown dropped it. I was perplexed. I figured he'd ask: If the approach wasn't successful, why did Thistletown continue bringing her to court a second, third, fourth, fifth and sixth time?

Dr. Gertzman also testified that every time Norma went home for the weekend, "It was extremely disruptive for her," and this disruption continued at the treatment centre for the remainder of the week. She noted that all the children in Norma's unit or house were sent home on weekends. Thistletown's rationale: to keep them from becoming institutionalized.

What was more likely was that the staff wanted to have their weekends off.

Meinhardt asked: "How many of those weekends were disruptive for Norma?"

Dr. Gertzman's answer: "Nineteen out of twenty."

Knowing this, why did Thistletown continue to send Norma home for the weekend? Why didn't the omniscient child care professionals simply keep Norma at the centre on weekends until some sort of understanding and calm could be established between Norma and her mother?

Meinhardt did not ask these questions.

Dr. Gertzman described Norma as "mentally ill" and said the girl suffered from "a personality disorder." This incredible statement was also left unchallenged.

Halfway through the psychiatrist's testimony, I was fuming. Thistletown was scoring big at its game plan, and the jury of five nice country folk was not getting the real picture. They were being inundated with psycho-babble and given little or no context.

At another point, Dr. Gertzman revealed that while Norma was at Thistletown, she had to be restrained while drugs were "forcibly" injected into her to control her behaviour.

Meinhardt's eyes narrowed. "What kind of drugs?"

Whoa! Finally a real challenge. I sat at the edge of my seat.

"Tranquilizers," she replied.

What kind of tranquilizers? What was the dosage? How often was she injected? Why did she need them? Why was she forcibly held down?

Meinhardt did not ask those questions.

I glanced at Mrs. Dean. She sat stiff and erect, looking tortured by what she was hearing. I felt terribly sad for the woman. She had lost her only child, and now these child care professionals were ripping her memory of her daughter to shreds.

The litany of horrors of Norma's stay at Thistletown continued. She was placed in "isolation therapy," Dr. Gertzman said, but she was taken out of it after "she complained about having hallucinations." Afterward, the psychiatrist added, Norma couldn't go to sleep unless a staff member was in the room because she was afraid of the dark and was having nightmares.

No one asked how long Norma was left in isolation. Nor was the Thistletown shrink asked why a patient whose problem, as they had defined and assessed it, was a deep fear of being left alone, deserted and unloved, why a patient such as this should be subjected to this form of punishment in the name of treatment?

The coroner called a lunch break. I walked over to Meinhardt and in a cynical tone asked: "What in heaven's name is going on here?"

"I don't understand," the prosecutor said.

"Yesterday, you were pretty tough on Dr. Danziger. Today, when it really counts, you're out here with a feather duster."

Meinhardt's face reddened. "You do your job and I'll do mine." With that he turned and walked out of the room.

Alone in the courtroom, I looked in front of me and saw a sheaf of documents almost a foot thick on the table Meinhardt had been sitting at. I sat down and began going through the files. They all related to Norma's short life. There were psychiatric reports, psychological assessments, social worker evaluations and teacher observations. If one thing could be said about Norma, she was certainly prodded and poked at by the child treatment profession.

I figured I had about forty minutes before people came back from lunch and the inquest resumed. Just enough time to look over the one document that I was particularly interested in. I rifled through the file folders looking for it. My pulse began to race when I found it near the bottom of the pile. It was a juvenile court file bearing Judge Stewart Fisher's name.

I flipped it open and began to read. As I had suspected, there was much more to the charge of break and enter than had come out at the inquest or in the thumbnail sketches offered up by Margaret Birch and John Smith in the Ontario legislature. What the public got was the bare bones. The juvenile court transcript added flesh.

My eyes raced over the court documents. I felt jittery. Meinhardt might walk in any minute and go ballistic. I read that the break-in occurred at the treatment centre in late June, 1976, during a weekend when Norma should have been home. Norma had found herself on yet another collision course with her mother. Wanting to avoid a fight, she left the house. And rather than hang around the streets, she ran to the safety and security of Thistletown. But the unit was locked and deserted. The staff had the weekend off. So Norma forced the door and went in. She stayed put the entire time, mostly watching television.

When the staff returned on Monday, they were seized by righteous indignation at finding her there. An emergency meeting was called, and after an intense discussion, the workers and the patients voted that the young "criminal" be charged with breaking and entering.

In the transcript, Judge Fisher asks Norma: "Why did you do it?"

Norma replies: "I wanted to stay there." She tells the judge she wanted to get back into her unit "because I didn't want to break anything at home if I got mad. I don't like hitting my mom and breaking things, but I get really mad."

Meinhardt had not mentioned this incredible sequence of events during the inquest. The court transcripts also described the first heinous crime for which Norma was dragged to court by her Thistletown keepers. It occurred during a weekend leave. She had come home on Friday at eleven and on Saturday at midnight. A clear violation of her ten o'clock curfew!

This transgression was enough to warrant a court appearance before Judge Fisher on June 7, 1976. The court record described her as "belligerent and unrepentant." She was sentenced to a week in a juvenile detention centre.

I figured with all the charges being laid by these sophisticated child care professionals, Meinhardt might have asked why a renowned treatment centre, whose primary responsibility is to treat disturbed children, would adopt the role of a cop. He did not.

Yet as a direct consequence of Thistletown laying charges against Norma and her subsequent consignment to the sordid ranks of convicted juvenile delinquent, it became possible to have her dumped into a training school.

I felt someone staring at me. I closed the binder and turned around. It was a Thistletown social worker.

"Just what do you think you're doing?" she boomed.

"Getting at the truth!"

"I'm going to tell!" she said, and stormed out.

A moment later, Meinhardt marched into the room. He glared at me but didn't speak. I shoved my notebook under my shirt for safekeeping and took out a new one for the afternoon session.

After lunch, the Thistletown troupe continued to play on Norma's negative behaviour. It became very clear to me what they did to her while she was in their care—they *created and exacerbated* Norma's negative behaviour. One child care worker recounted how a "negative response bracelet" was attached to Norma's wrist so she could "record her negative responses." They expected her to monitor her negative reactions throughout the day and record each and every one. She would do this by pressing a clicker or counter on the bracelet, which recorded the number of times she had a bad moment.

Quite an effective self-esteem-building exercise! I mused.

The stupidity didn't end there. A staff member was also given a clicker and dutifully followed Norma about the unit recording her "negative behaviour." At the end of the day, the worker and the patient would compare clicks.

"One day, Norma recorded a thirty-two," the worker told the inquest. The twelve Thistletown workers sitting in the courtroom nodded their heads in approval.

My God, I thought. The place was a freakin' cuckoos' nest! These fools put the girl in a monkey cage and didn't even realize she was clicking away to impress the keepers of the bananas.

Last to testify for the Thistletown team was social worker Glen French. He explained that the decision not to return Norma to Thistletown was taken on July 7. At that time, she was in juvenile detention for break and entry. "She was being very destructive and displaying antisocial behaviour. The recommendation was that we could not control Norma and that she required a controlled setting."

After her day in court, Norma was sent to the Oakville Regional Assessment Centre for yet another round of poking and prodding. Oakville, a clearinghouse, decided where each convicted delinquent should be placed after the judge passed sentence. On July 22, the Oakville assessment team recommended that Thistletown take Norma back.

At the inquest, French testified: "We told Oakville that her bed had been taken and there was no room. We also felt at the time it was not advisable that she should come back. We made it clear that we would not take her back immediately, but would consider it at a later date after monitoring the situation."

Day two finally drew to a close. As the Thistletown twelve were preparing to leave, I approached Dr. Gertzman. I wanted answers to a myriad of unposed questions.

"I have said all I am going to say about this case," she said flatly.

"There are a lot of questions that weren't asked, like why Norma Dean was —"

She cut me off. "I came here to answer questions for the inquest, not for the media."

"Well, the key questions were not asked!" I said angrily.

Dr. Gertzman turned and left with her retinue in tow.

One of the Thistletown cheerleaders broke from the pack, walked over and bellowed haughtily: "Just what is your problem?"

"*I* don't have a problem. You have a problem. Me!"

The woman huffed for a moment and stormed off.

On day three, Karen Jensen, a supervisor at the Oakville centre, took the stand and threw a wrench into Thistletown's version of events. Jensen said she felt strongly that the girl belonged in a treatment centre, preferably Thistletown. She definitely did not belong in a training school.

"The primary reason we felt Norma should go back to Thistletown was because she was halfway through her treatment program, and she did not need the strong external controls that a training school would give her. She still needed continued treatment, which she wouldn't get in a training school, but would get in a Ministry of Health treatment centre. She had serious emotional problems that needed to be worked through," she explained.

Jensen added that it was made quite clear to her by Glen French at the July 22 conference at Oakville "that Thistletown did not want to become reinvolved with Norma, even in the future."

Thistletown's conclusion was it had done all it could for Norma Dean.

Some of Jensen's testimony was at odds with the testimony of the treatment centre. The day before, Thistletown professionals testified that their progress with Norma was "minimal." Yet Jensen noted that when she reviewed the centre's reports, they showed "significant progress" during her stay there.

The contradiction was not explored.

Jensen recalled that when Norma arrived at Oakville, she felt "betrayed" by Judge Fisher and Thistletown. "She felt people had given up on her," but was under the impression she had been sent to Oakville "for a cooling-off period and that Thistletown would pick her up in two or three days."

After a full and detailed assessment of her case, Oakville staff concluded Norma's needs would be better met in a Ministry of Health treatment centre.

"The difference in a treatment setting is there are more professional people such as psychologists and psychiatrists to help and assist her. Training school is more involved in external and physical controls," Jensen explained.

The statement escaped the scrutiny of the jury members. Juvenile delinquents were sent to these institutions for punishment. Plain and simple! Most of the staff were guards. Their primary function was to maintain custody and security. They weren't hired to administer treatment or therapy. In Corrections, vocational courses were the key component in the rehabilitation of incarcerated delinquents. Keep them busy and you keep them out of trouble.

The Oakville assessment team knew the bleak realities of training school. So did Thistletown.

Once Thistletown formally refused to take Norma back, Jensen said, a frantic search was launched to find another treatment centre. Only one was willing to accept her: Youthdale, a bush camp 250 miles north of Toronto. The only problem was no space would be available for at least eight weeks.

"We felt that it would be detrimental to keep Norma locked up in Oakville," Jensen said. So a decision was made on July 25 to transfer her to Kawartha Lakes Training School until a Youthdale bed was freed up.

Michael John Martin, the head supervisor at Oakville, testified that Norma had threatened to kill herself and that rumours were flying around the centre that "there might be a suicide involving Norma. Some cottage staff mentioned that Norma would kill herself if she got angry enough. The feelings were there."

Martin said he made a notation on the girl's behavioural report because he didn't want to take any chances. He recommended that "she should be watched carefully and often. Having heard somebody say that, you can't ignore that in any child."

On day four, the coroner's jury piled into a van for a private tour of Kawartha Lakes Training School for girls. Inside, the jury and the coroner were shown the closet where Norma tied a macramé cord around a hook, slipped a noose around her neck and dropped to the floor.

The news media were not permitted to tag along.

That afternoon, a letter was introduced as evidence. It was written by Norma, in red ink, one week before she killed herself. It was found ripped in four pieces in the wastebasket in her room at the training school. Norma wrote:

Dear Karn [Karen Jensen],

Hi, just write you to say it was a big mistake to put me in here because the people are given me a ruf time and I'm not used to it but I won't tell the staff. Oh, Karn, I wish I was in Oakville or home. I hate this place. Please try and get me out of here. Sometimes I think of killing myself but I know it would hurt my mom more than it would hurt me.

In a postscript in large capital letters, Norma pleaded: "YOU JUST HAVE TO GET ME OUT OF HERE. SOON. PLEASE!"

Fred Koch, the superintendent of Kawartha Lakes Training School, said the note was found by a staff member who was cleaning Norma's room a week after her death. Koch confirmed that he had received reports from Oakville that Norma was suicidal and had read a notation of the girl's threat to kill herself while there. To my astonishment, he said he didn't consider the girl to be suicidal and as a result took no special precautions.

By this stage in the inquest, I wasn't surprised that his comment didn't trigger a simple follow-up question like: Why not?

Later, Meinhardt submitted a letter as evidence. It was addressed to Dr. MacKay, the coroner, and it was from Judge Fisher. In it, the judge explained the procedure in a juvenile court once a ruling is made to send a convicted delinquent to training school.

"The judge can only recommend what he feels should be done after listening to the evidence," His Honour wrote, adding that the moment a youngster becomes a ward of the Ministry of Corrections, "a judge loses all right of judicial review and the child loses all right to due process. This, of course, happened in the Norma Dean case."

Still, no matter what spin Judge Fisher tried to put on the case, the cold, hard reality was he was the one who sentenced Norma Dean to training school. And that meant only one thing to Norma — and every single kid ever sent to training school. It was the end of the line. No matter what colour the walls were painted, how the rooms were decorated or whether you wore your own clothes, training school was a prison, and losers were sent to prison.

Norma Dean suddenly saw her fragile world crumble before her. She was being taken far away from her mother. All the people at Thistletown who told her they cared and wanted to be her friend had deserted her. And with that abandonment came the final realization that her caregivers had conspired to get rid of her. Because of them, she ended up in a juvenile jail.

From the outside, Kawartha Lakes in no way looked like a prison for teenaged girls. There were no chain-link, barbed-wire-topped fences. A simple white picket fence surrounded manicured lawns and the sprawling red brick institution. Out back were a baseball diamond and a swimming pool. And during the daytime, the doors to the outside were left unlocked.

But the place was still a training school. There were strict rules and a strict regimen. Cross the line and there were punishments — privileges were removed or you were locked in an isolation room.

On day five, after a weekend break, the inquest resumed for a special session at the Kawartha Lakes institution. Several girls incarcerated at the institution were going to testify. The coroner told reporters that the girls would be identified only by a letter of the alphabet, to protect their identity. We were warned not to identify them in any way.

A stocky fifteen-year-old girl sworn in as Witness C testified that Norma told several girls on the morning of her death that she would hang herself. Witness B was tense and very nervous. She said that about an hour before Norma's body was discovered, "Norma was in crafts... pacing. She kept saying she wanted to go upstairs." Tears flowing down her face, the girl said that two days before Norma died, she had given her a photograph of herself. "She said, 'I want you to keep this. You seem to be a good friend. I want you to remember me.'" The witness broke down and ran out of the courtroom.

Testimony for Witness D was provided by Constable Ernie Walchuk, a Lindsay police officer. D, it seemed, had escaped custody and was on the loose. Walchuk read a transcript of a taped interview with the girl, who had befriended Norma at the training school. "Norma came to my room," Walchuk read. "She was upset. She looked like she had been crying. Then she came out and said: 'I feel like killing myself.' We talked for ten or fifteen minutes and during that time she did not say anything more about it." In the statement, the girl said she saw Norma later in the day in the art room. Then shortly after seven, while she was in the washroom, she heard a girl cry out, "She's dead, she hanged herself."

Witness A put up a cold, hard front. In a detached monotone, she testified that Norma "moped around" the day of the suicide. "She said once she couldn't wait to get out. She seemed depressed that day." Witness A then told how early in the evening she ran into Norma and asked her if she could borrow some baby oil. "Norma said, 'Come down to my room and borrow it in a few minutes.'" The girl said that when she got there, Norma wasn't in the room, and when she was leaving, the closet door suddenly flew open and slammed against the wall. She didn't go back to check on what caused the noise. "I didn't pay attention to it. We weren't supposed to be in other girls' rooms," A said.

The full weight of what the witness had revealed sank into each juror's head.

With so many girls seemingly aware that Norma was thinking of committing suicide, not one told a staff member. Shirley Hughes, a supervisor with the training school for more than thirteen years, attributed it to the code of silence among inmates. "In training schools, girls do not tell staff about problems with other girls. They are afraid of being called rats," she said.

Hughes was the person who discovered Norma's body. It was shortly after seven when she knocked on Norma's door and got no response. "I pulled open the door and she was hanging there, facing toward me. I was so shocked I called for another staff to get help right away. I yelled for someone to get scissors."

A Lindsay fireman and ambulance driver arrived ten minutes later, checked for vital signs but found none. Resuscitation was continued during the four-minute trip to Ross Memorial Hospital where Norma was pronounced dead on arrival.

In a brief address to the jury on the sixth and final day of the inquest, Mrs. Dean's lawyer, Sidney Klotz, slammed Thistletown. He pointed out that when Norma came into the treatment centre, "She was a child looking for care and understanding. The one facility that might have given that to her ended up discarding the child."

The lawyer argued that Thistletown "should have tried harder in working with the child," instead of dumping her off on another institution. "If a child is not making noise and staying quiet, they keep the child. But when children perhaps become a little rambunctious or difficult to handle, they pass them off," Klotz said.

Klotz finished with a suggestion to the jury that they consider a recommendation that professionals dealing with children "should be legally liable for their acts."

In his summation, Meinhardt shot down the recommendation and suggested the jury instead consider recommending that a single government ministry be created to deal with children. "It might make things a lot simpler . . . one authority which might coordinate all treatment of kids," the Crown said.

After deliberating for about two hours, the jury came back with four recommendations. They recommended that:

- Each succeeding professional dealing with a child should receive an overall case history on previous care.
- A yearly orientation program should be set up between the Ministry of Health and the Ministry of Correctional Services professional and supervisory staff to exchange information.
- If a child has been treated in a mental health, correctional or private psychiatric setting, pressure should be brought to bear on the parents or guardians to follow through on suggested aftercare treatment.
- As money is made available, priority should be given to mental health treatment centres.

I was steaming as I sped back to Toronto along Highway 401 to write the story. As far as I was concerned, the inquest had been a sham. It accomplished nothing—zip. The people who should have been challenged and held accountable were handled with kid gloves. The real issues got sidelined, and the jury completely missed the target.

At the office, I was slamming filing-cabinet drawers, kicking my desk and uttering ancestral Ukrainian curses when Joan Hollobon, the paper's no-nonsense medical reporter, screamed at me to knock it off.

"Write about it," Hollobon said. "That's the best therapy I can recommend. But if I hear you swear one more time, I'll wash your mouth out with soap. Do you hear me?"

"Yeah, I hear you." I looked around and realized most of the reporters and editors in the newsroom were staring at me. Then I saw Doyle standing with arms folded in the doorway of his office. He was glowering.

"Oh, shit," I muttered.

"Hey!" Hollobon warned.

Doyle wagged a finger at me and pointed to his office.

"You obviously have a problem, young man," Doyle began.

"I apologize for my temper, but the Norma Dean inquest ended this morning and the whole thing has pissed me right off. The stupid jury may as well have been on another planet with the inane recommendations they came up with. They missed the entire point. They never dealt with the key issue here."

"Which is?" Doyle interjected.

"Thistletown's role in charging the girl in the first place. That's the real point. If these so-called caring professionals really cared, they wouldn't have dumped her, and that's just what they did. They dumped her because Norma Dean didn't fit into their neat little package of how disturbed kids should act in their fancy, prim-and-proper treatment centre!"

"But she did commit a crime, didn't she?" Doyle asked.

"It was a trumped-up piece of garbage," I said. I explained the circumstances I'd gleaned from my quick read-through of the court transcripts sitting on the prosecutor's table.

Doyle listened intently. When I finished, he said quietly, "Stop kicking filing cabinets. Write about it. I want a carbon copy the moment you're done. I've got an editorial to write."

For two hours I pounded away at my typewriter, reviewing what I felt were the key points that were either missed or ignored by the inquest. I highlighted statements that went unchallenged and detailed Norma's so-called treatment at Thistletown. I pointed out that an inquest is not a public inquiry, that its function is to determine the cause of death. How far it goes beyond that is a matter of discretion. Then I questioned whether an inquest should have been the proper venue for investigating Norma Dean's death.

"Throughout the five days of testimony from some forty witnesses, the inquest failed to deal with probably the most important issue surrounding Norma Dean's committal to the Kawartha Lakes Training School," I wrote.

"Since when does an institution funded by the Ministry of Health for the *treatment* of disturbed children and adolescents become a *correctional* agency taking on a punishing, corrective function? The question was never asked."

I concluded: "Thistletown, described by the Ministry of Health as an outstanding mental health treatment centre for children, that receives $100 per day per child, that has all these highly qualified professionals attached to it, decided it had done all it could for Norma."

My half-page analysis was put on page eight under the headline: Questions Nobody Put. In the centre of the page was a stark illustration of a darkened clothes closet with a noose hanging from the clothes bar.

Doyle's editorial, under the headline There Was No Room at Thistletown, was a searing indictment of the treatment centre.

It began: "There was a place for Norma Dean in an Ontario Government treatment centre for disturbed children, but the centre wouldn't keep her. Toronto's Thistletown Regional Centre for disturbed children and adolescents gave up on her."

The editorial noted that the inquest "has presented us with an appalling string of facts with Thistletown mired in the midst of them." It pointed out that with all the treatment strategies employed by the centre, "the saddest strategy was the laying of criminal charges against Norma." Doyle concluded: "To treat Norma, Thistletown had made of her a juvenile delinquent. When the treatment failed, Thistletown turned its back, washed its hands. When the [Oakville] reassessment centre asked Thistletown to reconsider, the response was 'her bed has been taken.' With no one to care for her, her life has now been taken, too. It is a tragedy, an outrage, a life we didn't have to lose."

Late that afternoon, shortly after I had finished the news story on the inquest, I got an unexpected phone call. It was Frank Miller. I was surprised. I wasn't used to phone calls from Cabinet ministers.

Miller said he had just read a copy of the coroner's report and was concerned about the conclusions reached by the inquest jury. He was anxious to react to the recommendations, he said, but he couldn't because they were so vague. He wanted to know what I thought. We had a brief discussion. Actually, it was mostly a one-way conversation. I ranted. He listened.

An hour later, Miller reacted officially and forcefully. He issued an edict restricting the power of Ontario's treatment centres and psychiatric hospitals to lay criminal charges against children in their care. From now on, they would have to submit any request for such action directly to the health minister for approval. And as long as he was the health minister, they didn't have a hope of getting it, he said. The institutions were firmly reminded that no charges were to be laid simply out of a wish to relocate a child who is difficult to manage.

With Miller's statement in hand, I phoned Opposition leader Stephen Lewis for a reaction. He applauded Miller's move, describing it as "an excellent and brave step," and said the inquest jury's efforts were "weak." "What Thistletown was engaging in was one of the most damaging pursuits an institution can engage in," he said. "I was horrified that they would charge the girl. And in this regard, I was disappointed in the findings of the jury. The determinations were a little fuzzy."

I fired off a copy of Miller's edict to Doyle, and he inserted a comment in his editorial: "To his everlasting credit, Health Minister Frank Miller ruled yesterday that hospitals could no longer have unrestricted rights to lay charges against patients in their care. Thank God."

I left the office feeling sad, tired and proud. Sad for Norma Dean and her mother. Tired because it had been a long, tough and dirty fight. And proud that in the end, something came out of it. Norma Dean's death did not end up as a terse notice on the obituary page.

My investigation into her suicide was exactly the kind of journalism I wanted to pursue. I wanted to dig for stories that made a difference. I wanted to report on issues that affected the lives of people in a profound way, particularly the lives of children trapped in the child welfare system. I wanted to take on intransigent governments, boneheaded bureaucrats and the men and women who, claiming the cause of righteousness, inflicted suffering on helpless people.

As I headed home on the subway, I knew one thing for certain; the *Globe* was behind me. Doyle's editorial had made that clear.

CHAPTER FIVE

SERPENT RIVER

Elliot Lake was a blip on the map of Northern Ontario. It certainly wasn't a place I had ever contemplated visiting. But in late December 1976, Warren Barton, my meddlesome but sagacious city editor, suggested I pack my bags and head up to Canada's uranium capital with a view to unearthing a story. As always, there was more to Barton's plan. There had been a reshuffling and I'd been moved to a new beat.

"You're the new environment reporter," he pronounced with a grin.

"Warren, I don't give a damn about the effects of acid rain on car paint," I said with the energy of a flat tire.

"I'm not asking you to. It's your beat. Take it where you want."

I was sure I was being screwed over. Since the Norma Dean story, I'd continued to hammer away on children's issues and I had no desire to stop. I desperately wanted to keep up the pressure on the child welfare authorities. I complained to Barton and then to Clark Davey, the managing editor. But it was a management decision and whining wasn't about to change it.

The day after New Year, my plane headed north into an overcast sky while I muttered curses. I certainly didn't know it then, but it wouldn't be long before I thanked Barton for giving me this new beat.

My mission in Elliot Lake was to look into the mountains of toxic, radioactive tailings—the waste byproducts of crushed and refined uranium—that had been dumped for decades on the outskirts of the community by the two mining giants, Rio Algom and Denison Mines. The story was not a sizzler. But as we strolled across the grey, spongy dunes of tailings, a throwaway comment by Homer Seguin, an outspoken representative of the United Steelworkers union, caught my attention.

"This is like walking on the moon. Everything is dead and barren.

There was an attempt to grow grass here last year and it turned black. And they think that because this stuff is on land it won't get into the water system. Well, they're wrong. There's seepage from the snow and rain that makes its way into the creeks and streams," Seguin said.

I recalled seeing the putrid, discoloured lake water near the massive tailing mounds from the window of the plane as it circled over the town.

"That stuff is highly polluted and eventually it makes its way into Serpent River water," Seguin said.

I could feel a story coming on. "Is that where the town gets its drinking water from?" I asked.

"No, Elliot Lake's drinking water is piped in from a crystal-clear lake upstream," he said.

I felt the story start to fizzle.

"Now the folks who live downstream. That's a different story," Seguin added.

Not too far down river was the tiny, sleepy hamlet of Serpent River. Its residents, I learned, drew their drinking water straight from the belly of the beast. But before I began ringing any false alarms, I checked with the Ontario Ministry of the Environment in Toronto and the federal health department in Ottawa to find out exactly what was in the water.

I was told that recent tests carried out by their lab technicians showed the Serpent River contained radioactive contaminants that were more than double the safety standard set by the province. In fact, scientists had been warning for years that drinking water contaminated by radioactive waste can cause cancer and genetic defects.

I called Joseph Lafrenier, chairman of the water commission for the community of Serpent River. He said that 160 adults and 152 children drink water from the Serpent, and the only health measure taken by the water commission was to add chlorine at the intake pipe.

And "No, chlorine does not kill the radioactivity," Lafrenier said.

As I drifted through the village, I noticed a school bus dropping children off at the Rockhaven School for Exceptional Children. Lafrenier confirmed that the school was served by the same water pipe as the rest of the community.

I went to see the principal, Mabel MacAskill. She told me that she had never received any notice from the Ministry of Health or the Environment telling her the drinking water was unsafe. She added that none of the twenty-three mentally retarded children were from Serpent River. "They're bussed in from neighbouring communities — Elliot Lake, Spragg, Iron Bridge, Cutler."

Mrs. MacAskill said she'd heard rumours about radioactive contamination in the water but noted that "the health inspector comes here every month to test the drinking water from the fountain, and every time I ask him about the water, he always gives me the same answer, 'It's fine.' If he says it's fine, what else can a person do?"

I called the environment ministry office in Sault Ste. Marie, 107 miles to the east, and spoke to Jim Harmer, the district officer. He said residents had been warned several years earlier — and occasionally since then — not to drink the water. Harmer said he thought most residents were drawing their drinking water from wells and streams. "We didn't shut down their pipes because the water is okay for washing dishes and clothes."

I decided to do a random survey of a dozen households. I went door to door and found all the residents drank and cooked with the water piped in from the river. Not one had ever been warned not to drink it.

I then called Norman Giguere, an inspector with the Algoma Health Unit. He confirmed that from "a bacteriological point of view, the water is fine." He added that he had never tested it for radioactivity. "All we test for is bacteria. We don't have the equipment to do tests of that nature." Giguere also said he had not been advised by any provincial or federal government department about radioactive contaminants in the water. "Water supply is under the jurisdiction of the Ministry of the Environment. We haven't been advised by them about radiation."

I knew that I was onto a big story. Someone had screwed up big time. I decided it was time to phone the environment minister. George Kerr, his secretary said curtly, was not back from his Christmas break. She suggested I phone public relations. I figured this was an issue for the minister and it couldn't wait. So I trolled a few political contacts and got Kerr's home phone number.

The minister was not amused that I had his home number.

"Well, I think this is really important, Mr. Kerr. There are people in Serpent River drinking radioactive drinking water and according to the local health people, it seems your ministry is responsible," I said.

Kerr immediately became defensive — and sharp. "I can't believe our officials have not informed the local authorities that the water poses some problems. The information must be available in some way. I'm not a doctor but I would think if there are any health hazards, the local health officer should be aware."

"Well, he isn't. No one in the entire community is aware because no one in your ministry bothered to tell them."

Kerr's intensity level went up a notch. "I would think they would make it their business to get all the information they could. They just can't sit back and say they haven't heard about it. It's somebody's responsibility."

"Whose responsibility is it, Mr. Kerr?" I asked.

"Those responsible for the health of the people drinking the water — health officials!" the minister shouted into the phone.

"But if your people aren't telling them what's in the water, how are they supposed to know it's not safe?"

Kerr paused, and then reverted to the classic political comeback. "I'm going to investigate this whole business and get to the bottom of this once and for all."

Next, I tracked down Frank Miller, the Ontario health minister. He was congenial, wishing me a Happy New Year. Miller confirmed that his ministry had received some information on the drinking water from Serpent River that "indicated some testing had been done and everything appeared to be okay." The health minister added, however, that he suspected the tests were for common contaminants found in drinking water and probably did not include radiation. "Naturally, I would have to temper my reaction. I would hate to be an alarmist until I check further into this."

The banner story in the *Globe* on January 4, 1977, read: Northern Schoolchildren Drinking Radioactive Water.

That was all Tory Premier Bill Davis needed to see on page one with his morning coffee. The next day, George Kerr issued a press release announcing the immediate construction of a treatment plant to reduce the radiation contamination from the drinking water. In the written statement, Kerr noted that responsible medical authorities had indicated that there was "no immediate hazard" to the health of residents drinking the contaminated water.

Then why the scramble to build the plant? I wondered. I'd never seen such a quick reaction to a story. Something stunk.

Kerr's statement continued: "I am concerned, however, about the long-term effects on residents and I believe that it is necessary to reduce levels of radium contamination in the Serpent River drinking water to Ontario standards as soon as possible."

With this resolute statement of purpose, Kerr was showing the people of Ontario that his government was swift in its response to a health-threatening situation. But was this all a public relations show? I had a strong feeling it was. This issue didn't just happen overnight.

It didn't take long for the real story behind the story to surface. That morning I got a call from a ministry technician who worked in the water quality section.

"Congratulations and thank you," he said.

"What for?" I asked.

"We've been trying to get the government to build that plant for five years and could never get them to put aside the money. Your story gets it done in a day."

"What do you mean, five years?" I asked.

"The situation in Serpent River has been known a very long time. I'm not telling you anything I shouldn't. I suggest you come down to the ministry reference library and get a copy of a report called 'Water Pollution from the Uranium Mining Industry in the Elliot Lake and Bancroft Area.' It was published by the Ontario Water Resources Commission in October, 1971."

Needless to say, I went straight to the library. The document showed the Ontario government knew as far back as *1961* that drinking water from the Serpent River contained radioactive contaminants. And it strongly urged that "consideration should be given to alternate sources of drinking water supply for the homes which are supplied with water from the lower Serpent River... since any unnecessary exposure to radioactivity should be kept to a minimum." *And* the report was signed by then Ontario Water Resources Commissioner, George Kerr.

When I called, Kerr's secretary informed me that her boss wasn't in Toronto. Seems he had gone to Serpent River for a little politicking. He was going to make the official announcement of the new water treatment plant and show the concerned residents of Serpent River that the Tories cared about their health.

I grabbed the next flight.

As the meeting drew to a close, I approached the minister. He wasn't happy to see me.

"Can you tell me when you first learned that Serpent River residents were drinking radioactive water?" I said.

"It would be some time last year," the minister said a little too quickly.

"Are you aware of the Ontario Water Resources Commission report on the drinking water from October, 1971?" I asked.

"I don't know if I am aware of that specific..."

I pulled the document from my briefcase and waved it in front of his nose. Kerr hesitated a moment as his eyes focused on the document. "Yes, I've heard of that report."

"Based on this report, the first warnings about radioactivity were issued in 1971."

Kerr glowered.

"So why the urgency now over installing a water treatment plant when the problem has been known for so many years?" I pressed.

Kerr blathered on about local residents consuming the water for years — some as long as twenty-three years, and he was concerned about the long-term health hazards if they continued to drink it. "The sooner we get the treatment facilities installed, the better."

"But why did it take so long to initiate installation of the treatment plant?" I asked.

Teeth clenched, Kerr replied, "We didn't have the technology back in 1971. The technology, which will deal with the specific problem of reducing the radiation, was developed over the past six months."

I shook my head. I knew that he knew that I knew that was a load of crap. Nevertheless, he blundered on. His officials had repeatedly advised people in Serpent River of the potential health hazard in drinking the water over the years, he said.

Funny, I replied, that not one person in the community was aware of any such advice or warning! Kerr turned and left. The confrontation was over.

For the next few months, I continued to break stories about Kerr's bumbling ministry. It was like shooting a 12-gauge shotgun at the side of a barn. I couldn't miss. The department of the environment was colossally inept at dealing with environmental crises. It operated on reluctance. Reluctance to force Sudbury's nickel-mining giant, Inco, to clean up the pollution from its superstack; reluctance to stop the pulp and paper industry from dumping toxic chemicals into the river systems; reluctance to police the petro-chemical industry or keep track of where highly toxic liquid industrial waste was being dumped. The list went on.

Kerr did not appreciate the sudden attention his ministry was receiving from the *Globe and Mail*. My relentless hammering on environmental screw-ups infuriated him — and eventually drove him into making a mistake. He ordered the head of his communications department, a snarly ex–sports reporter named Bob Frewin, to put me in line. In late August, Frewin summoned me for a talk. Seated behind his desk in a black, high-back, leatherette swivel chair, he exuded self-importance. Before him, sitting erect and obedient, were three of his minions. There was an empty chair to their left. I felt as if I was walking into a set-up.

"You know, sonny boy, I used to be a reporter," Frewin began.

With those condescending words, Frewin set the tone. I felt like an indigent sharecropper in the Deep South who'd messed with the sheriff. Sonny boy, indeed!

Frewin continued. "We're concerned in the ministry about the way you do your job...about your negative reporting."

"I'm concerned about the way you do *your* job!" I snapped back. "Clean up the environment, and maybe I'll have something positive to write about."

Frewin ignored the interjection. "We've had a lot of complaints about you taking staff in this ministry out of context or misquoting them."

"Funny, *I* haven't received one complaint," I said.

"We've received several."

"Name one!" I challenged.

"That is not the issue here."

"I'm not going to defend myself against phantom accusers."

"They exist, all right. And I've instructed everyone in the ministry not to talk to you. All your queries are to be referred directly to me. I'll deal with you from now on."

"So you're telling me that no one is allowed to talk to me anymore," I repeated.

"That's right, sonny boy." Frewin leaned back in his swivel chair and grinned. His minions grinned.

Suddenly, I lost it. "The name is Malarek! And don't you forget it! I'm not your fuckin' sonny boy, and I won't stand for some fat-ass jerk like you talking down to me."

"Get out of my office," Frewin bellowed. "I'm going to give Clark Davey a call about you! He and I go back a long way. We're old friends."

Old friends or not, Davey backed me up. He called me into his office and asked me about my "meeting" with Frewin. I told him what had happened. "I'll deal with it," he said, and wrote Frewin a terse letter, with a copy to me, that read:

> I gather that a number of ministry officials have been called on the deputy's carpet or the minister's rack for telling Mr. Malarek and the taxpayers of Ontario the truth.
>
> As you know, we make every effort to get the ministry's side of any story we publish. If you are unavailable or less forthcoming than the knowledge-able officials of the department...then the responsibility for any breakdown in communication between your ministry and our readers must be borne by the people who applied the gag.

I regarded this incident as a true test case. It was my first *mano-a-mano* standoff with a government ministry and, to my relief, the *Globe* had backed me all the way. Their support made me confident, cocky even. Kerr was going to have me to kick around for some time yet.

Two months later, on October 25, 1977, the testy minister was responding in the Ontario legislature to another embarrassing story in the *Globe* with my byline, about his officials secretly incinerating hazardous PCB wastes in a cement kiln in Mississauga, just outside Toronto.

In a heated exchange during Question Period, Hugh O'Neil, the Liberal member for Quinte, asked if it was true that someone in Kerr's ministry had requested that a confidential report be compiled on the reporter who wrote the story.

Looking beleaguered, Kerr confirmed that his officials had indeed compiled a file. He said the action was taken to deal with complaints by ministry staff about my stories. "I'm really not sure who gave the orders or who made the decisions," he said lamely. And yes, he'd look into the matter.

Later, Robert Frewin told a gaggle of reporters that he had com-piled the file after receiving a letter from Clark Davey in which "Mr. Davey, by implication, accused us of trying to gag Mr. Malarek."

Frewin then handed the reporters an unsigned report dated September, 1977, that stated: "Many ministry staff consulted by Mr. Malarek in the preparation of his articles have claimed, to the information services branch, significant instances of misquoting or misrepresentation of the ministry position as they stated it."

As well, Malarek's stories "seem to be negative," Frewin said, adding that there was "nothing personal in all this. It's an analysis of his work."

Yeah, right.

Frewin added, "He's very difficult to talk to. We don't always talk calmly, and you can quote me on this—I've had him shout at me in my own office. I found him to be very intense and aggressive, which is to his credit as a reporter."

Thanks a lot, Robert.

While the Queen's Park news hounds were chasing me down for a quote, I got busy on the phones calling every technical member of the ministry staff I had interviewed. My questions were terse and I tape-recorded the answers.

"Have I ever misquoted you?"

"Have I ever taken you out of context?"

"Have there been inaccuracies in any of my stories?"

The responses were a resounding NO! Some said they had never even spoken to Frewin. Others said they had been told never to speak to me again. No reasons were given. All asked that their names not appear in the *Globe*. The atmosphere in the ministry was poisonous. I played their comments back to *Globe* editor-in-chief Dic Doyle.

Outside the legislature, Kerr conceded to reporters that the incident should have been handled differently. "It is not the type of thing I would favour in the future and I don't expect it will be done again."

The besieged minister soon found himself with another *Globe* writer on his case. The following day, Norman Webster, the paper's Queen's Park columnist, lambasted the government's "vicious assault on freedom of the press." In his column, Webster wrote that by the end of a stormy session of Question Period on the Malarek file, "You'd have thought Bill Davis had the gumshoes out checking into the sex life and questionable habits of critical reporters, in order to bring them to heel."

Webster likened the government's tactics to former U.S. president Richard Nixon's harassment of the press:

"Investigations, wiretaps, use of income tax records—the whole range of Nixon-administration dirtiness—is clearly intolerable, but surely politicians and civil servants have every right to be nasty to reporters they feel are being unfair to them and their story.

"They can legitimately cut them dead at the symphony, make obscene phone calls, write letters to the editor, make statements in the House, threaten libel action or, as Mr. Kerr's people did, send an unfriendly analysis of a reporter's stories to his editors....

"In Mr. Malarek's case, the report from Environment was noted by his superiors, given the weight it deserved—one buzzard feather—and duly forgotten. Mr. Malarek remains on the beat, disturbingly unintimidated."

Kerr knew he was beaten. Two days later, he made a brief statement to the House. The ministry had no intention of muzzling or intimidating anyone, he said. His ministry wanted only to improve its working relationship with the newspaper and its representative. Outside the chamber, I was intercepted by a Davis aide. The premier wanted a brief word with me, he said.

Davis was pacing in his corner office puffing on a cigar. He offered me one.

"No thanks, I don't smoke," I said. I was uncomfortable and so was he.

"I just want to tell you that I had nothing to do with the compilation of that file and I apologize for any embarrassment it caused you. If there's anything I could do?" the premier asked.

"Thanks," was all I could come up with. We shook hands and I left.

For the next year and a half, I pounded away at various ministries—Environment, Labour, Community and Social Services, Health, Corrections, the Solicitor General. Being let loose on the environment beat had opened my eyes to a raft of issues unrelated to my major preoccupation as a reporter—child welfare messes. My tales of corruption in high places, and blunders and disasters filled pages. Nobody ever called or wrote to complain that I'd misquoted them. And no one ever compiled another file on me.

Then, in early 1980, the managing editor raised the stakes. He wanted to see how I would handle an international crisis. I was dispatched to the other side of the world as a foreign correspondent to

cover the Soviet invasion of Afghanistan. It was an astounding experience and a harrowing adventure, one I had never imagined. I was forced
to tap into survival skills I'd learned on the backstreets of Montreal.
My rough-and-tumble training ground had prepared me for what was
to come.

CHAPTER SIX

WAR STORIES

In the spring of 1980, the Islamic fundamentalist regime of Ayatollah Ruholla Khomeini began expelling foreign journalists from Iran for reporting unflattering stories. Topping the list of those getting the boot were American reporters, followed closely by Brits and West Germans. The exodus was worrisome to editors at many U.S. newspapers who wanted to keep a close eye on the big story — the fifty-two American hostages being held by Khomeini fundamentalists at the U.S. Embassy in Tehran.

But I had an ace up my sleeve — a valid visa to enter Iran as a foreign correspondent. I had wangled it out of the chargé d'affaires at the Iranian Embassy in Ottawa the previous January, just before heading off on a four-week assignment to cover the Soviet invasion of Afghanistan. The official Iranian Islamic revolutionary seal had been stamped in my passport just days before Kenneth Taylor, the Canadian ambassador in Tehran, smuggled six American diplomats out of Iran on forged Canadian passports. The Americans had secretly taken refuge with Canadian officials when three thousand Iranian students, demanding the return of Shah Mohammad Reza Pahlavi to face trial (he was in exile in Egypt), stormed the U.S. Embassy on Sunday morning, November 4, 1979.

I'd gone after the Iranian visa because the American hostage drama was one foreign story I wanted a piece of. I figured it wouldn't hurt to be prepared just in case the *Globe* decided it wanted to get directly involved. And now, in May, 1980, rumours were flying that something big was about to break. Since Canada had become a major player in the drama, it made sense for the *Globe* to have someone there.

Dic Doyle and Clark Davey decided I should go.

My arrival at the Tehran airport touched off a flurry of activity. My Canadian passport was not a welcome sight. I was led to a room, strip-searched and held for several hours. Then I was driven to a bleak government building in downtown Tehran. On a doorway outside was a sign in Persian and English. The English part was straight out of George Orwell. It read: Ministry of National Guidance. Inside, I received a stern lecture on press corps etiquette.

My instructor was Abolhassem Sadegh, Iran's chief handler of foreign journalists. Sadegh was a dour man with a three-day sprinkle of salt-and-pepper whiskers on an ashen face. He made no attempt to hide his distrust and suspicion of Western scribes. Truth was, he had no choice. The hard-line mullahs were tightening the noose, and Sadegh was a man under siege.

Dressed in a bland, two-piece grey suit and white shirt buttoned at the collar with no tie, Sadegh perched behind a wooden desk almost hidden by stacks of foreign newspaper and magazine clippings and transcribed texts of radio and television dispatches.

"Why should I allow you to stay in Iran?" he asked as he scrutinized my passport.

"I have a visa. It's legal," I replied calmly.

"Your country is no longer represented here by an embassy. You are aware of that?"

A subtle threat, perhaps? "Yes, I'm aware of that," I replied. "If I have any problems I'll take them to the British Embassy."

Sadegh shoved my passport under a desk lamp. "You can understand why we might have a problem with this travel document, I'm sure?"

I shrugged. I was dead-tired after twenty-two hours in airports and on airplanes and was in no mood to be drawn into a long-winded, no-win discourse. I figured whatever Sadegh said I'd just nod—keep my responses short and neutral.

After several minutes, he seemed convinced the document was bona fide and tossed it on the desk in front of me. Then, without skipping a beat, he levelled a measured broadside at the Western news media.

"It seems the foreign press are not interested in reporting the truth. They are deliberately distorting life in Iran and the revolution. They have conveyed the impression there is violence and chaos in the streets. It's true something may be happening in one spot—"

"Like at the American Embassy," I interjected.

"Yes. But life is also going on normally in ninety percent of the streets of Tehran. You could walk down the streets of Tehran and feel more safe than on the streets of New York City."

"Well, I hope I'm given the opportunity to find out."

Sadegh glared at me. He continued. "Foreign reporters write about the long queues for bread and meat. I live here and I haven't seen them. Occasionally, when a shop is about to open, there is a lineup in front of it, but is that not normal?"

"See it all the time back home," I said, keeping my voice as neutral as I could manage.

"Instead, some make it seem like we are suffering shortages when we are not. We can buy and get anything we need. They make things look a lot worse than they really are, especially television, especially *American* television."

The bureaucrat yammered on. I was in his corral and he was doing his job. I knew I was obliged to suffer him gladly or hop on the next plane home. He gave me "guidance" for three hours during which he took potshots at NBC, CBS, ABC, the *New York Times*, the *Washington Post, Time* and *Newsweek* magazine. I sat and listened, occasionally nodding and feigning interest.

"And as for *Newsweek*. Now here is a magazine that feeds its readers what it wants from what it has created."

On and on he harped, until at last, through the drone, I could sense a change in pitch. His stamina was flagging. I leaned forward and tried to focus on his words.

"I must warn you that we will be watching you and reading your dispatches. If you take the same tack as your colleagues, you will be expelled," Sadegh said firmly.

"I understand, and thanks for the informative talk," I said.

Sadegh then led me to a room where a tiny black-and-white head shot was taken of me and fitted under plastic in a spanking-new press pass. It began: *In the name of Allah.* Then read: Islamic Republic of Iran. Ministry of National Guidance. On the back was a series of scribbles in Persian, along with Sadegh's signature.

"If there is any problem, show this press pass," Sadegh said, handing the pass to me. "It should solve most difficulties, unless you are somewhere that is strictly forbidden. Then it is your own doing and your own problem."

He pointed to a map of Iran on the wall with red tags dotting virtually every town and city with the exception of Tehran and the holy city of Qom, home of the Ayatollah.

"Those red tags are to notify foreign journalists these areas are off-limits. If you go to these places, you will be arrested, detained and expelled from Iran. Is that understood?" said Sadegh.

"Just Tehran, Qom, and that's it," I said.

He nodded. "You will require special permission to go elsewhere. Do not contravene any of our regulations. You are in Iran and subject to Iranian law. I hope you understand that."

"I understand."

He eyeballed me sternly as we shook hands. I was free to go.

It took me less than twenty-four hours to discover firsthand just how deeply Iranians resented Western journalists that spring of 1980. The next morning, I headed for the U.S. Embassy. It was Women's Day in Iran, and a women's rally was taking place in front of the most reviled building in Tehran, the American Embassy. A sea of women completely covered in black *chadors* — brows knitted, fists jabbing the air — screamed contempt for the U.S.A. and President Jimmy Carter. As a surge of shrieking women pushed toward the entrance of the compound, I snapped a picture. I was positioned in front of the embassy gates, which were guarded by heavily armed *pasdarans*, Khomeini's trusted and loyal revolutionary guards. A teenage *pasdaran*, clutching a Belgian G-3 machine gun, rushed up behind me and jabbed the muzzle into my ribs. I dropped my camera on the pavement. He ordered me to pick it up and open the back. Nervously, I obeyed him. He ripped out the film contemptuously, warning me as he did so not to take any more photographs showing revolutionary guard positions around the embassy.

A few days later, I ventured onto the grounds of Tehran University hoping to find out what the students thought about the revolution. I figured this would be a place for stimulating, informed debate and exchange of ideas. I was never more wrong. Within minutes, I was surrounded by a hostile crowd of young men.

"You have come here to write a farce about Iran," a weasel-faced student shouted, waving an accusing fist inches from my face. "All you Americans are pigs!"

Like thousands of Canadians mistaken for Americans round the world have done, I trotted out my Canadian identity. "I'm not American. I'm Canadian and —"

"Your country, Canada, is just like the U.S. You are one and the

Above Victor Malarek and Philip Gillis in 1961: My unofficial foster brother.

Below Investigative reporter in the making: on the police desk at the *Montreal Star,* circa 1971.

Top Roland Michener, Jeanne Sauve and Victor Malarek:
Award for meritorious public service to journalism for series
on immigration and refugee issues. *GOVERNMENT HOUSE*

Above 1988: Another Michener Award, for the Lang Michener story.

Below January 1980: In the Khyber Pass during my six-week stint covering the Soviet invasion of Afghanistan.

Bottom Iranian women, dressed in chadors, demonstrate in front of seized U.S. Embassy in Tehran, in support of Women's Day. VICTOR MALAREK

Top General Qassemlou (left) with one of his peshmerga bodyguards in the mountains of Kurdistan—at his hideout bunker. VICTOR MALAREK

Above Mohammed—my peshmerga bodyguard, in Saqqez. VICTOR MALAREK

Right Old Kurd reflects on the war in his homeland. VICTOR MALAREK

Top Dr. Santokh Singh, accused of masterminding the assassination
of Rajiv Gandhi.

Above Mahmoud Muhammad Issa Mohammad—convicted Palestinian
terrorist enters Canada as a legitimate permanent resident.
DIANA NETHERCOTT, *THE GLOBE AND MAIL*

Above Mark Salvail talks with Somali refugees in the Ogadan Desert in Ethiopia.

Right A Somali refugee family shelters from the sun. VICTOR MALAREK

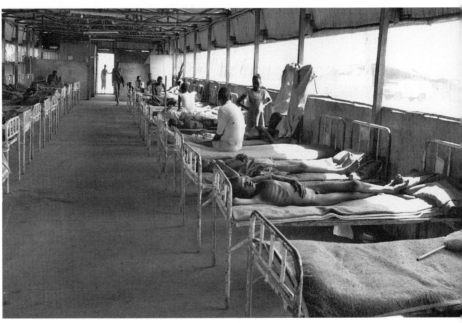

Top Posing with Dinka boys in 1989—in the world's largest open-air orphanage.

Above Hospital ward in Dinka refugee camp.
VICTOR MALAREK

Top, left Martin Pilzmaker, disbarred lawyer, runs from a Toronto courtroom. PETER LEE, *THE GLOBE AND MAIL*

Top, right Thomas Douglas: Lang Michener's "moral" conscience.

Above, left Small-time drug dealer Alain Olivier—sentenced to 100 years in a Bangkok prison.

Above, right Derek Flanagan, killed in Thailand in a botched drug bust. *RCMP* same. You are not interested in the truth about the Iranian revolution. You are simply interested in making us look ridiculous in the eyes of the world."

I realized that debate with fundamentalists was a pointless. The student's verbal lashing got louder. His contorted face, red with rage, was inches from mine. His breath was hot.

The ever-growing crowd outside the library, which was plastered with revolutionary posters, wildly applauded. I was becoming very nervous. I sensed the situation was getting dangerously out of control. I kept my feet planted firmly and my eyes focused on the crazed student. Then someone in the crowd grabbed my camera, pulled out the film and tossed back the camera. I started to walk away, not too quickly, at a pace that I hoped would not trigger a reaction from any of the hotheads in the crowd. As I retreated, the students laughed and jeered. Somebody spit on me. But no one chased after me.

Later, at the Intercontinental Hotel, I bumped into a CBC news crew. A few days earlier, I learned, the cameraman, Dennis Packer, and the soundman, Bill Payne, had been shooting a May Day demonstration when rocks began to rain down on the entire press corps. Within seconds, they were surrounded by a pack of hostile protesters.

The situation looked grim, Packer recounted. "This guy grabbed me, put his face up to mine and said, 'I'm going to kill you.'"

Payne was attacked by another ranting protester and received a couple of bruising blows to the kidneys. The man also threatened to kill him.

"We just turned and calmly walked away," Packer said. "The next day there were a lot of guys walking around the hotel with bandages on their heads. Some reporter is going to get killed here. You can sense it."

During my forays into the heart of Tehran, I also learned that many Iranians despised the hard-line mullahs and silently wished Khomeini dead. These people's lives had been completely turned upside down by the revolution, and all they could see was black clouds on the horizon. They had had it with the fundamentalists shoving their firebrand version of religion down their throats. And they had grown weary of the political rhetoric and sabre-rattling against the West.

Those hurt worst by the revolution were the affluent, Western-educated Iranians who lived in the posh north end of Tehran at the foot of the snowcapped Alborz Mountains. In private gatherings at expensive homes, they complained bitterly about their impending doom. They knew they were roundly detested by the self-righteous majority because their families had made their fortunes during the thirty-eight-year reign of the reviled Shah Mohammad Reza Pahlavi. The "King of Kings" fled Iran on January 16, 1979, at the controls of his Boeing 727 jet, fitted out with its infamous gold toilet, leaving his loyal subjects to fend for themselves. Many members of the upper-middle classes desperately wanted to escape fundamentalist Islamic Iran. But no nation wanted them. Largely because of unflattering and slanted media reports, the world wanted neither the religious extremists from the new regime nor Iranians tainted with the Shah's era.

"Many, many of my friends and relatives want to leave Iran. We are very unhappy," a twenty-three-year-old computer programmer confided. "But where can we go? What country will take us? Because of this government and its attitude to Western governments, I cannot get a visa for any country. I flew to Britain, West Germany and Copenhagen as a tourist and tried to get a visa to stay but could not. I went to the American Embassy and your embassy while I was in those countries. They, too, are not interested in Iranians even if we say we oppose this government!" The young man's hands nervously worked a string of lapis lazuli worry beads. "I am not a fundamentalist. I am not a fanatic. I have no future in my country."

For Seyyed Algar, a twenty-eight-year-old U.S.-educated engineer, there was nothing left in Iran to feel good about. "I am not that religious. I am a Moslem but not a fanatic like some of those in the government. I miss the nightlife, the discos. Since they closed down the nightclubs and movie houses in Tehran, there is no more fun. Now all we have is one television station full of religion and propaganda about the revolution."

Since the Shah had gone into exile, both his supporters and his foes had tried to rewrite the history of his reign. The former portrayed him as an enlightened modernizer and reformer, the latter as a villainous dictator worse than Adolph Hitler.

The truth was somewhere between. True, the Shah supported progress, Western-style. But he used bullets and torture to silence his opponents. In 1956, with the help of the U.S. Central Intelligence Agency (CIA) and the Israeli spy service, he formed Savak—a dreaded force of thirty thousand secret police that systematically employed arbitrary arrest, imprisonment, torture and execution to crush his suspected enemies. At the same time, he led Iran into the modern age. He fashioned something of an economic miracle in Iran. He brought a measure of stability to a formerly turbulent country, he fostered Western liberal values (the human rights of his opponents excepted) and he encouraged higher education. In so doing, he improved the lives and expanded the cultural perimeters of many Iranians.

The Ayatollah undid all that with his cruel, narrow brand of authoritarianism and fundamentalism. The aging cleric who became absolute ruler of Iran in January, 1979, sought to return Iran to medieval times and a regime of puritan virtues, holy scriptures and godly warfare. Now firmly at the helm of his theocratic republic, the Ayatollah established a reign of terror that went beyond the Shah's worst excesses. Anyone who opposed him was arrested, jailed, tortured and summarily executed.

The intensity of the propaganda was chilling, absurd and hateful. Sitting in my hotel room one night, I turned on the television for a taste of Iranian fundamentalist programming. A public-service cartoon aimed at the children of Iran began innocently with a white dove flying happily through a clear blue sky. Then it spied Uncle Sam's top hat, all decked out in red, white and blue with a band around the brim festooned with stars. It was such a dazzling sight that the bird couldn't help but swoop down to take a closer look. As it approached, a menacing black claw lunged out of the hat, snared the squawking, frightened bird and yanked it inside. There was a loud clanking of steel, and the stripes were suddenly replaced by jail bars. The frightened dove slumped over, weeping, but perked up when it heard laughter and the jangle of spurs coming toward it. The footsteps were those of U.S. president Jimmy Carter, dressed in full cowboy regalia and packing loaded six-shooters. The president looked at the bird, laughed wickedly, pulled out his guns and blasted away at the helpless creature. Then he turned and strutted off, cackling hideously. The dead dove's blood oozed from the cage onto the ground while a message in Persian appeared on the screen: "America ... America, death to your trickery. Our martyrs' blood is dripping from your hands."

For five weeks, I wandered the streets of Tehran looking for stories while rumours about the imminent release of the hostages ebbed and flowed. I was amazed that the walls of virtually the entire city of six million had been covered with propaganda. Every day, students and political and religious activists barrelled down the streets carrying open tins of red, black, blue and white paints or armfuls of posters and pots of glue. They crouched and stretched, trying to squeeze their message into whatever space they could find on the poster-plastered, slogan-painted walls. Some of the messages were religious, with generally one theme — *Allah-o-Akbar* (God is great). Others were pointedly political — *Marg Bar Shah, Marg Bar Carter* (Death to the Shah, Death to Carter). There were even some posters calling for the establishment of a Marxist government. But those were usually torn down and replaced with *Marg Bar Marxist*.

Posters plastered on walls throughout the city denounced Carter and the American government for its involvement in Iran during the Shah's reign. A particularly grotesque colour poster showed a human skull wearing Uncle Sam's top hat. The skull was feasting on the intestines of a dead child killed by so-called U.S. imperialist plots and aggression. The child's eyes were open.

Another poster showed stars falling from the U.S. flag into a bomb-like configuration, where they turned into Stars of David. Another depicted President Carter vomiting the Shah from his mouth; yet another superimposed Carter's face against a pair of fangs, dripping blood, on the body of a snake coiled around the globe.

One afternoon, I was driven 120 kilometres to the holy city of Qom, hoping to catch a glimpse of the seventy-nine-year-old Ayatollah. The town was teeming with turbaned mullahs and heavily armed revolutionary guards in green military uniforms. Outside a magnificently tiled mosque, I joined a throng of young religious zealots. In my jeans and blue T-shirt, unshaven, and with my dark complexion, I blended imperceptibly with the crowd.

The procession snaked its way through an impoverished neighbourhood of mud and stone dwellings. Then we crammed into a narrow alleyway, at the far end of which was a modest two-story home — Khomeini's residence. It was a far cry from the Shah's opulent palace and not at all what I had expected. I waited for several hours, hoping to catch a glimpse of the Ayatollah.

Finally, the crowd and I got what we had been waiting for. I felt a chill as Khomeini, dressed in an earthy brown robe and black turban, made a brief appearance in a window. His face was ashen; he looked tired, and his black eyebrows gave him a foreboding appearance. His white beard and age notwithstanding, there was nothing warm or grandfatherly about this man. He looked cold — possessed by his single-minded mission. He reminded me of fire-and-brimstone French Catholic clerics from my Quebec past.

Upon seeing Khomeini, the crowd went into hysterics. They began chanting their undying devotion to the Imam—the leader. Many beat themselves, smashing their fists into their chests.

Back in Tehran, I spent the next few weeks attending press conferences and writing about the upcoming national election, as rumour after rumour raced through the city that the hostages were about to be freed. I was growing bored and impatient. I had come for action, and all I was getting was a steady diet of staged protests. Day after day, like clockwork, there were demonstrations in front of the American Embassy compound. They were so scripted, it wasn't worth the effort to show up. Thousands of men, women and children squatted on the pavement and waited, sometimes for hours. Then the alert would go out—the television cameras were approaching! The fuses were lit and what followed made outstanding television. Unshaven, rabid-eyed men, wearing white sheets with blood-red bandannas tied around their heads, jumped and jerked like crazed hyenas while beating themselves with leather belts or slamming their fists into their chests. You could feel the compression from the collective thud. Women shrouded in black *chadors* shrieked. Everyone chanted: Death to America! Death to Carter! Down with American Imperialism! Death to the Shah!

It was theatre of the absurd and the international press corps lapped it up. End of story. Or was it?

It was not. I was about to stumble upon a large group of people who would happily choose death over mingling within Khomeini's obedient flock. They were the Kurds.

Throughout Iranian Kurdistan—a harsh, ragged region in the Alborz Mountains northwest of Tehran—the Ayatollah was flexing his muscles with bullets, mortars and bombs. A state of undeclared war was in force. Pitched battles were raging in the streets. The city of Sanandaj, the capital of Kurdish Iran, had been blasted into submission. Neighbouring Saqqez was under siege, and Banez was being reduced to rubble.

A colossal herd of journalists languished just a few hundred kilometres away in posh hotel rooms in downtown Tehran. And the Western world was almost oblivious to the distress of the Kurds. This was ten years before the Gulf War. Only then did Kurdistan become an identifiable place in an atlas for most North Americans. At this time, I knew nothing about the Kurdish cause. But I smelled a good story.

In the middle of downtown Tehran—in a location the rat pack of

Western journalists could hardly miss — was a one-room, Spartan office, the headquarters of the beleaguered Kurdish Friendship Society. Here a ragtag band of patriots churned out press releases on the daily carnage in their homeland and passed them out to indifferent Western journalists. As far as the reporters were concerned, the story they'd been sent to cover was the American hostage crisis. What was happening in some far-off mountain province was of little or no consequence. Who the hell were the Kurds, anyway?

At first, I was no different from anyone else in the pack. But when I get bored, I get impatient. And I was very, very bored.

As I walked by the Friendship Society early one morning, a young man with a pleading look buttonholed me. He introduced himself as Jamal and grabbed my hand. I was trapped. I grudgingly agreed to hear him out. But only for a few minutes, I said. I was in a hurry, I added.

"We are twenty-five million people with no homeland," he began. "Our country was divided after World War I with pieces going to Turkey, Syria, Iran and Iraq. We are neither Arab, nor Persian, nor Turk. We Kurds have lived in the mountains for more than four thousand years. We are not allowed to exist as a people. Our language and culture have been banned."

As he lectured, my gaze fixed on a montage of photographs on the walls of the tiny office. They depicted horrifying scenes of death, dismemberment and devastation.

"Where were these taken?" I asked.

"Sanandaj. This is what the Iranian Army has done to the Kurdish people with their bombs and mortars and rockets."

"When?"

"This past week," Jamal replied.

I stared at a picture of a hysterical mother carrying a little boy. He was dead, his legs hanging, almost severed by shrapnel.

"We are asking simply that we be allowed to live in peace in our own homeland," Jamal said. "Instead, we are torn apart by four nations. We will not submit. We will never submit, so they try to exterminate us." Jamal stared directly into my eyes.

"The Kurdish people have a saying: Kurds have no friends."

He was right. Nobody knew the Kurds even existed. I couldn't recall one demonstration or one word uttered in Canada about the Kurdish cause. I had never even seen Kurdistan on a map before coming to Iran.

"If Kurdistan wasn't on the Iranian government's no-go list, I'd probably go there," I proffered. I knew I was being disingenuous, and from the expression on Jamal's face, so did he.

"You don't need the government's permission," he said. "You are invited by the Kurdish Democratic Party. There is a bus leaving from the bazaar this afternoon for Tabriz in the north. I will have someone meet you there to take you into Kurdistan. You will see for yourself what is happening. That is, if you care about truth and justice."

It was a pitch, no doubt, that Jamal had made to scores of reporters before I happened across his threshold. He went on insistently. "There are hundreds of journalists here for the American hostages. I am certain one will not be missed."

"What if the hostages are suddenly freed and I'm up in Kurdistan? I'd be in deep shit with my editor," I argued.

"The hostages will not be set free for many more months. The people who hold them are zealots. They want to make a point and they will take their time in doing so. You will be in Kurdistan reporting on a genocide."

Again, I glanced over at the photographs on the wall. For several minutes, I was transfixed by one picture. The corpses of more than a dozen young men riddled with bullets lined a blood-soaked concrete floor. Some of the bodies' eyes were open.

At the bus terminal, Jamal pointed to a sign atop the front window of a colourfully painted bus crammed with passengers.

"It is going to Tabriz," he said.

"When I get there, what then?"

"You will be met by a friend. I will pass a message along."

It took twelve hours to get to Tabriz. The bus wound its way through a string of villages and towns. As we drove along the edge of rocky foothills deeper and deeper into the country, we passed green hills dotted with flocks of sheep and blood-red hills covered with a tapestry of poppies. I stared out the window, wondering who was behind the booming opium harvest in Iran.

It was almost two in the morning when I stumbled off the bus onto a deserted street in Tabriz. From the shadows of a rug merchant's shop, a stocky man wearing a black-and-white *kaffiyeh* motioned me to follow him. I felt as if I'd been thrust into a low-budget spy movie. The man led me to a teahouse, where he introduced me to two swarthy men who spoke no English. We shook hands, had a cup of very sweet, black tea and then headed out into the night. We were going to Mahabad. The first leg of the journey was by Jeep through the bumpy foothills. It was slow and arduous. We drove with no lights to avoid detection. I was dead-tired and running on adrenaline.

We'd been motoring for about two hours when the driver shut off the engine and coasted to a stop. I looked at my watch — 4:10 a.m. It was time to walk. As we trekked up a steep mountain path, I was grateful that I had stayed in shape. For four years, I had been dancing with a Ukrainian dance troupe in Toronto known as the Black Sea Cossacks, and my legs were as powerful as truck pistons.

As the first rays of dawn poked over the mountain peaks, one of my escorts led me to the side of a ridge and pointed to a valley below. In the greyish-blue darkness, I could make out a massive Iranian military bivouac, its front flank defended by wall of rocket launchers, tanks and artillery. They were all pointing in one direction.

My guide pointed in the same direction. "Mahabad," he said.

As we got closer to the town, we were intercepted by rifle-toting *peshmergas* — Kurdish freedom fighters. There were firm handshakes, bear hugs and kisses on the cheeks. Again, no one spoke English. We leapt into a Jeep for the short ride to town.

Nestled in a picturesque valley, Mahabad was one of the few towns in Kurdish Iran that had not yet been attacked by Khomeini's soldiers. It was the stronghold and headquarters of the Kurdish Democratic Party, which claimed to have twenty-five thousand heavily armed *peshmergas* fighting in various parts of the hotly disputed territory with Iran.

The first thing I noticed as we drove through the town was the absence of posters singing the praises of Ayatollah Khomeini and the Iranian revolution, and of graffiti damning Carter and the American imperialist pigs.

Mahabad appeared to be a cheery place, filled with warmth and a strong sense of belonging. Children played in the courtyards. Striking olive-skinned women in bright robes, their faces uncovered, shopped in the busy bazaars and markets. Fiercely proud men, in colourful turbans and sashes, baggy pants and loose-fitting shirts with military collars, strolled hand in hand. Elderly men with white beards and leather-skinned faces sat close together in packed teahouses chatting amicably as they thumbed their worry beads.

Yet while everything appeared serene, there was a strange, uneasy feel. The reason became clear when I looked up.

Atop the mountains around the town, the Iranian Army was poised to strike. Dozens of artillery pieces were perched on the crags. Helicopters ferried in fresh supplies daily, as well as ammunition and reinforcements. For the moment, there was calm. But all that was needed was a spark and Mahabad would be reduced to a pile of rubble and death, like so many other towns and villages in Kurdistan.

My escorts brought me to a building that looked like a government office. I sat on a hard wooden bench in a dank corridor desperately trying to stay awake. I was utterly exhausted. After an hour, a portly man emerged from an office and warmly grabbed my hand.

"I say, it's so good to meet you, old chap. How may I be of help to you?"

I was surprised to hear him speak with a measured British accent.

"I'm here to find out what is happening in this part of the world. I was told there's a war going on."

"Quite so, and I suppose you would like to meet General Abdulrahman Qassemlou, the leader of the Kurdish Democratic Party?" he said.

My eyes lit up. "If it could be arranged, that would be great," I said. Jamal had told me that Qassemlou was the head of the outlawed KDP and an archenemy of the Ayatollah and his mullahs.

"That can be arranged. But first, you should have something to eat and get some rest. Come with me."

"What's your name?" I asked as we walked down the street.

"My dear chap, you can call me Colonel," he said with a wry grin.

"Can I ask where you learned to speak English?"

"I was a prisoner in the Shah's prisons for seventeen years, and every day from my cell I would monitor the BBC for news of the world. I learned to speak English from the radio."

"That's incredible!" I now understood the accent. He sounded just like a BBC radio news announcer.

"Not really," he said matter-of-factly.

The colonel took me to his home. There I met his wife, a slender woman, much younger than the colonel, with blue eyes and long black hair. We entered a room that could have come out of *The Arabian Nights*. The entire floor and all the walls were covered with magnificent, hand-knotted Persian rugs. Dozens of finely embroidered pillows were propped against the walls, and a large brass antique samovar stood in a corner.

"We will rest here," the colonel suggested.

I dropped onto the floor, leaned against a pillow and instantly drifted into a deep sleep. I awoke to find a beautiful, dark-eyed little girl staring curiously into my face. Startled, I smiled. The little girl giggled.

"She's five years old—my youngest," the colonel said. "I trust you had a good sleep."

"Yes. I was really tired."

"I have arranged for you to be picked up here early tomorrow morning. You will be taken to meet General Qassemlou at his bunker. I'm sure you can understand why he is not in the town."

"Does he speak English?" I asked.

"Not very well. But he speaks French fluently. He taught economics at the Sorbonne in Paris in the mid-1970s. And he speaks some Czech and some Russian."

"I speak French," I said. "I'm from Quebec. It's a French-speaking province in Canada."

"Yes, I'm well aware of the struggle for independence by the people of Quebec."

"The BBC?"

The colonel grinned. "Quite so!"

I laughed. "Tell me a little about General Qassemlou."

"Back in 1960, the Shah of Iran sentenced him to death. Qassemlou escaped and fled the country. He lived in Czechoslovakia until 1976 where he taught at the Charles University in Prague. Then he went to Paris to teach at the Sorbonne. A few months before the Shah was sent into exile, he returned to Kurdistan to lead the party and the people in our struggle. He is deeply committed to the Kurdish cause."

"How did your men get all these weapons?" I asked.

"When the Shah went into exile, the country was thrown into disarray. The Kurdish Democratic Party of Iran saw an opportunity. During demonstrations throughout Kurdish Iran, we seized the weapons from army barracks and police stations."

"But things don't seem to be going too well for the cause," I said.

"They're not," the colonel said somberly. "It's ironic. The Shah used American-built jets and helicopters to oppress us. Now the bombers are flying the green flag of Islam with Khomeini in the cockpit. He has killed more Kurds in one year than the Shah killed in almost forty years."

The ride to the general's secret bunker over extremely hilly terrain took about three hours. I wasn't required to cover my eyes. There was no need for such precautions since I had no idea where I was and could never have found the place again if my life depended on it.

The hideout was ringed by heavily armed *peshmergas*. Slung across their shoulders were Russian-made Kalashnikov assault rifles, and strapped to their sides were pistols and revolvers. Grenades and bayonets dangled from their waists. They were ready for battle.

Qassemlou looked much older than his forty-nine years. The brutal losses on the battlefield had taken their toll. His face was tired, lined with worry and profound sadness. The situation for his troops was grim. Every battle had been lost, the death toll was heavy, the suffering and devastation massive. He was barely holding on.

Within moments of our introduction, he got down to business. He had a message he wanted delivered to the outside world. The battle strategy was about to change. The *peshmergas* were pulling out of all towns and villages and were heading for the hills.

"We are going to fight a guerrilla war from this moment forward," Qassemlou announced. "We will decide when and where to strike. We are not going to fight any longer in the towns and villages. The people have suffered enough. We are going to fight from the forests and the mountains. We will be an unseen enemy. The government of Iran will no longer choose the time and place for fighting. We will."

Qassemlou's words made good copy. But the hard truth was that he was retreating. He had lost. More than two hundred thousand Iranian troops had dug into military fortifications throughout the region, and there was little the five million Kurds of Iran could do except submit.

I asked him about life under the Ayatollah since the overthrow of the Shah. He shook his head in dismay.

"Even under the regime of the former Shah, conditions in Kurdistan were never as brutal as they are now. Under orders from the mullahs, the Iranian Air Force use Phantom jets and helicopter gunships to bomb and strafe small towns and villages. And the *pasdarans*, the revolutionary guards, are vicious. They are fanatic Moslems who have been given a license to kill by Khomeini. These *pasdarans* are racist. They are Shi'ite Muslim. We Kurds are Sunni Muslim. The *pasdarans* go into our towns and villages and massacre and torture people simply because we are Kurdish. The Shah was never so brutal."

Qassemlou looked out the window at a band of young *peshmergas* crowded around a Jeep, laughing and joking. He was a proud father admiring his sons. "These men are *peshmergas*. Do you know what that means?"

"Freedom fighters," I offered.

"It is much more than that. It is a term of honour. To be a *peshmerga* is to make a pact with death. Your life becomes the struggle. You have no time for anything else."

The general drew a deep breath and sat down.

"I am very happy to be back with my people," he said after a long silence. "But I am tired of the fighting. I want it to end so that we can get on to building a free and democratic Kurdistan."

He was close to defeat and he knew it. The Iranian Army was just too powerful. The Ayatollah's *pasdarans*, assured of martyrdom and instant elevation to paradise, were ready to wrap their young bodies in white funeral shrouds and sacrifice themselves to Allah, advancing in waves as cannon fodder.

I stayed at the bunker that night chatting with Qassemlou about the dreams and aspirations of the Kurdish people. It was a memorable history lesson, rich in folklore that went back four centuries before the birth of Christ. It was a story of a people that in many ways reminded me of my grandfather's Ukraine. A country that seemed forever destined to be under the hammer of one foreign power or another. Like Ukraine, Kurdistan was caught in the crossfire of invading armies. The Kurds, twenty-five million strong, had been carved up and held in oppression by a succession of intolerant rulers — Turks, Syrians, Iraqis and Iranians.

At dawn, Qassemlou assigned three battle-seasoned *peshmergas* to take me to the latest front line, the town of Saqqez. For more than two months, Saqqez had been the scene of a bloody battle between the Iranian Army and Kurdish rebels. Hundreds of people had been killed, even more wounded, and it wasn't over yet because the Iranians had not managed to rout out all the *peshmergas* who by now were the only people left in the town.

We drove through tough, hilly terrain for almost six hours. In the middle of the afternoon, one of my *peshmerga* bodyguards, a wiry fighter named Mohammed with steely eyes, droopy mustache and huge hands, stopped the Jeep and leapt out. The road was heavily cratered with holes the size of large mixing bowls. In a ditch were the charred, mangled remains of two minivans. They'd been hit by machine-gun fire from Iranian helicopter gunships. Three Kurds trying to bring desperately needed supplies to the people of Saqqez had been killed.

Mohammed sketched a crude map in the dust with a bayonet, conferring with his sidekicks as he did so. Then he sat down on the ground cross-legged and yanked a huge, compressed, dark brown glob out of a sack. He gnawed off a hunk and passed the glob to me, grinning widely. I was not about to insult my hosts. I tore off a corner with my teeth and began to chew. It was pasty, gritty and very sweet. The guys laughed. Silently, I prayed I wouldn't be struck down with a case of dysentery. But I was hungry, and the dates were a welcome treat.

After the break, we split up. Mohammed stuck with me; his cohorts disappeared down a steep hillside. He instructed me to keep a short distance behind him at all times. Then he moved over to a ridge overlooking Saqqez. A couple of seconds later, I followed. Mohammed released the safety catch on his Kalashnikov, dropped down on his stomach and crawled to the edge. I was close behind. He placed two fingers on his right shoulder and pointed at two mountaintops. I nodded, indicating that I understood there were Iranian outposts on them.

In the valley below was Saqqez. From a distance, it looked like a placid, picture-postcard town. We stealthily made our way down the mountainside. My palms were sweaty and my pulse was racing. Odd, I thought as I looked up: the sky was so blue and the sun so radiant, it just didn't seem like the kind of day for a battle.

Sporadic machine-gun fire smashed the afternoon calm as we approached the outskirts of the town. We darted from building to building, using the walls for protection, trying to make our way to the town centre.

Saqqez was in ruins. The streets and alleyways were deserted, pockmarked with craters of all sizes from mortar shells and bombs, littered with glass, rocks and wood and strewn with deadly shards of shrapnel. Most of the buildings were destroyed by grenades, mortars and artillery shells. We moved deeper into the empty town, stray cats, packs of hungry dogs and an occasional rat scuttling in our wake.

Mohammed stayed about twenty feet ahead, darting skillfully from building to building and then turning to wave me onward. From time to time, we chanced upon a couple of *peshmergas* tucked behind obscured, well-fortified, sand-bagged bunkers.

Then came true terror. Mohammed had waved at me with a gesture

I didn't understand. I continued to creep forward. Just as I was about to cross a road, he charged and tackled me to the ground. He pointed to a machine-gun nest at the far end of the street. I had almost walked into the direct line of fire.

We lay there for a few minutes while I tried to regain my composure. I was shaking. I vividly imagined machine-gun bullets slamming into my body.

We'd been lucky. The Iranian sentries had not spotted us.

We crept around the town for almost two hours before we came across the first of several surprises. In a tiny, boxed-in square in the heart of the main bazaar, we happened on forty or so very frightened people huddled together. Most were old. One elderly man with a snow-white beard and holding a cane sat dejectedly beside a blind man. A teenaged boy stood rigid against a wall, staring blankly into space. Four elderly women, draped in black mourning shrouds, whispered to each other in a corner. On the street, a handful of ragged children, maybe ten or twelve years old, played marbles.

In a dusty stall in the centre of the square, a large, dented, nickel-plated samovar stood like a beckoning statue. Steam spouted from its top. A single, open kiosk displayed bags, plastic pots and wooden crates filled with dried beans, fruits and nuts. It was all that was left of a once-bustling market place.

As we entered the courtyard, Mohammed was besieged by the shell-shocked townsfolk. A man with a grizzled beard locked onto his arm and began pleading with him. Tears streamed down his weathered cheeks.

Mohammed shrugged. His face showed no emotion. He didn't have any answers for the shell shocked townspeople.

Qassemlou had told me that most of Saqqez's sixty thousand inhabitants had fled to other towns and villages. Almost half were in Bukan, twenty miles away. Those who remained were too sick, too old or too frightened to leave.

The huddle of survivors shepherded us to the wooden stall where the samovar bubbled. They offered us tea, then rice, potatoes, onions and thin flat bread. We politely and repeatedly refused the food. These hospitable people were offering us their meagre rations. We accepted only the tea, black and heavily sugared. I drank it slowly, savouring each sip.

I had just swallowed my last mouthful when an elderly man grabbed my arm and began pulling me toward an alleyway.

"Mosque, mosque, bomb!" he shouted in broken English while pointing to the sky. His eyes were filled with indignation. Aided by a clutch of elders hovering by his side, he told in sign language how a bomb had slammed into the two-story stone and wood mosque where they were praying on a Friday, the Moslem Sabbath. Seven people were killed. Several more were injured. The tall, slender green minaret, from which the mullah called the congregation to pray, had collapsed through the two floors. One of the elders seemed almost possessed as he scrambled through the debris, tearing madly at the burned beams and shattered walls.

"Koran, Koran!" His breathing was laboured as he scooped up charred pages of the Moslem holy book and held them in his clenched fist.

The man ran to me and began stuffing the burnt pages into my jacket pocket. "Koran, Khomeini. Koran, Khomeini. *Allah-o-Akbar!*"

"*Allah-o-Akbar,*" the other elders intoned, dropping to their knees.

Mohammed finally reappeared and extricated me from the elders' passionate display amidst the ruins of the mosque. We continued our sortie through the town. As we scurried down a back alley, my foot caught a metal object. I tripped, falling hard on the ground. Mohammed doubled back and helped me up. What I saw made my knees buckle. It was an unexploded mortar shell, jammed four inches into the hard-packed dirt road. My heart pounded as I imagined the deadly explosive detonating under my feet.

Mohammed motioned to me to take cover behind a building. Then he crouched behind a pile of rocks and took aim with his Kalashnikov. He blew up the shell on the second shot. The explosion was deafening. Dirt, rocks and debris rained down on us. As the echoes ricocheted in the distance, Mohammed suddenly looked toward the sky and put his fingers to his lips. My ears immediately picked up a low, flapping drone coming from one of the mountaintops. Then we saw it. A green helicopter gunship heading straight for us.

Mohammed charged toward an abandoned house, kicked down the bolted door and dove in. I was right behind. For what seemed an eternity, the helicopter buzzed the town, the propellers thundering overhead as it whizzed by, searching for a moving target. I chewed nervously at my fingernails. My guardian calmly sat back and puffed on a Winston. Then the sound of the blades grew distant. I looked at Mohammed and forced a weak smile. His eyes shot to the ceiling. He placed his hands on his head and motioned me to duck down near the wall.

In the distance, I heard a hollow pop. A second later, a fast-approaching whistle. Then an explosion shook the ground. It was followed by another and another and another. A mortar landed just outside the house, sending a shower of dirt, glass and rock down on us. Then there was a lull.

Mohammed pulled a revolver out of his holster and handed it to me. No, no! I motioned, vainly trying to explain that I would not get involved in the shooting. Mohammed shook his head and roughly grabbed my face with his hand. He placed his fingers on his shoulders, sign language for the Iranian Army. I nodded to let him know I understood. He put his arms behind his back as if he were taken prisoner. Again, fingers on his shoulders. He unsheathed his bayonet and pretended to slit my throat and then his. Finally, he took the revolver and pointed it to his head.

I felt the blood drain from my face. I understood what he was trying to tell me. Rather than be taken prisoner, he was suggesting a quicker and less painful alternative: suicide.

I nodded weakly and took the gun. The steel was cold. The reality was terrifying. I felt numb. Then a mortar slammed into a building behind us, and I was rudely shaken into consciousness.

The mountainsides opened with machine-gun fire. The army blasted away, raking the town indiscriminately. Lead slammed into walls, tore through doors, shattered windows and ricocheted off the roads. The *peshmergas* returned fire.

It was my first experience in a real battle. I was petrified. Months earlier, in Afghanistan, I had been witness only to the aftermath of war. The Soviets hit their targets with lightning quickness and lethal precision. I had arrived in their wake, when all that remained was destruction and the stench of death.

Now, in this forgotten Kurdish town, a single thought echoed through my mind. I was going to die in this hellhole. How would anyone ever find out I was killed? Would my body be dumped in a hole and never found? Who would tell my beautiful Anna? Who would tell my mother and my brothers that I was dead? Then my self-pity turned to rage. I had put myself into extreme jeopardy — and for what? A story! An adventure! A chance to dance on the edge of a cliff.

"I am a goddamned idiot!" I shouted.

The gunfire intensified. Bullets pinged off the walls and streets. Mohammed returned fire through a hole in the wall. He never wasted a bullet. He watched, waited, found a target and pulled the trigger. I hugged the ground and tried to find religion with a 45-caliber revolver in my hand. I was soaked with sweat, and my hands were shaking.

Then suddenly, it became very quiet. We remained still for a long, long time. It was dusk when we crept out of our hideout, I saw that a mortar had gouged a huge crater into the street. A few metres more and we would have been blown to bits.

Mohammed smiled and gave me a reassuring slap on the back. We headed toward the bazaar. Some of the townsfolk were stumbling into the alleyways, shaking off the dirt and dust. We couldn't tell if anyone had been killed in the latest barrage.

Mohammed and I waited for complete darkness before making our final dash out of the town. Once in the Jeep, we made a beeline for a safe haven.

Bukan was awash with refugees from Saqqez and Baneh. Thousands of children, women and men had poured into the town. Hundreds were lined up in front of a food station waiting for a meagre handout of potatoes, rice and onions. About three thousand families were living in a tent village on a soccer field on the outskirts of Bukan. Another thousand refugees were crammed into two schools. Many more were given shelter by families on the floors of their homes.

That night, I slept on a floor along with six battle-weary soldiers in a house belonging to the local doctor. I was totally exhausted and passed out as soon as I lay down on the rug. Late into the night, I was jolted by a terrifying nightmare. I dreamt I had been captured by the *pasdarans*. I was tied to a chair, and they were torturing me. Mohammed, his shirt ripped open, sat slumped in front of me, a macabre expression on his face. His eyes were open and defiant — but he was dead. His throat had been slashed from ear to ear. Blood dripped down his chest. Then the cold steel of a bayonet pressed against my neck.

My eyes popped open. My skin was clammy, and I was breathing in erratic gulps. I gazed around the room at the shadowy mounds snoring on the floor and realized where I was. Shaken to the core, I couldn't fall back asleep. I stared at the ceiling until the first rays of dawn filtered through the window.

In the morning, I had some tea and a bowl of starchy rice with raisins. Mohammed informed me in sign language that he was returning to Saqqez to try to rescue the remaining townsfolk. He had assigned a new guide to get me back to Mahabad.

When I got back to Tehran, I was told by a hotel clerk that the Revolutionary Guard had dropped by on four separate occasions looking for me and that I had been summoned to the Ministry of National Guidance. I sensed I was in deep trouble. I thought fast and hard about my options. I knew one thing: I wasn't up for National Guidance.

I decided to move quickly. I checked out of my hotel and booked into another one. I found out through a couple of journalists that a British Airways flight was due to land the following afternoon in Tehran. It would be an excellent opportunity to leave the country, they pointed out, because it was a Moslem high holiday and all government offices would be closed. It would be next to impossible for airport security to get a reading on my departure status.

Early the next morning, I packed my things hurriedly and headed for the airport. At passport control, a junior clerk was on duty alone. He telephoned repeatedly to the Ministry of Foreign Affairs, trying to raise someone to check the bona fides of my departure. I played to his youth and inexperience and kept insisting, in tones I hoped sounded authoritative, that I had every right to leave. Since I was not Iranian, I explained, I didn't have to submit my passport to government authorities three days before departure. The young clerk looked dubious. Clearly he was suspicious over my Canadian passport, as was everyone else at the airport. Everyone from the baggage handlers to the armed sentries had scrutinized it.

I was beginning to get very worried. Then I remembered my trump card. I pulled my Iranian press pass from my pocket—the one Sadegh had given me, issued by the Ministry of National Guidance, which introduced me "in the name of Allah."

That did it. The clerk was convinced I was a bona fide Canadian journalist with a right to leave the country. But for good measure, he ordered me to be strip-searched. I was taken to a cubicle behind a curtain and told to open my mouth, put my arms over my head, spread my legs and bend over. Every single piece of my clothing and all my possessions were examined. The guard questioned three shards of metal I had wrapped in a pair of socks. I picked them up off the street, I lied. He dropped them back in my case. The metal was shrapnel that had exploded outside my hideout in Saqqez.

My interrogation and strip-search took three hours, three of the longest hours in my life. The most nerve-racking moment came when the officer started going through a half-dozen books I had in my suitcase. One of them contained the negatives from my trek into Kurdistan. All film had to be cleared by National Guidance censors before leaving the country. The inspector started going through a book on the revolution. It was filled with pictures of Khomeini's triumphant return to Iran from his exile in France. He wanted to keep the book, he said, and as we argued over it, I managed to move the novel containing the negatives into the cleared pile.

At last, I was given the green light. My passport was stamped, and I headed for the departure lounge.

The moment the British Airways jet lifted off the ground, I ordered a double vodka straight up.

"Sorry, sir," the flight attendant replied. "I can't offer you an alcoholic beverage while we are still in Iranian airspace."

Oh, my God, my ordeal isn't over yet! I thought.

A few minutes later, as we were passing over a mountain range, the pilot announced over the intercom that Mount Ararat was on our right.

I knew my geography. I rang for the flight attendant.

"We're in Turkey," I informed her. "I'll have that double vodka, please."

POSTSCRIPT

On July 27, 1980, the Shah died of cancer in exile in Egypt. He was sixty. On January 20, 1981, after 444 days in captivity, the fifty-two American hostages were finally freed, the same day Ronald Reagan was sworn in as the fortieth president of the United States.

On June 3, 1989, Ayatollah Khomeini died of old age. He was eighty-nine. And on July 13, 1989, one month and ten days after the death of Ayatollah Khomeini, Qassemlou arrived in Vienna, Austria, for a hastily organized secret meeting with three Iranian diplomats. It had been arranged with the aim of bringing an end to ten years of fighting between the *peshmergas* and the Tehran regime. Qassemlou, the respected and internationally recognized leader of the twenty-five million Kurds in Turkey, Iraq, Iran, Syria and the former Soviet Union, had signalled publicly his willingness to negotiate after Khomeini's death.

Shortly after seven that night, Qassemlou, along with two close advisors — Abdallah Ghaderi and Fadhil Rasoul — embraced the Iranian delegation in friendship at a downtown Vienna apartment. As the fifty-nine-year-old Kurdish leader sat down in an armchair, the Iranians pulled out silencer-equipped revolvers and began firing. Qassemlou was killed instantly, hit three times in the face and head at point-blank range. His associates were also assassinated. The suspects fled the country under the full protection of diplomatic passports. The Austrian authorities did nothing to stop them.

CHAPTER SEVEN

MONTREAL INTERLUDE

It was trumpeted as a promotion, a reward for my hard work. After returning from Afghanistan and Iran, I was named Montreal bureau chief for the *Globe*. I was excited, at first, because I was going home. I had never been able to get Quebec out of my blood. I was a loyal *Canadien*, and from the moment I left Montreal in 1973, I pined for it. I fantasized about la Belle Ville. It was cosmopolitan. It had adrenaline. It had passion. It had a soul. Nothing, in my mind, could surpass my hometown.

From the moment I arrived in Toronto, I'd steadfastly refused to let it seduce me. Toronto wasn't in the same league, I decreed. Toronto was just a pit stop—for professional purposes only. I was frantic to make my escape.

But my return to Montreal in April, 1981, was a splash of ice-cold water in my face. In the years I had been away, there had been a dramatic change. My beloved city had gone from cosmopolitan to provincial. It had lost its international charm. Bill 101—the French-only language law—had irreparably altered the landscape. Everything that was not French was considered second-class or was not permitted to exist. The mood had soured, and the gulf between the two solitudes had widened. And in the wake of the victory of René Lévesque's separatist party in 1976, a lot of my old friends had packed up and moved away.

All of which I might have come to terms with, eventually.

But there was one thing I couldn't adjust to. My new job! In my mad scramble to get out of TO, I hadn't bothered to weigh the demands. Really, I was going back to general reporting—day-to-day news events. Granted, I was also about to cover a major turning point in Canadian history: Prime Minister Pierre Trudeau's patriation of the Constitution in 1981 and Quebec's ultimate refusal to sign it; the rise of Brian Mulroney; the astounding resurgence of Robert Bourassa, the Quebec premier who had been soundly humiliated by René Lévesque and the Parti Québécois in the 1976 provincial election. Yet despite my front-row seat for these momentous events, I felt like a scribe again. And I hated it!

I was not cut out to be a stenographer, scribbling down the verbal meanderings of politicians. And covering Brian Mulroney's speeches was like floundering in a vat of maple syrup. With his baritone blarney, he dragged speechmaking and politics to a new low.

Still, there were moments worth reporting, if only for the unalloyed delight of having the occasional banner story on the front page. But in my heart, I wanted to dig up stories that mattered. And as Montreal bureau chief, grandiose as the title sounded, I was at the beck and call of my editorial masters in Toronto. They wanted me glued to the polit-ical-reporter pack—watching, jotting and recounting the government news of the hour and of the day.

By the spring of 1984, I had had it with Montreal. Much as I hated to face up to the hard truth, I was prepared to beg to go back to Toronto. And not only for the job they could offer me there. Toronto had changed. Even I realized it had become a truly interesting, cos-mopolitan city. Fortunately for me, the recently appointed managing editor, Geoffrey Stevens, was only too happy to get me out of Montreal. Not to make *me* happy. Quite the contrary. During my stint as bureau chief, Stevens was the national editor, and I had managed to rub him very much the wrong way. National bureau chiefs across Canada reported to him, and he liked to keep close tabs on them. In my case, close tabs meant telling me where to be, when to be there and how to do my job. And I liked a long leash. Truth was, I could only work when I was given a long leash. Stevens and I had a few heated exchanges and, if the *Globe*'s new editor-in-chief, Norman Webster, had not gone to bat for me, I'm certain Stevens would have fired me.

Upon my return to Toronto, the peripatetic John Fraser, now the national editor, intercepted me as I bounded into the newsroom. He calmly exhorted me to keep my cool. Stevens, he warned me, was not looking forward to our face-to-face meeting.

"You make him tense," Fraser said.

"He makes *me* tense," I replied.

I walked into the managing editor's office. What a difference from that first time eight years ago, when Clark Davey sat behind the desk! Stevens and I didn't shake hands. We barely made eye contact. I'm not sure which of us was more uncomfortable. Brushing his blonde hair from his forehead, Stevens got right to the point. He suggested I might be the perfect candidate to start up a multiculturalism beat. The pierogi beat!

"I'm so happy to be a Ukrainian in Canada," I responded sarcastically.

My direct boss was Paul Palango, the new city editor and a Stevens protégé. I figured my days at the *Globe* were numbered. But Palango surprised me. He talked tough, and he had a hard, provocative edge to him. He loathed lazy reporters and measured every reporter by a simple yardstick: Can I remember a story he or she has done? If so, the reporter passed muster. If not, forget it. Needless to say, Palango did not remember stories based on regurgitated press-release rewrites or press conference reports. His first love was investigative reporting.

Palango's advice to me was curt and frank. "If you want to break stories, I'll back you. If you want to sit on your ass, join the general reporters and don't moan to me about your assignments."

I smiled. I knew I had come home.

CHAPTER EIGHT

TERRORIST IMMIGRANTS

There was something odd about the call, and almost from the start, I felt an uneasy twinge. I knew when I got that feeling I shouldn't ignore it. But in this case I almost did, because the tip was dynamite. A sure-fire front-page banner story!

But first the caller wanted to set the ground rules. He demanded a guarantee of complete anonymity and a promise I would not tape-record the conversation. The guy obviously had media savvy.

"Do I have your word?" he asked.

"Yeah. You've got my word. I won't tape any of this," I said. "And on the first point, I don't even know your name," I added.

There was a pause. That short, tense moment where a caller either wades in or hangs up. He cleared his throat.

"The man's name is Bagga. He's a former major in the Indian Army. External Affairs has information he was involved in a plot to assassinate Rajiv Gandhi, the prime minister of India."

I jotted down the information in my indecipherable shorthand. I could feel the adrenaline surge through my veins.

"Bagga is also wanted for the murder of the Indian Army general who led the attack on the Sikh Golden Temple in Amritsar back in June 1984," the caller continued. "And for inciting an entire regiment of Sikh soldiers to desert and take up arms against the Indian government at the time the army was laying siege to the Golden Temple."

"This is incredible!" I said.

"Then you can understand why the Indian government wants Bagga extradited. This man is a terrorist and a killer."

"How did he get into Canada?" I asked.

"He literally walked across a farm field from the U.S. into British Columbia."

"When?"

"June, 1986. And the first thing he does is claim he's a refugee fleeing persecution in his homeland," he said, a caustic edge to his voice. "Claims he's a Sikh holy man who simply wants to live a religious life of meditation seeking God."

There was something in the caller's sardonic tone that triggered my built-in crap-detecting radar. For some unexplained reason, this amazingly generous news offering felt contrived — as if it had been sanitized and carefully filtered through a controlled vetting process before being "leaked" to me.

Then came the particulars.

Name: Santokh Singh Bagga.

Date of birth: 15/7/1936.

Place and date of entry into Canada: Vancouver, June 20, 1986.

The last bit of information was the first real clue that something just didn't add up. Here it was Monday, May 10, 1988, and this supposed bad guy was still in the country after almost two years. If he was so dangerous, I wondered, why wasn't he arrested upon his arrival, detained and quickly turfed? Ottawa could have declared him persona non grata and moved for immediate deportation on the grounds that he posed a serious threat to national security. Or the Indian government could have demanded his extradition to face criminal charges back home for murder, sedition and treason.

The caller had more titillating information to impart. Bagga entered Canada accompanied by two people. A son, Gursev, date of birth October, 1967, and a woman, Jasbir Kaur, date of birth September, 1952.

"Our information shows that Gursev Singh was involved in the armed siege in Amritsar. He was holed up in the Golden Temple with a bunch of Sikh extremists who shot it out with the Indian Army. Somehow, he managed to escape during the military mop-up, and he's now being sought by Indian authorities for his part in the shoot-out."

An added bonus, I thought. Two terrorists! The story just kept getting better.

Then the kicker. "You'll be getting some paper on this very soon to back up what I've just told you." The caller hung up.

I glanced over my notes and began typing the lead paragraph based on the information I'd been given. I stored it in a locked computer file.

A Sikh terrorist who is alleged to have been involved in the assassination plot of India's Prime Minister Rajiv Gandhi and the murder of an Indian Army general recently slipped into Canada claiming to be a refugee, a federal government source told the *Globe and Mail*.

I couldn't believe it! This was the second anonymous tip I'd received in five months about a terrorist sneaking into Canada. My story on the first, a Palestinian, had set off fireworks in the House of Commons and outrage in the Jewish community. It also unleashed vitriolic accusations from the Arab community that I was a dupe of the Israeli secret service, the Mossad, and a telephone threat on my life, purportedly from a member of the Palestinian Liberation Organization.

I knew from the moment I got the information about the Palestinian that it was solid. It had the feel of truth, and after a few days of digging, I was able to prove it.

It was late Wednesday afternoon, January 13, 1988. A telephone call. A disembodied voice flushed with anger and indignation. He said he had some highly sensitive information that would blow the lid off Immigration. But before he shared the details, he wanted assurances. I had to promise not to divulge his identity.

"That's simple," I said. "Just don't tell me who you are."

"Then how can you trust what I'm saying?" he asked.

"Even if you told me your name, I'd be a fool to take you at your word. My job is to prove what you tell me and not just take your allegation and print it as fact."

"Well, here goes," the caller said. "On February 25, 1987, a guy named Mahmoud Muhammad Issa Mohammad landed at Toronto's Lester B. Pearson International Airport."

He paused.

"And?" I asked.

"He's a convicted PLO terrorist."

"Convicted of what?" I interjected.

"Murder. He killed a Jew in a terrorist attack, and now he's in Canada wanting a better life for himself and his family."

"So he's claimed refugee status in order to stay here." I said cynically.

"No. Not at all. No refugee-status claim here. He and his wife and three children came here as landed immigrants."

"If this Mahmoud guy is what you say he is, how did he manage to slip by the RCMP or CSIS (Canadian Security Intelligence Service) security check?" I asked. "You'd figure every intelligence agency in the Western world would have his name in their computers. Did he lie about his identity or change his name?"

"No. That's what's so amazing. Apparently the man didn't even try to hide his identity. He is who he said he was," the caller maintained.

"But someone along the way must have asked him if he had a criminal record?" I said.

"Yeah. And he told the immigration counsellor at the Canadian Embassy in Madrid that he didn't have a criminal record."

"What did this guy do?" I asked.

"I'm not exactly certain. I haven't seen the file. It's stamped Secret, and access is need-to-know only. But I was told he was a member of a PLO terrorist group that staged some sort of attack in Europe several years ago. I also heard an Israeli man was killed in that attack. The only hard facts I've got at my fingertips right now are his name, date of birth and date of entry into Canada."

"How did you get that information?" I asked.

"It's on the front-line computer. No trouble getting that. Anything more will definitely trigger alarm bells."

"How are you so sure this guy is the terrorist? You might have the wrong man. Mohammad is a very common name throughout the Middle East," I pointed out.

"Because the shit has really hit the fan over this case. Last June, there was a high-level meeting in Ottawa with senior officials from External Affairs, Immigration, the solicitor general and CSIS," he said. And afterward, he added, a top-secret report was prepared for External Affairs Minister Joe Clark, Solicitor General James Kelleher, Employment and Immigration Minister Benoit Bouchard and junior Immigration Minister Gerry Weiner.

"Have you seen the report?" I asked.

"Like I said, it's top secret! There's a record of whoever puts their hands on it, and I've got no reason to be asking for it."

"Can you get access to it?" I asked.

"Probably. But I could get in serious trouble if I was found with that file in my possession."

"I don't want you to take any undue risks," I said. "Look, I'll see what I can do from this end. I've got a few good sources in Immigration and at External and CSIS. If you hear anything more, give me a shout."

I quickly enlisted Amanda Valpy, the paper's omniscient librarian, to help me run down Mohammad. She tapped into the newspaper's computer database, which went as far back as 1978, but the screen came up No Match. I parked myself at a table in the library and began sifting through stacks of envelopes stuffed with yellowed newspaper clippings on the PLO and terrorism. I went all the way back to 1975. Again, nothing.

My next move took me to even older clippings stored on microfiche. After several hours in front of a projector, I was depressed. I had gotten absolutely nowhere in a search that took me back to 1972, when the Palestinian terrorist group Black September killed eleven Israeli athletes at the Olympic Games in Munich, Germany. The name Mahmoud Muhammad Issa Mohammad had drawn a complete blank. Fed up, I went home.

Early the next morning, I was back in the library digging into the past.

In 1971, nothing.

In 1970, suddenly, pay dirt!

Mohammad's name jumped off the microfiche screen. It was an article about his conviction by a Greek criminal court on March 26, 1970, of wilful manslaughter. Mohammad and another terrorist, Maheb Suleiman, had attacked a New York–bound El Al Boeing 707 jetliner in Athens on December 26, 1968, and shot to death an Israeli man in a hail of machine-gun bullets. The airplane was destroyed by a grenade Mohammad had tossed into one of the jet engines. Both terrorists were overpowered by Greek police. In a separate story, the Syrian-based Popular Front for the Liberation of Palestine claimed credit for the attack. From its base in Beirut, Lebanon, the PFLP announced in a press release that the two Palestinian commandos had been sent to Athens under orders "to destroy an Israeli plane and kill Jews."

At his trial in 1970, Mohammad, who was identified as a teacher and Palestinian refugee, was sentenced to seventeen years and five months in prison. He was twenty-six. Sulieman, a twenty-two-year-old student, got fourteen years and three months.

I dug around a little more and found an obscure story about a hostage exchange in early 1971 in which seven Palestinian terrorists were released from Greek jails. Mohammad was one of them. Once freed, he retreated to the land of Jordan.

My background research was done, but I needed a lot more before I could run with the story. That afternoon, I called a highly placed source and left my code name (I never gave my real name when I phoned any of my key government sources) and left a message with their secretaries, assistants or switchboard operators. In Ottawa, "Malarek" on a pink message slip was a red flag.

A short while later, my source called back. He drew a short, sharp breath at the mention of Mahmoud Muhammad Issa Mohammad.

"How the hell did you find out about him?" he asked.

"Sources!"

He laughed.

"What about this guy?" I asked.

"He's here, all right. He's been here for about a year. He came with his family last February as a landed immigrant. Apparently, though, when he was in the air on his way over, Immigration got an urgent telex about Mr. Mohammad's past, and an alert was put out at Pearson International Airport to intercept him the moment he landed."

"Was he intercepted?" I asked.

"All Canada Customs and Immigration staff were told to keep their eyes open. But the flight arrived during a shift change, and the new shift wasn't informed about the alert until it was too late. So Mr. Mohammad was welcomed to Canada and allowed to enter with no difficulty."

"Immigration screws up again!"

"I see it as CSIS screwing up. I find it incredible that a cursory security check wouldn't have picked this man out. I'm certain the moment he was arrested in Greece, his name, mug shot and fingerprints were fed into the computers of every single intelligence agency in the Western hemisphere. All CSIS had to do was type in the name, and bingo, you've got a match!"

"How did Ottawa suddenly discover that Mohammad and the terrorist were one and the same man and that he was on an airplane on his way to Canada?" I asked.

"The CSIS agent at the Canadian Embassy in Madrid fired off the telex," the source said.

"I don't get it. Are you telling me CSIS suddenly found out Mohammad was a terrorist on the very day he's winging it to Canada?"

"The Mossad tipped CSIS!"

"Great spy service we've got," I said sardonically. "So Mohammad just walks through the doors at Pearson Airport and he's in."

"CSIS finally caught up to him at his cousin's home in Brantford [Ontario]. He denied he was involved in the El Al attack. Claimed he was a victim of mistaken identity and said the terrorist in question was a cousin with the same name."

"What happened then?"

"The RCMP got hold of Mr. Mohammad's immigration application and ran his photograph and fingerprints through Interpol and confirmed he was in fact the man involved in the terrorist attack."

"Then why is this terrorist still in Canada after almost a year?" I asked.

My source laughed. "That's a question for the immigration minister!"

I needed more confirmation. A couple of not-for-attribution conversations with sources were not enough to go with a story this explosive.

Over the weekend, I worked the phones, calling contacts in External Affairs, the RCMP and Immigration. I was circumspect because I didn't want to set off alarm bells. But I could tell from their reaction that they couldn't, or wouldn't, help me out. This case was too sensitive.

Then, early on Sunday afternoon, a brown envelope with my name in bold block letters was dropped off at the security desk in the *Globe* lobby. I opened it and smiled. It contained a number of highly sensitive and secret government documents about Mohammad. It was the confirmation I needed. I immediately photocopied them and hid a copy in an obscure filing cabinet far from the newsroom. Being in possession of secret government documents was grounds for an official visit by the RCMP.

One document, stamped Top Secret, stated that CSIS headquarters in Ottawa had information in its files that in November, 1986, Mohammad was living in Spain. However, the agency had no indication the man was about to apply to immigrate to Canada, "so the information was not shared" with the CSIS liaison officer overseeing screening operations in the region.

Shades of bumbling cops, I mused as I absorbed the contents. One memorandum, dated July 18, 1987, was prepared shortly after the high-level meeting of government officials in June, which the first caller had told me about. It dealt in part with a proposed response should the *news media* stumble onto the story. Written by Deputy Immigration Minister Gaetan Lussier to Benoit Bouchard, the document stated that although Mohammad "has been identified as a potential security threat and person known to have been involved in a terrorist action, CSIS does not consider him an immediate threat to the safety of any Canadians." If questioned about the department's failure to detain the man, the response would be: "Because Mr. Mohammad had a wife and three children in the country, there was no intention of arresting him until the Immigration Department was ready to proceed to a full inquiry to deport him." Well, at least I knew what the official government line would be when I called.

However, Lussier noted that Mohammad could delay deportation proceedings by making a claim for refugee status. Through various appeal stages, he could stall his removal for five years or longer.

And there was another problem, the deputy minister added. "As a stateless Palestinian with a Lebanese travel document, it is unknown if Lebanon or Spain—where he last resided—would accept him back. Unfortunately, Mr. Mohammad could remain in Canada for some time."

While the July memo played down Mohammad's possible threat to the safety of Canadians, another Lussier memorandum to Bouchard, dated October 27, 1987, pointed out that Mohammad was "an important figure" in the PLO and "is considered by CSIS as an organizer of terrorist activities" although not likely "to commit actual violent acts." Fat difference! I thought.

Lussier also said CSIS was worried that PLO "sympathizers may be tempted to take Canadian hostages abroad" if it appeared Canada might deport the man to "an unfriendly country," such as Israel. In fact, the document stated, Israel had already expressed, to the Department of External Affairs, an interest in extraditing Mohammad. Lussier's memo suggested that the Israeli government, while quietly trying to deal with the case through diplomatic channels, "could try in some manner to embarrass Canada if we appear to move too slowly."

The deputy minister was saying that Canada was caught between a rock and a hard place. If we let this guy stay, we would offend Canada's Jewish community and Israel. If we kicked him out of the country, a particularly rabid faction of the PLO might exact some sort of revenge on a Canadian target. But the bottom line was: this man was a convicted murderer and he had to go.

On Sunday afternoon, I phoned a house in Brantford and asked for Mr. Mohammad.

"Who is speaking?" a suspicious male voice asked.

"I'd like to speak with Mahmoud Muhammad Issa Mohammad," I said. There was a long pause. Then another man got on the phone.

"Who is speaking?" he asked.

"Victor Malarek."

"Who are you?"

"I'm a reporter with the *Globe and Mail*."

"There is no one here by that name," the man said firmly, and hung up.

I knew I had the right place and I knew I had the right guy. I started writing the story.

On Monday, January 18, 1988, the banner headline read: Terrorist Got Through Immigration Net.

The story set off the predictable wild and vehement debate in Parliament. The Opposition MPs demanded to know who was asleep at the switch in allowing the Palestinian terrorist entry into the country, and what the Mulroney government was going to do about it. Gerry Weiner, the flaccid junior minister of immigration, was left juggling a very hot political potato. With the voice of a wannabe gladiator, he vowed that Mahmoud Muhammad Issa Mohammad would be deported from Canada in six months — tops! Yeh, sure, I thought. In an interview with Barbara Frum on the CBC's *The Journal*, I predicted: "Mahmoud will still be here six years from now."

And now, five months later, I had been told that another alleged terrorist had broken through the CSIS screen.

My search of the *Globe*'s computer database turned up nothing on Major Santokh Singh Bagga.

The next day, Tuesday, May 11, I phoned a solid contact in the immigration enforcement unit and asked him to run Bagga's name through the security computer. Moments later ... bingo! It popped up along with a date of birth, date of entry into Canada and, more important, a current address. The Sikh was living on a rural route outside the tiny hamlet of Princeton in southwestern Ontario along with his son, Gursev, and Jasbir Kaur.

By this time, I was tense and impatient. Every hour, I checked with the mail room and at the security desk in the lobby to see if an envelope had been dropped off. Without a piece of concrete evidence, I was stuck.

While I waited, I hunkered down in the library and did some background research on the Sikh situation in India. In particular, I looked into the 1984 siege of the Golden Temple — the Sikh equivalent of St. Peter's Basilica in the Vatican or the Great Mosque in Mecca. The standoff at the seventy-two-acre temple complex had been led by Sant Jarnail Singh Bhindranwale, a thirty-seven-year-old charismatic holy man, who had moved into the temple with a group of armed followers in mid-December, 1983. Bhindranwale had feared the Indian government was planning a commando action to kidnap him and put him in prison. He entered the temple for sanctuary believing the army would never dare attack this most holy place.

He was wrong.

On June 3, 1984, Prime Minister Indira Gandhi gave the nod for Operation Blue Star. All approaches to Amritsar were sealed off. No journalists were permitted in the area. More than twelve thousand ordinary Sikhs — men, women and children — had crowded into the court-yard of the Golden Temple to commemorate the martyrdom of the fifth guru, Arjan Dev. Early the next day, the army attacked. About four thousand crack Indian troops mounted a brutal frontal assault. Heavy artillery, including tanks and howitzers, blasted away at the complex. When the guns fell silent seventy-two hours later, *officially* four hundred ninety-two Sikhs, including Bhindranwale, his corpse riddled with bullets, and eighty-four government soldiers, lay dead. *Unofficially,* the toll among innocent Sikh pilgrims was as high as eight thousand.

India's fifteen million Sikhs were outraged and scandalized that the army had defiled their most scared shrine. The biggest insult was the damage to the Akal Takht, the seat of Sikh temporal authority. The sheer wantonness of the attack drove many formerly moderate Sikhs into the radical camp; some clamoured for revenge.

On October 31, 1984, at 9:15 a.m., as Indira Gandhi strolled through the garden behind her house, two of her trusted Sikh bodyguards shot her. The assassination unleashed a four-day bloodbath during which angry mobs of Hindus throughout India rounded up thousands of Sikh men, women and children and murdered them. Some were hacked to death, others were burned alive in the streets. Men had their beards set on fire. Women were raped. Sikh homes, places of worship, shops and vehicles were set ablaze. In Delhi alone, according to official figures, more than three thousand Sikhs were killed. Unofficially, the death toll exceeded five thousand. The police, the army and high-ranking government officials did nothing to stop the carnage. In some cases, they even exhorted the mobs. In the rest of India, thousands more suffered the same fate.

Like most Canadians, I had seen Sikhs on the city streets but I knew little about them and nothing about their religion. It was time for some enlightenment. I learned that Sikhism was founded by Guru Nanak in India in the fifteenth century, and although it is a unique religion, it shares features of Hinduism and Islam. One of the main tenets of Sikhism is the rejection of the Hindu caste system and idolatry. As word spread of Guru Nanak's quest, people came to listen, and those who accepted his teachings were called Sikhs, or devoted followers. After Guru Nanak came nine successive gurus, or teachers. The fifth guru, Arjan Dev, set about compiling the Guru Granth Sahib, or holy scripture of the Sikhs. It was the tenth and last guru, Gobind Singh, who gave the religion its final militaristic form. He created a brotherhood of Khalsa — the pure of faith — and decreed the so-called "Five Ks," a standard of dress that includes *kes,* unshorn hair kept neatly under a turban and a full beard; *karaa,* an iron bracelet that continuously binds the Sikh to God; *kachhairaa,* breeches, like underwear, which represent modesty and chastity; *kangaa,* a small wooden comb worn in the hair as a symbol of physical and moral cleanliness; and *kirpaan,* a small sword that demonstrates a Sikh's resolve to fight against evil and unjust forces of oppression.

As I was poring over the material, the interoffice paging system jolted me out of my seat. "Victor Malarek. There is a package for you at the security desk."

There was no return address, but I could clearly make out an Ottawa postmark. Inside the large brown envelope were three documents classified Secret, all dealing with the case of Santokh Singh Bagga. Two were letters written by Joe Clark, Secretary of State for External Affairs. They were addressed to Benoit Bouchard, Minister of Employment and Immigration. The third document was a memorandum to Bouchard from his deputy minister, Gaetan Lussier. I sat back in my cubicle and began reading.

The first letter from Clark to Bouchard was dated April 1, 1987.

In it, Clark waxed indignant that he had been informed, not by Canadian officials, but by the Indian High Commission, that Major Bagga, his son, Gursev, and Jasbir Kaur had filed a refugee claim in Canada.

Amazing, I mused. The refugee procedure was supposed to be closed and confidential, and yet a foreign government had got word of three claimants.

Clark pointed out that Major Bagga was wanted in India "because of his suspected involvement in a conspiracy to assassinate the Indian Prime Minister and a number of other subversive activities. Bagga is also alleged to maintain close association with known Sikh activists in the United States and Canada. The Indian authorities have made strong and repeated representations for his return to India."

Clark noted he had heard that the refugee claims by all three individuals had been recently rejected by the Refugee Status Advisory

Committee (RSAC). But he was concerned that the RSAC was reviewing this decision "with a view to granting refugee status. I would find it somewhat irregular, if indeed, there is accuracy to the report that the RSAC" is reconsidering the claims, Clark wrote. "This is particularly the case considering that no claims for refugee status made by Indians of Sikh faith have been accepted by the RSAC. In view of this and in the context of our bilateral relations with India, I would be concerned if this individual was to be granted exceptional and unwarranted treatment."

Bouchard urgently dispatched Clark's letter to his deputy minister for immediate action. A week later, on April 7, Lussier sent his boss a sizzling memorandum. It explained: "Major Bagga was in the Indian Army from 1956 to 1982. Apparently he and his son Gursev Singh, who is also a refugee claimant, were involved in a large scale army desertion and mutiny by Sikh soldiers on June 10, 1984 as a result of the Indian Army's invasion of the Sikh Golden Temple. The mutiny resulted in a battle with loyal troops and both sides had fatalities. Court martials and prison sentences resulted. Major Bagga claims to be an intimate of the late fanatical Sikh priest and martyr, Jarnail S. Bhindranwale, who died leading the Sikh defense of the Golden Temple and General Jaswant S. Bhuller, another well known Sikh extremist. Major Bagga is also an associate of R.S. Malik, a millionaire Canadian who is believed to finance the fanatical Sikh group, Babbar Khalsa."

Lussier noted that the Indian government had asked the Department of External Affairs and the RCMP to return Major Bagga to India where "he is wanted for his involvement in the Army mutiny and is implicated in the assassination of the Indian Army general who led the army assault on the Golden Temple, and in an attempt to assassinate Prime Minister Gandhi."

The deputy minister concluded: "In my opinion, based on the information we have received on Major Bagga, I believe he is a threat to Canada's security as well as possibly being a fugitive from justice in India. Therefore, I recommend even if he is found to be a Convention Refugee[1] we make every effort to return him to India."

[1]Convention Refugee refers to the United Nations definition of a refugee as a person who has "a well-founded fear of being persecuted for reasons of race, religion, nationality, membership of a particular social group or political opinion." The 1951 UN Convention on Refugees was signed by about one hundred nations, including Canada.

Attached to the deputy minister's memorandum was a "case summary," which contained more details of Santokh Singh's activities in India. For example, it said Singh's military career began in July 13, 1956. It gave the reason for his premature retirement on January 12, 1982, as: "discrimination against Sikhs."

The memo noted that Bagga lived in Poona, India, where he preached Sikhism and baptized Sikhs. The 14th Punjab Regiment was also stationed in the town and "Bagga was one of five holy Sikhs who baptized Sikh soldiers" in the regiment. It went on to say that Sikh soldiers in the unit "deserted from Poona on 10 June 1984 to march to Amritsar to defend the Golden Temple following Operation Blue Star."

The summary concluded that "no criminal charges have been laid against Bagga in India to date," according to the RCMP and Interpol. "He is, however, wanted under the India Terrorist and Disruptive Activity (Prevention) Act and the Indian Passport Act and Foreign Exchange Regulations."

There were two points in Lussier's memorandum and summary that set off warning buzzers in my head. First, if Bagga was such a dangerous man, involved in all these heinous plots and terrorist activities, why had no criminal charges been brought against him in India? Second, if the man was a threat to Canada's national security and a fugitive from justice in India, why didn't the Canadian government arrest him and put him behind bars?

Clearly, something else was going on here.

Clark's second letter to Bouchard, dated June 2, 1987, partially answered my suspicions. In it, Clark made clear his displeasure with the immigration department's recent decisions to recommend in favour of Sikh refugee claimants. For the external affairs minister, the overriding concern appeared to be Canada's "bilateral relationship with India," and not whether Sikh refugee claimants had a genuine fear of persecution in their homeland. Clark accused extremist Sikhs "of using Canada as a base for their violent advocacy of a separate Sikh State, Khalistan."

Clark also pointed out that while he fully appreciated the "independent nature" of RSAC, he found it "most disconcerting to learn that a number of Indian Sikhs were recently recognized as refugees" by the board. He once again noted his "considerable embarrassment" that the "information on these decisions was initially received by my department from the Indian Government," and strongly encouraged his Cabinet colleague to "seriously consider" foreign policy concerns and potential security threats when evaluating recommendations by RSAC on Sikh refugee claims. Clark suggested that Bouchard urge immigration officers to work closely with officials at External Affairs in finding "legal solutions through which problems...concerning Sikhs may be overcome."

The Sikh terrorist story was taking on a more complex and sinister dimension. It was orbiting in the celestial sphere of *bilateral relations* between India and Canada. And from what I could determine, a senior minister of the Crown was blatantly interfering in the operation of the RSAC, which was supposed to be a quasi-judicial, independent, decision-making body.

I placed a call to Joe Stern, RSAC's chairman. I had met with Stern on a number of occasions and knew him as a true champion of refugees. I could hear him draw breath over the phone when I mentioned Santokh Singh Bagga. It was obvious from his reaction that I was the last person he wanted to speak to about the case. He refused to discuss it but strongly advised me to be careful with the information I'd been sent.

"There is much, much more to this case that you should be aware of," Stern said. "I wish I could help you but my hands are tied."

I decided to hold off for at least a day. Stern's warning and the contradictions in the leaked documents made me uneasy. That night, I called a well-placed Ottawa source at his home. He was hesitant about saying anything at all about the case but finally gave in to my entreaty after exacting a promise that our conversation was not for attribution. He informed me that the case had been discussed behind closed doors at senior management meetings in Immigration and at the highest levels at External Affairs.

"Shades of Mahmoud Muhammad Issa Mohammad," I said.

"That's for sure. Everyone's running around on this one because Joe Clark has his nose out of joint. He fired off a heavy-handed letter to Benoit Bouchard demanding explanations. Clark definitely wants this Sikh man kicked out of the country. Apparently, the case has become a diplomatic embarrassment for External Affairs. The bottom line for Joe and the boys at External is they don't want any Sikhs accepted as refugees. For them it's a question of how it would look for Canada to be acknowledging that India, the world's largest democracy, is a violator of basic human rights. You see, *that* wouldn't bode well for bilateral relations."

"There's that phrase again," I interjected.

"What?"

"Bilateral relations."

"Well, it's very important when you're trying to sell India Canadian technology like a CANDU reactor for a billion dollars," the source pointed out. "Look, Victor, this is all very troubling. I can't believe someone leaked you those documents. It's select information and only tells part of the story. I'm going to ask you to sit on this for a couple of days while I dig around and find out what's going on here."

"I don't know about that," I said. "This stuff could have been leaked to the *Toronto Star* by now, or the *Ottawa Citizen*, or the CBC. I don't want to be scooped by them."

"I don't think it's been leaked to anyone else. The material is too sensitive. I think you were targeted for a controlled leak. Think about it. The story appears on the front page of the *Globe* and outraged Canadians will be clamouring for the man's immediate deportation. It won't matter one bit whether he's a bona fide refugee and had been set up by the Indian government. The federal government will be forced to act, and this man will be deported to who knows what—prison, torture, execution. And for what?"

"Bilateral relations," I replied. "But I've got to tell you, I'm really worried I'll see the story in another paper tomorrow morning."

"You won't. I'm sure of it. If some other reporter had gotten the information, it would be out by now, or at the very least, inquiries would have been made to the minister's office, and I would definitely have heard about it," he said firmly. "Look, Victor, I'm going to tell you something that you have to keep totally off the record for now. I have to have your word on it."

"You've got it."

"I know for a fact that the man and his son were recommended by RSAC for Convention Refugee status and it was a unanimous recommendation by a three-member panel of highly respected experts in the field. But I've been told there was some strong-arm backroom political maneuvering to reverse the decision. If you just hold off for a couple of days, I'm sure I can get my hands on something that will put this whole issue in proper perspective. Give me a day or two, and I'll see what I can do."

"All right. I'll hold off. But I really need something—and soon."

For most of Wednesday, I sat on my thumbs. By late Thursday, I was afraid to even glance at the competition newspapers or watch the

CBC or CTV national news. When the phone rang, I grabbed it on the first ring and snapped at family and friends for calling me at work. I wanted the line free! Every thirty minutes or so I paced the short distance between my mailbox and my desk, hoping something would suddenly appear in my slot. Nothing. By Friday morning, I had had it. It was time to call Santokh Singh Bagga.

I jotted down a few terse questions I would *try* to ask once I got him on the phone. I was fairly certain I wouldn't get anything more than the standard "no comment" or the familiar "call my lawyer" before the line went dead.

I dialed the number. A young man answered. I identified myself and asked for Mr. Bagga. Moments later, a soft-spoken man came on the line.

"I am Dr. Santokh Singh. How may I be of service?"

"Santokh Singh Bagga?" I inquired.

"I am Dr. Santokh Singh. I no longer use the name Bagga."

"Fine. That's no problem," I said. "The reason I'm calling is I'm working on an article about your presence in Canada and there are a number of questions I would like to ask you."

"I would be only too happy to answer any questions you have, sir," he answered.

"The matter I want to deal with is quite serious. It has to do with certain of your *alleged* activities in India," I said, stressing the word "alleged". I didn't want to scare him off by having him think I had bought the party line.

"Then I think it would be better if we met face-to-face. Why not come to my home and we could discuss the matter in person?" Dr. Singh replied.

I was completely taken aback. I certainly hadn't expected that response, and given the time frame, it put a serious crimp in the deadline I had set for myself. I had wanted the story in Saturday's *Globe,* at the latest. Dr. Singh's invitation dashed any hopes of that. There was no way I could make the weekend paper if I headed off to Princeton.

But I was committed to go. We made arrangements to meet at 3:00 p.m. at his home. I asked if I could bring along a photographer. "I have no problem with that. Your photographer would also be welcome," Dr. Singh said.

As I was rushing out the door for the ninety-minute drive to Princeton, a mail boy shouted my name and tossed a brown envelope on my desk. I raced back and ripped it open. In it were six more documents dealing with Singh. They were the missing pieces of the puzzle. While *Globe* photographer Fred Lum drove west along the 401 highway, I read intently.

The package contained three memos between Joe Stern and James Bissett (the executive director of immigration, who reported to Deputy Minister Lussier), plus an explosive memorandum from Lussier to Bouchard.

My contact was dead on. These documents certainly added a new and unsettling perspective to the case.

In Stern's first memo, dated June 2, 1987, and classified secret, the RSAC chairman presented a very strong, credible case claiming that Santokh Singh Bagga was not a threat to Canadian security and would face almost certain imprisonment, torture or death if he were deported to India.

Stern stated that he wanted to clear up "misinformation" around the handling of the Bagga case and correct "inaccurate" statements made by Lussier to Bouchard about the refugee process.

I could almost envision Stern's memo frying in Bissett's hands. Stern rubbed senior bureaucrats like gritty sandpaper. He was overweight, balding and scruffy. But behind the dishevelled appearance was an astute, articulate intellect that commanded the respect of community leaders who worked with refugees. He was a man who would never sell out or bend to pressure.

In his memo, Stern took pains to explain the workings of the refugee process in detail so there would be no misunderstanding or confusion. He pointed out that the *first* assessment of a refugee claim "is an informal procedure," meant to expedite cases that have no merit whatsoever. At this stage only one RSAC member reads a transcript of the case and makes the decision. He noted that certain safeguards had been established to ensure a full consideration by a three-member RSAC panel. This would occur if a *second* read-through by a minister's delegate, a member of the United Nations High Commission for Refugees or the chairman of RSAC came across "meritorious aspects" that may not have been taken into consideration during the first pass.

In that first, cursory, assessment, Bagga's claim had been rejected as "manifestly unfounded." But in a second pass, the minister's delegate disagreed. He felt there were meritorious aspects to the claim. So he sent the case to RSAC for a full review by a three-member panel.

Stern also took Bissett to task for improperly interfering with the

RSAC's autonomy. The RSAC was a tribunal set up to provide independent advice, he said, and immigration officials had no business interfering with this process. Stern continued: "A panel was constituted consisting of William Barton, our former Ambassador to the United Nations, Yvon Beaulne, our former Ambassador to the Vatican and Representative to the United Nations Human Rights Commission, and Dr. Ed Ziegler, former chairman of the RSAC. I meticulously avoided indicating to them any personal views I might have of the case and the panel has reached a decision. The Committee has unanimously recommended to the Minister that the claimant be found to be a Convention refugee."

The panel decided that Santokh Singh deserved Convention Refugee status because they had found him to be "a dedicated Sikh separatist, convinced that the goal of the Indian Government is the extermination of Sikhdom," Stern wrote. "It is therefore understandable that in the eyes of the Indian Government he is an enemy of the State."

The panel committee buttressed their recommendation that Santokh Singh be given refugee status with Amnesty International documents and United States Country Reports containing unequivocal, damning evidence of arbitrary arrest, imprisonment, torture and execution of Sikhs in India. Should Santokh Singh return to India, the committee concluded, he would run the risk of "being summarily dealt with by the army, the police and the courts." In other words, he would be tortured and probably executed.

The panel ruled that Dr. Singh's son, Gursev, also should be accepted as a Convention Refugee. "The claimant is a young dedicated Sikh, the son of a Sikh leader ... who the authorities evidently regard as hostile to the Indian government. The claimant was present at the time of the raid against the Golden Temple but he asserts that he was not involved in the fighting. However, he asserts that as a witness the authorities would imprison him."

I turned to the second memo, dated September 3, also written by Stern to Bissett. Stern tossed the ball into Bissett's court. In light of "the extreme sensitivity of the case," Stern wrote, Bissett should consider handling it himself, as a "Minister's Delegate."

The next piece of correspondence was the memorandum from Lussier to Bouchard. It was dated February 10, 1988, and was stamped Secret. In it, the deputy minister briefly revisited the extremely serious allegations put forward by Joe Clark.

Then he made a stunning revelation: "As you know, the Right Honourable Joe Clark wrote to you on April 1, 1987 advising you that Bagga is wanted in India because of his *suspected* involvement in a number of subversive activities including a *suspected* conspiracy to assassinate the Prime Minister of India. In addition, Mr. Clark suggested that the Canadian Government's granting of Convention refugee status to Bagga would have a negative effect on Canada's bilateral relations with India."

Then came the kicker.

Lussier informed his boss that both the RCMP and CSIS "have recently advised us that they have no evidence or intelligence which indicates that Bagga is inadmissible or represents a threat to Canadian security."

In other words, there was no proof of the very serious allegations leveled at Santokh Singh by Joe Clark! Something sinister was going on. I was sure of it.

The deputy minister added that although Indian government officials advised the RCMP in April, 1987, that they were considering extradition, "they have not pursued this matter with either the RCMP or External Affairs since that time."

I picked up the last document in the package. As I read it, I realized that it further confused the issue. It was a reply from Bissett to Stern. Bissett claimed that Santokh Singh would not face certain persecution, torture, imprisonment or execution were he to return to India. He based his claim on information he had received from three *hand-picked* immigration officers who had reviewed Santokh Singh's refugee claim on behalf of the minister of immigration.

Bissett's three immigration officials claimed reports by Amnesty International and United States Country Reports of imprisonment, torture and death focussed on the exception rather than the rule in India. Such "abuses may be attributed to lack of control over police forces in certain areas rather than to government policy," they opined. I stared in disbelief at their choice of phrase — *lack of control over police forces in certain areas*. They were trotting out the old "a few bad-apple policemen" argument! They concluded, "The Indian judicial system [in general] is functioning in a fair manner."

I wondered what these men had been smoking. It was documented that the Indian government had enacted a Draconian law giving police the power to arrest and jail suspects for up to a year before charging them and taking them to court.

The three officials' final statement went over the top. "The treatment afforded to other persons involved in the desertion of the 14th Punjab Regiment would seem to confirm this opinion," they wrote. "The accused have been tried in a fair manner, the guilty have been given relatively light sentences, those who were discharged from the army were reinstated, and full insurance benefits were provided to the family of those who were killed during the events."

I was sure this had to be a press release issued by the Indian government, repeated verbatim by the three immigration officials. If this was *not* the case, on whose benighted information were these Canadian officials relying? I knew that at least thirty-five soldiers from the regiment had been shot dead and that several more were tortured and jailed.

The trio concluded: "Consequently, we feel that subject's fear of persecution on the basis of his religious or political opinions is not founded."

Their names were illegible scrawls at the bottom of the page. The document was dated December 15, 1987.

The gray and blue *Globe* staff car pulled into a narrow, gravel lane dividing a modest, two-storey white farmhouse and a large, red barn. A weathered Indian man with a wispy salt-and-pepper beard, wearing a white turban and charcoal suit, came down the laneway to greet us. With him was a tall, slightly built, much younger man wearing wire-rim glasses and a bright orange turban.

We shook hands. "Welcome, sir. Welcome to my home. I am Dr. Santokh Singh, and this is my son, Gursev Singh."

They ushered us into the back room, where we removed our shoes before entering the house. We entered a spacious living room furnished with mismatched, utilitarian sofas and armchairs. On the walls were colourful prints of Sikh gurus, and historic Sikh leaders in full uniform with proud military bearings, some on horseback, all carrying swords and daggers.

Santokh Singh sat down directly in front of me and smiled warmly. "How may I be of assistance to you?"

I looked at him closely. What I was seeing so far did not jibe with the government documents I had been reading about this man. But then, I thought, killers come in all shapes and sizes. Mahmoud Muhammad Issa Mohammad had been a middle-aged, slightly overweight businessman in a three-piece suit. He certainly hadn't stood out in a crowd as a terrorist and a murderer.

"I'll get right to the point, Dr. Singh," I began. "I've received some information about you that alleges you're a terrorist."

I watched his face for a telltale flinch of nervousness or tension. He remained calm.

I continued. "In fact, I have a letter written by External Affairs Minister Joe Clark that says you're wanted in India as a suspect in a conspiracy to assassinate Prime Minister Rajiv Gandhi."

That got a reaction. Santokh Singh sat bolt upright and stared at me wide-eyed. I passed him a copy of the letter. He read it very slowly, every so often shaking his head. From the corner of the room, I could hear the motor drive humming on Fred Lum's Nikon camera.

"I have never been involved in such a thing," Dr. Singh began as he handed me back Clark's letter. "I have by no utterance ever advocated violence or terrorism or the violent overthrow of the Indian government. I am a peaceful man. A man of religion. I have been a very spiritually inclined person since the age of seven."

"Then where would Mr. Clark get this kind of information?" I asked. "These are extremely serious allegations."

"I do not know why Mr. Clark would write such wicked things about me. They are simply not true," Dr. Singh replied.

"You entered Canada illegally on fraudulent passports?"

"That is true."

"Why?"

"I could not obtain a passport in my name. The Indian government was searching for me, and I was told by a person I knew in the military services that the army was to shoot me on sight because I was a religious activist and I had expressed in my writings that the only way for Sikhs to survive with respect and dignity was to have their own state. I also exposed the government of India in its plan to commit genocide against Sikhs and exterminate Sikhs and even to conspire against Sikhs by accusing them of being terrorists. For me, there was no other way to escape but through fraudulent departure. I could not obtain a passport in my name. It was the only way to save our lives."

"Why would the Indian government issue shoot-on-sight orders?" I asked.

Dr. Singh said he believed the reason he was so reviled by the government of India was the clandestine publication of a book he had written entitled *The Only Option for Sikhs*. It was the summer of 1984, and Singh was living underground in Bombay. "I wrote the book to counter the mischievous and malicious propaganda of Indian government-controlled television, radio and anti-Sikh media," he said. The publication of the book sent Indian government censors and the secret police into a frenzy, he added.

"I wrote under the name Dr. S.S. Dharam to escape the persecution that would follow as a result of exposing the Indian government's sinister design to exterminate the Sikhs," Dr. Singh said, stressing that while he did not advocate violence, "I very much believe in the creation of a Sikh state. I believe it is morally and physically impossible for Sikhs to exist in India today."

"The problem I have is why Joe Clark's signature would be on documents that label you a terrorist and a murderer," I said. "You say these allegations are not true. He maintains they are. I don't see what would be in it for Clark to make these things up."

Dr. Singh took a deep breath and thought for a moment. "I think that when Joe Clark went to India in 1988, the Indian government somehow or other got to him. Whatever they fed him, he took blindly and decided that he wanted to be for them and against Sikhs. And when he came back to Canada, he was totally against Sikhs getting refugee or immigration status. So it makes me wonder whether this man, Joe Clark, is the secretary of state for external affairs of Canada or India's foreign affairs minister?"

"Have you ever been questioned about these allegations by any Canadian officials from External Affairs?"

"I have never been questioned by anyone. Joe Clark has never taken the time to ask for or listen to my side. He has not even given me a chance to defend myself. It is really intellectual bankruptcy to listen only to one side. I feel that Joe Clark has sold out to India. He is selling my blood and my son's blood for the sake of his own benefits."

"Again, I've got to tell you I find it hard to understand what would be in it for Joe Clark to go after you," I persisted.

"Maybe you should ask yourself this question: If I was this dangerous person that Mr. Clark says in these letters, if I was such a great risk to India, then why didn't the Canadian government move to deport me from Canada right away instead of waiting two years? A moral and prudent person would have moved right away to deport me instead of using such an underhanded method."

At that moment, a demure woman in traditional Punjabi dress entered the room carrying a tray of tea and cookies. Dr. Singh introduced her to us. She was Jasbir Kaur, the woman who had come to Canada with Dr. Singh and his son.

"Jasbir Kaur has a Ph.D. in philosophy," Dr. Singh told me. "Her thesis was on the concept of man in Sikhism. She is a very spiritual woman."

"She fled India with you?" I asked.

"No. She escaped from India in April, 1985. She went to Delhi to arrange for the defense of the soldiers who deserted from the 14th Punjab Regiment, and while she was there, she learned that the police and army in Poona were looking to arrest her."

Later I learned that Jasbir Kaur had gone first to Hong Kong, then to Taiwan and Japan before ending up in the United States in July, 1985, where she joined Dr. Singh and his son.

After we finished our tea, Dr. Singh suggested we continue the interview while on a stroll around his 20-acre farm. All this, Dr. Singh said proudly, would one day become a retreat where Sikh children, teenagers and adults could visit to escape the contaminating influences of city life. Here, he explained, they could connect with their cultural roots, learn about their religion and get in touch with their spiritual side through meditation and prayer.

One day, God willing, Dr. Singh said, the fallow cornfield would be a lush forest with an open, oval patch in its heart where the devoted could come and meditate in the tranquillity and peace of nature. This was his dream, he said, one he knew he would not be around to enjoy — at least not in his physical state of being.

I struggled to maintain my professional skepticism. I also mused about Joe Clark and the boys at External Affairs accusing this "terrorist" Sikh of planting a forest so that one day his band of "religious followers" could carry out paramilitary exercises aimed at the overthrow of the Indian government.

While we walked, Dr. Singh expounded on his political views. He said he strongly favoured the creation of Khalistan, an independent Sikh state. But he also felt it should be done "by pressure of world opinion" and not through violent acts. "I have suggested legal, persuasive and peaceful ways to solve the problems," he said.

I listened intently to what he was saying, waiting for a slip, a contradiction. Dr. Singh said he had a doctorate in philosophy and had published a score of books on Sikh issues and religion. His main quarrel with the Indian government was its manipulation of world opinion against Sikhs. "They have cooked up conspiracies that show Sikhs to be terrorists that want to divide the country, that kill innocent Hindus. This poison is being deliberately spread by the Indian government to make certain that Sikhs are hated outside India."

"So are you saying these allegations that you instigated a mutiny, a mass desertion of Sikh soldiers in the 14th Punjab Regiment, are a deliberate pack of lies?" I asked.

Dr. Singh laughed. "I did no such thing. These men mutinied and left their posts to go to Amritsar to defend the Holy Temple. This happened on June 10, 1984, after the Golden Temple had been attacked by the army. Sikh soldiers in about ten regiments throughout India mutinied when they heard of the attack on their holiest shrine. I had nothing to do with their decision. It is true that I baptized hundreds of soldiers from 1982 to 1984. But I never told them to desert their post."

"The soldiers of the 14th Punjab Regiment were in the town of Poona where you lived and preached? You're saying you had nothing to do with instigating the desertion?"

"The soldiers of this Punjab regiment were baptized by our group. When the 14th Punjab mutinied, the army blamed me, whereas, in fact, I had done no such thing."

"So why did they desert and head off for the Golden Temple?"

"They got an emotional trauma because their holiest shrine had been attacked by the government of India. They got religiously shocked, and as a result of the trauma, they left their place of duty with arms and went to Amritsar to defend it against the government, that is, to fight against the government."

"Were you not in command of this regiment?" I asked.

"No. I was a retired army major living in the vicinity of this regiment at Poona where it is located."

"Didn't the army come looking for you after the desertion only to find you had disappeared?"

"That is true."

"Where did you go?"

"I had left Poona to find out what had happened to my son, Gursev. After his high school exams, he and some friends travelled through Punjab to visit Sikh temples. On June 1, he came to the Golden Temple, and while he was there the curfew was imposed by the army, and nobody could come out of the Golden Temple. Nobody could escape, so he was caught up in the melee. I left Poona to go to Amritsar to find out if he was alive or if he had been killed. Luckily he and many others escaped. They made a hole behind a wall and escaped from there."

"What happened after you found him?"

"After I traced him, I contacted some friends in Poona and was informed that my house has been encircled by army soldiers and army officers. Even though I had nothing to do with the 14th Punjab Regiment's desertion, the army wanted a scapegoat."

"Maybe they wanted the person responsible for causing the troops to desert," I said.

"As I have already told you, I did not do such a thing," he said calmly, looking directly into my eyes.

"What happened next?" I asked.

"I did not return to Poona, knowing I would be arrested if I went there. I went into hiding. After a month or so, I was informed that my house was broken into by these soldiers. All my baggage was confiscated and removed. My station wagon was also confiscated by the government. I remained underground in Bombay."

"What did you do while you were underground?"

"I was hurt by what had happened. That is when I wrote *The Only Option for Sikhs*, telling all I had seen in Punjab, what the government was doing and what was their policy to exterminate Sikhs."

I turned to Gursev. "Why did you go to the Golden Temple?" I asked.

"After my high school exams, I and two other friends decided to travel to Punjab with a view to visit Sikh temples and historic Sikh *gurdwaras*," Gursev replied. "On June 1, 1984, we reached Amritsar and went to pay homage at our holiest shrine, the Golden Temple."

"Did you go there to fight, to take part in the siege?"

"No. We were in the process of settling down when the government troops started firing with machine guns from various positions around the Golden Temple," Gursev went on. "We came out of the Guru Nanak Niwas, which is the rest house in the Golden Temple complex, and found that many pilgrims who had gone to pay their homage in the Golden Temple lay dead in front of the temple and around the Pool of Nectar."

Like thousands of pilgrims who had come to pray at the temple, Gursev said, he was trapped by the fighting. "Anybody who dared to move out of the Golden Temple was shot dead by the Hindu army soldiers who had encircled the complex."

"And you didn't go there to fight?"

"No. I went there to pay homage."

"You must have known trouble was brewing? The entire town was crawling with Indian soldiers."

"I never expected the army would attack the Golden Temple. I never thought that such a thing would happen, that the government would ever attack the temple," Gursev said.

"Did you see armed Sikhs in the temple?"

"Yes, there were some men with rifles."

"Didn't that alarm you?" I asked.

"Not at all. They had been there for quite a while. Carrying arms in Punjab was nothing unusual."

"The government of India says there were hundreds of armed Sikhs in the temple," I said.

"That is not true. There were at most forty to forty-five members carrying weapons."

"So you never went there with the intent to fight?" I persisted.

"No. Not at all. Never. I had summer holidays and I went there to visit and pay homage and learn more about my religion and culture."

"Tell me about the attack," I said.

"I remember when it started. It was in the early morning hours on June fourth. There was a rain of bullets coming from all four sides of the Golden Temple," Gursev recalled. "Hundreds were killed as a result of the sudden mass firing, and they lay dead in the Parikarma; that's the path for walking around the Pool of Nectar.

"The following day, the army opened up with artillery and tanks. The fighting was fierce. Until the time I got out at 1:00 a.m. on June sixth, about three thousand Sikhs lay dead inside the courtyards of the Golden Temple. One thousand alone were killed around the Pool of Nectar."

"How did you escape?" I asked.

"Me and my friends tried to find a way out of the Golden Temple. We found a wall behind the rest house and broke through into a back alleyway. Later we managed to sneak out of the city and for eighteen days hid in surrounding villages."

Gursev said he remained underground until he fled India in November, 1984, "after seeing the horrifying massacre of thousands of Sikhs who had been killed by burning and other horrifying means in Delhi after the assassination of Prime Minister Indira Gandhi."

He headed for the United States with a passport issued under a phony identity. His father, who also witnessed the mob attacks on Sikhs in New Delhi after Gandhi's assassination, decided that to survive, he, too, would have to escape from India.

Dr. Singh picked up the conversation. "I realized I no longer had a future in India. I obtained a passport."

For about a year, Dr. Singh travelled through the United States as a Sikh holy man, escorted by followers wherever he went. On June 20, 1986, he flew to Seattle, Washington, and walked across a field into Canada with his son and Jasbir Kaur. At 10:50 a.m., on September 12, 1986, under oath, he told his story to Mariette L'Heureux, a senior immigration officer at the Canada Immigration Centre in downtown Vancouver. At noon, the hearing concluded, and Dr. Singh was informed that the transcript would be forwarded to the immigration minister for a decision on his refugee claim.

Back in his living room, I asked Dr. Singh if he had ever been informed of that decision.

"No. I am still waiting for news."

"I was told a letter was sent to you last month, informing you that your claim for refugee status had been rejected," I said.

"I have not received such a letter. Maybe they sent it to my old address, but I sent them a change of address on October 15, 1987," he said, producing a copy of the form he had filed with the department.

When I informed him that his claim had been rejected as unfounded, Dr. Singh was visibly shaken. He said he could not understand the decision. But the real shock for him was to learn that his original claim had been unanimously accepted as bona fide by a three-member panel of the Refugee Status Advisory Committee.

"I was never informed of this decision," he said, shaking his head. "I do not understand what is going on here. Why has this been allowed to happen?"

"That's what I'm trying to find out," I said.

I left Dr. Singh alone in his thoughts for a moment and racked my brain, wondering why Joe Clark had moved so decisively against a man neither he nor any of his officials had ever met or spoken to. In the few hours since I had met Dr. Singh, he had impressed me as a man of integrity with a deep sense of commitment to his religion and his people. He seemed a profoundly religious and spiritual man who had thought deeply about life and had decided to place his soul in God's hands. And now, for whatever reason, he had become an expendable pawn on the chessboard of international politics.

Dr. Singh broke the silence. "I do not know what to make of all this. Mr. Clark is just telling lies and not caring at all about justice. In my life I have never tried to offend anyone. My pursuits in life have been religious and spiritual. I feel Mr. Clark has sold out one hundred percent to the Indian government for whatever pressure is on him, whether it is commercial gain with India or because he wants to maintain a close friendship with the Indian government."

"I don't know what his motivation is but I hope to find out," I said. "I really have only one more question. The RSAC decision said that your getting landed status in Canada hinged on your obtaining security clearance from the RCMP and CSIS. Has anyone from the RCMP or CSIS ever visited you?"

"I have been visited on several occasions by CSIS agents, and they informed me that I had been cleared by them and that their finding was passed on to External Affairs and the immigration department."

As I got up to go, Dr. Singh took my hands and looked directly into my eyes. "I know that in India they are looking for my flesh and blood. They will surely put me in jail and torture me if I am sent back. And I will surely be killed."

"When this comes out in the *Globe and Mail*, I don't think the Canadian government will be sending you anywhere," I said. "At least, not in the short run."

I said goodbye and left.

Landing a one-on-one interview with Joe Clark was not an easy task. His handlers wanted to know the topic before agreeing to serve up their political master on a platter. It was the weekend, and finding a bureaucrat at work in Ottawa was next to impossible. After a few persistent calls, however, I tracked down Georges Rioux, a designated spokesman for Clark.

"Mr. Clark is in Calgary for a conference on Canada-India relations and is too busy with engagements to comment on the case," Rioux said tersely.

What an ironic twist of events, I thought, Clark attending a conference on bilateral relations with India.

"Well," I said to myself, "if Joe's too busy to comment, then he can deal with the fallout when the *Globe* hits the streets on Monday morning."

I turned on my computer and began typing the lead paragraph.

External Affairs Minister Joe Clark has intervened to have a former Indian Army major refused refugee status even though the man was declared a bona fide refugee by independent officials.

Government sources and internal federal documents obtained by the *Globe and Mail* indicate that Mr. Clark's concerns have more to do with bilateral relations with India than with the merits of the refugee claim.

On Monday, May 16, 1988, the *Globe's* front-page story was headed: Clark Intervened To Block Refugee Status.

That afternoon all hell broke loose during Question Period in the House of Commons. The Opposition Liberals and New Democrats were appropriately scandalized by Clark's actions, and they were demanding answers.

The charge was led by Sergio Marchi, the Liberals' bombastic immigration critic. "My question," he began in a deliberate, measured tone, "concerns the extraordinary interference of the Secretary of State for External Affairs in the independence of the refugee determination system over the case of Santokh Singh."

Marchi ponderously recounted the details of the *Globe* story. Was Clark "the External Affairs Minister for Canada or the Foreign Minister for India?" he concluded, his voice laden with sarcasm.

With Clark absent from Question Period, the debate degenerated into a boisterous free-for-all. Indignation from the Opposition ranks was repelled by wave after wave of obfuscation from the government side. The Tories, bless them, had been overcome by a sense of moral duty to Dr. Singh. They argued it would be inappropriate to discuss the case because of the possibility of an appeal by the claimant. How noble of them! I thought. Someone should have thought about that before interfering in the operations of a quasi-judicial tribunal.

Meanwhile, several thousand miles west in Calgary at the conference on Canada-India relations, things were not going well for Joe Clark. What should have been a day of pomp and protocol had been tainted with a whiff of scandal and international intrigue.

S.J. Singh Chhatwal, India's high commissioner to Canada, left the beleaguered external affairs minister to fend for himself. Chhatwal, looking the consummate diplomat with silver hair and wearing a navy Nehru suit, haughtily denied that the Indian government had ever sought the extradition of Santokh Singh. And, he insisted, his government had never put any pressure on Canadian officials to have Singh's application for refugee status rejected. In fact, Chhatwal concluded, "there is no case" against the former Indian army major.

Clark's handlers, standing at the back of the room, cringed. They realized their man was in desperate need of a spin doctor. Somehow, they had to find a way to dig their hapless boss out of this very deep hole.

Chhatwal pointed out that the *only* information sent from the Indian government to the Canadian government was that Santokh Singh had entered Canada with false identification and that there was some talk of his encouraging Sikhs to desert the Indian Army.

"We knew that the gentleman had false papers, and there was some suspicion that he was involved in the desertion of Sikhs from the armed forces.... [But] how you grant refugee status, we don't come into that. It is your law and your procedure," the Indian diplomat said sternly.

When Clark stumbled to the podium at the hurried press conference, he knew he had a serious problem on his hands. Yes, he had intervened in the Santokh Singh case, he confirmed — because it carried "a security dimension."

But now, in the face of the *Globe* story, Clark went on, his chins underscoring his indignation, the importance of the Santokh Singh extradition case paled in comparison to another, much more serious issue: the leak of sensitive, secret correspondence between Cabinet ministers. "This letter did carry the classification Secret, and for this letter to carry that classification means that someone somewhere has broken the law of Canada, and that is something we are going to look at!" the minister blustered.

Clark flatly dismissed charges that his interference showed Canada was more interested in friendly relations with India than in maintaining a consistent refugee policy. "There has been an impression developed out of this that concerns of other governments are a priority ahead of Canadian policies. I am here as a minister of the Canadian government, and we are making Canadian decisions for Canadian reasons!"

He steadfastly refused to deal with any questions about his interference in the Santokh Singh case, citing the restrictions of national security and privacy legislation.

In the wake of my *Globe* piece, Clark came under heavy fire from refugee advocates and Sikh organizations. They, too, wanted answers. Michael Schelew, an Amnesty International spokesperson specializing in refugee issues, said Clark's interference in the independence of RSAC undermined "the integrity and credibility of Canada's refugee determination process. He appears to be forgetting that a human life is at stake." Several Sikh groups accused Clark of discriminating against Sikhs. Among them, Parminder Singh Parmar, a spokesman for the World Sikh Organization, said that by intervening in the refugee case, Clark had shown Canadians how a foreign country can influence Canada's immigration system. "He sits with the Indian politicians and he has been brainwashed by them," Parmar said.

On day two of the Santokh Singh affair, the *Globe*'s banner headline read: India Denies Pressure in Refugee Case. The news media across Canada were leading with the story of Clark's meddling and India's unequivocal denial that it had anything to do with the matter.

Question Period degenerated into another bun fight. The government rode out the storm by resorting to high rhetoric and windy retorts, never once providing a straight answer to a single question put to them.

But the scent of vengeance permeated the corridors at immigration headquarters. Santokh Singh, his son, Gursev, and Jasbir Kaur were going to pay dearly for allowing their confrontation with Ottawa to be dragged into the news media — even though they had absolutely nothing to do with it in the first place.

Like many stories, I figured this one would be played out somewhere down the road, probably when the appeal was heard. Regrettably — I speak with hindsight — I went on to other stories and let it slide, thinking that if anything significant happened I would get a call.

I learned all the sordid details of what happened four and a half years later, in October, 1992, when I reconnected with Dr. Singh. He came to see me with his son, Gursev. By this time, I was no longer with the *Globe*. (In July, 1990, I joined the CBC as co-host of the investigative current affairs show *the fifth estate*.)

As Dr. Singh recounted his agonizing odyssey through the immigration system, I felt my blood pressure rise. The events had taken their toll on him. Physically, he looked worn, almost broken. He couldn't comprehend why he was being put through this mental anguish. Gursev's eyes mirrored his concern for his aging father. His life was also in a state of limbo. He was in university studying for a teaching degree. He was doing well but he felt dislocated, not knowing whether he would ever be able to call Canada home.

Dr. Singh had kept copious notes on all correspondence, phone calls and dealings with a long list of immigration officials. Referring to his notes from time to time, he filled me in on the details.

The appeal the Tories had so sanctimoniously concerned themselves with in Question Period never happened, despite the fact that Dr. Singh had filed an application with the Immigration Appeal Board on May 17, 1988. Instead, the case was shoved into a void called the Refugee Backlog Clearance Program, which was supposed to deal with an estimated hundred thousand refugee cases sitting in limbo. The title was an exercise in Orwellian newspeak. It should have been labelled the Backlog Burial Program.

Theoretically, cases shoved into the Refugee Backlog Clearance Program would be assessed individually on *humanitarian and compassionate grounds*. Those who passed were given landed immigrant status. Those who bombed were referred to a full, rigorous refugee hearing.

The Singh and Kaur files gathered dust on some bureaucrat's desk for three years. Then, in August, 1991, they were assessed "on humanitarian and compassionate grounds" by an immigration officer in the department's London, Ontario, office. And surprise, surprise! All three were summarily rejected. Their files were sent to the department's Mississauga office on September 3 for further action. That office was to arrange for an oral hearing to determine whether Santokh Singh, Gursev Singh and Jasbir Kaur had a credible basis for refugee status in Canada.

Again, they were shoved through the bureaucratic meat grinder.

In the first week of September, 1991, Dr. Singh was informed that he would be called in for his oral hearing within a month. When he had heard nothing for more than three months, he called the London office and was curtly told to contact the Mississauga office, since his files had been transferred there. He did, and was told that his files were not in the Mississauga office. After repeated calls to London and Mississauga, he was told the files were "untraceable." Dr. Singh persisted. In the first week of March, 1992, he informed the London office that he was going to approach the immigration minister about the missing files. That apparently lit a small fire under a lowly bureaucrat, who sent a fax to the Mississauga office asking about the files.

On March 9, Dr. Singh received a phone call from Jim Oldreive, assistant manager of the Mississauga office, who informed him that while he was still trying to trace the missing files, instructions had been given to the London office for the issuance of work permits. Three days later, Oldreive phoned Dr. Singh and told him the files had been found and that oral hearings for refugee status would take place within the next couple of months.

Six months passed with no word about the hearings. In mid-October, frustrated and upset, Santokh Singh came to see me.

Angrily, I picked up the phone and called Peter Harder, the associate deputy minister of immigration. I outlined the situation tersely. I was really pissed off.

"I don't understand what is going on here. These people don't deserve this kind of treatment. Nobody deserves to be screwed around like this. Enough already!" I said.

"I promise I'll look into it, Victor. I'll get back to you before the end of the week," Harder said.

He was as good as his word. Harder called back three days later and told me that all three files had been approved for landed immigrant status because their refugee claims were found to be credible. That decision, he said, had been made on September 30 in Toronto. Yet for some reason no one had bothered to tell the claimants.

I figured they were in good hands with Harder. So once again, I didn't follow up. Then in late April, 1994, I got a phone call from a friend of Santokh Singh's who told me that the three still were not landed. I couldn't believe it. I called Dr. Singh immediately and asked him why he hadn't let me know what was happening.

"I did not want to bother you," he said.

His voice was filled with anguish as he recounted his, Gursev's and Jasbir's ordeal. There had been a series of phone calls between Dr. Singh and a succession of immigration officers at the Mississauga office before the three were granted an appointment to finalize their immigration papers, in the last week of October, 1992. But when they arrived for the appointment (a ninety-minute drive from their home), they were summarily dismissed by an abrupt official. The appointment had been cancelled, he said. He offered no reason. Dr. Singh phoned Jim Oldreive to complain about the treatment. They were called back to the office about a week later. They filled out a sheaf of immigration forms and had their photographs taken. Then they each paid $450 to process their applications for landed immigrant status. They felt confident that the nightmare was ending at last.

But their hopes were dashed yet again. They were told they could not be landed that day because CSIS had not cleared them. But CSIS and the RCMP had given them a clean bill of health in 1988! Dr. Singh protested. The immigration officer assured them that the CSIS clearance would take about six weeks. Landed immigrant status would be granted, at the latest, by mid-January, 1993, he said.

January came and went, and nothing happened. In March, Dr. Singh contacted Andrew Rustja, an immigration officer at the Mississauga office, for an update on his case. Rustja informed him that they had not yet received security clearance from CSIS and that he had sent the domestic spy agency another urgent reminder.

More than three months passed. On June 30, 1993, the Mississauga office was shut down. A Kafkaesque twist! All the files were transferred to an office near Pearson International Airport in Toronto.

Then, silence.

Dr. Singh was now convinced that what was happening wasn't mere coincidence or bureaucratic ineptness. He believed it was deliberately orchestrated.

And so did I.

"I'm going to make a few calls and get to the bottom of this," I said. "What has happened to you makes me ashamed to be Canadian. I'm going to call Sergio Marchi's office."

"I have already written to Mr. Marchi since he became minister of immigration," replied Dr. Singh. "I wrote to him on the thirteenth of February of this year. He has not yet responded."

"Typical. When in Opposition, rant and rave about human rights abuses. When in power, do nothing," I said.

That afternoon, I phoned Marchi's office and explained the case to one of his special assistants. I reminded her that Marchi had vociferously championed the case when he was the Liberal Party's immigration critic in Opposition.

"This harassment is going to stop now," I said in a firm voice. "It's deliberate and it's perverse. I was told two years ago by Peter Harder, your deputy minister, that these people would be landed within the month. Well, something better happen and soon."

"I'll look into it," the assistant said.

"I suggest you do more than look into it. I'm serious about this. This has gone on long enough. You tell Marchi he's got to put a stop this freakin' torture!"

A day later, the assistant phoned and said the landing would take place on May 5. It did, but oddly, only for Dr. Singh.

The next day, I called Marchi's office and angrily asked why Gursev Singh and Jasbir Kaur weren't landed at the same time. The assistant was befuddled. A week later, she called back and announced they would be landed on June 5. This time, only Gursev got landed. Jasbir Kaur was left out in the cold. Her file, it transpired, was lost, and for the moment couldn't be traced. Finally, on August 12, she was called into the immigration office in Toronto and landed. The immigration officer handling her file had gone on vacation and forgot to pass on her file.

POSTSCRIPT

There were many layers to the Santokh Singh fiasco. On the most mundane level, it was a classic example of bureaucratic bungling and ineptitude. Lost files, offices closed, messages misinterpreted or not delivered, civil servants going on vacation. On another level was bungling by our security and intelligence forces, the RCMP and CSIS. Then came the government and Joe Clark. What was the agenda here? Where was Clark coming from? Why did he go to such great lengths to get this man tossed out of Canada? Was Clark genuinely misguided? Did he simply mess up? Was he duped by the Indian government? Or was he willing to turn over a genuine refugee for the sake of bilateral relations and trade considerations?

The answer probably lay in a statement made by one of Clark's officials in External Affairs the day after the Santokh Singh story ran in the *Globe*. Robin MacNab, a deputy chairman in the trade development division, told the *Globe*'s Robert Matas that close relations with India could bring several multimillion-dollar contracts to Canada within the next few years. "There's no question about it. Obviously, in awarding big projects, politics is important," MacNab said.

So important that earlier in the year, going through old newspaper files, I discovered Clark was on record expressing concern about maintaining warm relations with India when he urged provincial premiers to boycott activities of three Canadian Sikh organizations that support an independent homeland for Sikhs. And at about the same time, External Affairs officials intervened in an application for a $300,000 grant to establish a chair in Punjabi literature and Sikh studies at the University of British Columbia. They maintained that support for the education program "could harm bilateral relations with India."

Clark countered at the Calgary press conference that his intervention in the Santokh Singh case did not show Canada is more interested in chasing trade dollars than maintaining a consistent, fair and independent refugee policy. But he wasn't about to give an answer on the more worrisome question that remains unanswered to this day: Who provided him with the serious allegations about Dr. Singh? He was satisfied with simply clouding the entire sordid affair by diverting the attention to the security leak. Well, he never found out the source of that leak.

If there was a hero in this affair, it was Joe Stern, the white-knight chairman of the Refugee Status Advisory Committee, who would not back down in the face of heavy political and bureaucratic pressure. Unlike Clark, Stern understood the importance of independence in the refugee process. In the end, however, Stern lost. When the new refugee board was created in 1989, his contract was cut short by the Tory government and he was given the heave-ho because he wouldn't toe the party line.

Meanwhile, not for the first time, bureaucracy had spun out of control while going after the wrong target. The real terrorist, Mahmoud Muhammad Issa Mohammad, is still in Canada! On January 18, 1988, the day my story came out in the *Globe* about his presence in the country, the Tory government vowed to rid Canada of this convicted killer within six months. More than eight years have passed, and Mohammad is still living quietly with his family in Brantford, Ontario. He's used every legal maneuver and loophole in Canadian law to maintain his residence in this country.

CHAPTER NINE

NIGHTMARE ON BAY STREET

Martin Sheldon Pilzmaker hung out his shingle on Toronto's powerful Bay Street, just a kilometre away from the *Globe*. But I first heard his name fifteen thousand kilometres away, in Hong Kong. He practiced exclusively in the lucrative field of business immigration, specializing in the importation of ultra-wealthy Hong Kong families into Canada. Pilzmaker was not your run-of-the-mill lawyer. At thirty-six, he was worth an estimated $40 million. He rode around in a convertible, chauffeur-driven Rolls-Royce Corniche and he lived in a sprawling, fourteen-thousand-square-foot mansion on the Bridle Path in Toronto's north end. He wore Italian silk suits, tailored monogrammed shirts, Gucci loafers and a diamond-encrusted, twenty-two-karat gold Rolex watch.

Pilzmaker grew up in Outremont, an upper-middle-class, largely French-Canadian and Jewish neighbourhood of Montreal. At Outremont High School he was looked down upon by his classmates as a loathsome, fat geek. Now, in Toronto, Pilzmaker was no longer a social outcast. Surrounded by hangers-on, he held court at fine restaurants where he took pride in always picking up the tab. He charged everything on his platinum card, which he signed with a stubby, solid-gold Le Blanc fountain pen, and his credit-card charges were between $30,000 and $40,000 a month.

He threw lavish parties at his home. Expensive liquor flowed freely, although he personally never touched a drop of alcohol. Rémy Martin cognac at $140 a bottle was standard fare. Surrounded by partyers, Pilzmaker remained aloof and sullen in a dark corner of his living room, watching his guests drink, schmooze and let loose. Later, he'd skulk around the mansion peeking into rooms where guests had sneaked off for a romp in the sack. He was a voyeur and, when he went

to bed, he would barricade his bedroom door in case one of the inebri-
ated women wandering the hallways got any ideas.

People speculated about what made Pilzmaker tick. The fact that he
never married and was devoted to his mother (he dispatched her on several round-the-world vacations, accompanied by one of his secretaries)
fuelled the predictable rumours that he was gay. If he was, he was deeply
in the closet. His solitariness, counterpointed by his taste for Gatsby-
esque parties and lavish spending, reflected a desperate attempt to buy
affection and friends.

But despite his garish lifestyle, he remained elusive. He avoided
reporters like the plague. Unlike his media-hungry colleagues, Pilzmaker
didn't return any of my phone calls. Nor did he offer a single comment
on Ottawa's Entrepreneur Program for well-heeled immigrants — in
sharp contrast to other lawyers, who panned this patch of immigration
law. They never missed an opportunity to pontificate in Canada's
national newspaper. It meant free and valuable advertising for them.

Not Pilzmaker. He didn't want a drop of ink. And he certainly didn't
want his picture in the paper. It was precisely this that put me on his
trail. I smelled corruption. I set out to find out everything I could about
him.

I began with a simple paper chase. By looking up records on the incorporation of Pilzmaker's firm, I got a home address. I searched the title
on his property on the Bridle Path and found the magnificent mansion
was worth a cool $4 million. He was paying upwards of $50,000 a month
in mortgage payments and another $50,000 a year in property taxes.

Through the Ontario Ministry of Transportation, I got the description and license-plate numbers on all six of his cars — a Rolls-Royce, a
Jaguar, a Ferrari, a Cadillac, a Porsche and a four-wheel-drive Jeep. The
Law Society of Upper Canada directory listed him as having received
his LLB degree from McGill University, class of '75. He was a B student
who (a classmate told me later) sat at the back of the room wisecrack-
ing and zinging paper spitballs.

One of my contacts at the Canada Commission in Hong Kong told
me about the seminars Pilzmaker had held in sumptuous hotels to
recruit Chinese businessmen in search of Canadian passports. His reputation in the colony's sleazier business circles was solid gold. The word
on the street was, Martin Pilzmaker could make things happen.

At this early stage in the hunt, I discovered that Pilzmaker had been
wooed by Lang Michener, an august Bay Street law firm in Toronto

that boasts former Governor-General Roland Michener as one of its founding fathers. The firm also had Jean Chrétien, then the leading contender for federal Liberal Party leader, on its roster of 180 lawyers.

Odd place for a guy like Pilzmaker to park his attaché case, I thought. This was a stuffy, upper-crust, old boys' firm where grey suits, silver hair and orthopedic shoes ruled the boardroom. Yet these proper barristers had pursued Pilzmaker like ardent suitors. Why? Because Lang Michener yearned for a piece of Pilzmaker's action — a chunk of the bountiful harvest of business immigrants from Hong Kong.

Pilzmaker was willing to share the wealth in exchange for the recognition and prestige he craved — seeing his name embossed on the letterhead of a prominent, old-school Toronto law firm.

He had approached Eddie Goldenberg, an associate at Lang Michener and a fellow Montrealer, to suss out the possibility of joining the firm. Goldenberg (now Prime Minister Chrétien's chief political advisor and confidant) told the boys at Lang Michener about Pilzmaker and the incredible money he was making in Hong Kong.

The boys were truly impressed. They were willing to hold their noses and suffer Pilzmaker's crude conduct in return for an entrée into the teeming Pacific Rim. The senior management group voted to make him a full senior partner with a starting salary of $400,000 a year. It was the first time a new lawyer coming into the firm had parachuted right into the gold circle. Not even Jean Chrétien, their prime minister-in-waiting, rated that kind of carte blanche treatment. All he managed was associate status, $100,000 a year and an office in Ottawa.

But Pilzmaker, who showed up for an initial meeting with the Lang Michener brass wearing a $20,000 fox-fur coat and a frizzy perm — definitely *not* the Lang Michener uniform! — was calling the tune. One of his conditions was that two of his associates, Gary Wiseman and Lloyd Ament — plus his trusted secretary, Jeanne Ramsay — come with him. The boys agreed. Pilzmaker was invited to join the firm in January, 1985.

During his first ninety days, Pilzmaker fulfilled Lang Michener's wildest expectations by billing $300,000. By the end of the year, his billings topped $1 million. The senior partners were aglow with excitement. But it wasn't long before Pilzmaker's style started to rub people in the firm the wrong way. He would arrive and leave in his chauffeur-driven Rolls. He'd saunter around the office boasting about his billings. In the spring of 1986, he paraded through the corridors showing his partners his 1985 tax return, which indicated a gross earning of $2.1

million. Then he waved a cheque made out to the Receiver General of Canada for $1.4 million for taxes. Pilzmaker also crowed he had a numbered Swiss bank account with $3 million in it. "That's my rainy-day fund in case anything ever goes wrong," he'd say.

In mid June, 1988, I phoned the firm and asked to speak to Martin Pilzmaker. The switchboard operator curtly informed me that he was no longer with Lang Michener, and no, she didn't have a forwarding address or a phone number for him.

At first, I took Pilzmaker's departure at face value. The mix of flash and brash probably had been just too much for the traditionalists at the firm and there had been a parting of the ways. But after I made a few calls, it occurred to me that there was something unsettling about the departure. It was oddly hush-hush. Everyone at the firm refused to talk about it, almost as though they had been ordered to keep their mouths shut. Then one lawyer, first extracting a sworn promise of anonymity from me, spilled the beans.

"Pilzmaker was expelled by the senior partnership," he said. The expulsion had occurred in September, 1986, after a vote by the entire partnership.

Then came the bombshell: On June 8, 1988, the RCMP had quietly raided the offices of Lang Michener at First Canadian Place and carted away several boxes containing 149 of Pilzmaker's files. At the time of the raid, the firm's outside lawyer sternly warned the Mounties about the sanctity of solicitor-client privilege, and the police had sealed up all the documents without looking at them.

My insider revealed that in the brouhaha following Pilzmaker's expulsion, the firm had locked up several of his filing cabinets containing a number of important client files. The unprecedented move had something to do with a money dispute. Pilzmaker in turn slapped Lang Michener with a lawsuit in an effort to retrieve his files—and the firm countered with a suit of its own.

"So there's a court action," I said to my informer.

"If I were you I'd pay a visit to the Ontario Provincial Court and look up the court record," the lawyer suggested. "I would also check with the Law Society of Upper Canada. Rumour has it that Pilzmaker is being investigated by Stephen Sherriff."

Sherriff was the law society's top gun. He was hired on as senior counsel of the society's discipline committee in 1981. He took on the job as chief investigator at a time when complaints about crooked lawyers were on the increase and public trust about the society's will to police its members was on the wane. His mandate was clear: crack down on unscrupulous solicitors.

I wasn't sure I could get to Sherriff. The word on the street was he didn't like me. I'd been told he'd blown a gasket over a feature I'd written for the *Globe* in July, 1985, that described the law society as nothing more than an old boys' club that existed to protect its members from their clients instead of protecting consumers from bad lawyers.

I decided instead to tap into my RCMP contacts. I phoned Staff-Sergeant Ty Watts, who confirmed the June 8 visit to the firm. However, he was reticent to offer details because no charges had been laid. But Watts didn't leave me empty-handed. He said the raid had to do with alleged offenses that took place between April, 1986, and November, 1987, and that the investigation centred on four people. He refused to name them. However, the Mountie noted that the search warrant listed the following offenses: uttering forged documents; aiding and abetting Hong Kong citizens to come to Canada by reason of fraudulent or improper means or misrepresentation of material facts; and counselling persons to make false representations in connections with applications for Canadian citizenship.

"You should give Stephen Sherriff at the law society a call," Watts suggested. "From what I hear, he's also looking into this matter."

Sherriff cocked his gun the moment I identified myself. "I'm busy protecting lawyers from their clients and the public," he said caustically.

"I wrote it the way I saw it," I countered. "Anyway, that was then. Maybe now you can prove me wrong. And if you do, I'll eat my words — or a least a copy of the *Globe*."

"I'd pay to see that," Sherriff said.

"I'm told you're investigating Martin Pilzmaker. Is that true?"

"I am not going to confirm any investigation regarding a specific lawyer," he replied noncommittally.

"Well, there's a great start to our new and improved relationship. Then can you tell me if you're investigating alleged wrongdoing at a specific Toronto law firm?"

"What do you want to know?"

"Are you investigating Lang Michener?"

"We've been informed that a lawyer at Lang Michener was approached by another lawyer and offered a home interest-free for three years if he allowed a Hong Kong client to appear to own and live in the house. The lawyer rejected the offer as being unethical and reported it to his superiors at the firm," Sherriff said.

"So what does this have to do with your investigation?"

"Our investigation is centring on allegations that certain Hong Kong businessmen would buy homes in Toronto and appear to take up residence. The mortgages, utilities, Ontario Hospital Insurance Plan and drivers' licenses, for example, were all paid from Toronto addresses. But in fact, these homes were occupied by Canadians a lawyer had arranged as caretakers so there would be the paper appearance that Hong Kong citizens were living there, when in fact they weren't. The Canadians got their rent or mortgage free for cooperating in the scheme."

"I don't get it. What would be in it for a Hong Kong businessman?" I asked.

"On paper, it appears that the man had lived in Canada continuously for three years and on that basis he received his citizenship. In fact, the man was rarely in Canada for much of the required three-year period because he was operating a business back in Hong Kong."

"You can't name the lawyer behind the scam?"

"No. But I can confirm that we've begun disciplinary procedures to have a lawyer disbarred for professional misconduct. That's all I can tell you for the moment. The investigation is continuing."

I called Lang Michener for a comment about the investigation. After a frustrating runaround, Michael Eisen, a senior partner, was designated by the executive committee to deal with me. Clearly uncomfortable in the role of spokesman, Eisen pointed out that he was reluctant to discuss a case currently before the law society. He did confirm, after some prodding, that a former Lang Michener lawyer had been "requested to retire." That was all he was willing to share.

Later that afternoon, I got an unexpected phone call. A voice I didn't recognize claimed to be in the know about what he coined "the Lang Michener affair." He offered to help me out from time to time by pointing me in the right direction. What he wanted was complete anonymity.

An hour later, a courier handed me an envelope. I put my feet on my desk and ripped it open. In it was a law society document and a letter written by Pilzmaker to one of his Hong Kong clients. In the letter, Pilzmaker explained that he was "in the process of suing" Lang Michener "and it seems to me that they are doing whatever they can to

destroy my reputation." He stressed that he firmly believed "the outcome of any investigation would indicate there has been full compliance
with the law."

The law society document detailed some of the allegations against
Pilzmaker. The most serious involved "orchestrating the fraudulent
acquisition of duplicate passports by clients to maintain the illusion of
residence in Canada." It also contained a reference to "the approach"
that Sherriff had talked about earlier. The so-called approach, my source
said, was made to Brian McIntomny, a young associate at Lang Michener
in July, 1986. McIntomny didn't bite. He was troubled by the scheme
and told his supervisor at the firm about it. Eventually, after a long and
acrimonious battle in the Lang Michener boardroom about whether to
keep the matter under wraps, it was reported to the law society.

I was sitting on very hot stuff. But if I hit the papers now with what
I had unearthed, there was a strong probability I would blow any chance
of getting at the real story. I figured no one would be willing to open up.

I discussed my concerns with Paul Palango, my editor for the past
year. Normally, he was supportive. His eyes widened as I recounted my
findings.

"We can't hold this. We go with it tonight," he said.

I was dismayed.

"But what about the bigger story?"

"You can still chase it. But this is news, and that's our business."

"Yeah. But what if a reporter from the *Star* or CBC gets onto this?"

"That's the chance you'll have to take. It just means you'll have to
work that much harder to make sure someone else doesn't take the
story from you."

I made the standard attempt to reach Pilzmaker for comment. He
wasn't hard to find. He'd ensconced himself in private practice in pala-
tial digs in the Eaton's office tower on Queen Street. His secretary took
a message. He didn't call back. I was not surprised.

On Tuesday, June 21, 1988, the *Globe* ran its first front-page story
on the Lang Michener affair. The headline read: Lawyers' Aid to Hong
Kong Immigrants Investigated by RCMP and Law Society. In the article,
I wrote that the Mounties were investigating four people—three
lawyers and a secretary—for allegedly creating false Canadian resi-
dences and bogus business intentions so that as many as 149 of their
wealthy Hong Kong clients could get landed status and, eventually,
Canadian citizenship. I revealed that the Law Society of Upper Canada

had begun disciplinary procedures to have "one of the lawyers, a former partner at Lang Michener," disbarred for professional misconduct. The *Globe*'s lawyers had gingerly lifted Pilzmaker's name out of the article.

The next day my source called with an interesting sidebar.

"Just wanted you to know that two of Pilzmaker's colleagues, Lloyd Ament and Gary Wiseman, were forced to resign from Lang Michener last month after they were privately reprimanded by the law society for professional misconduct."

"What was the misconduct?"

"Failing to report the unethical conduct by a colleague. Guess who?"

"Pilzmaker?"

"You got it. But all Ament and Wiseman got was a slap on the wrist from the discipline committee. I think they struck a deal with Sherriff to cooperate in the law society's action to have Pilzmaker disbarred."

I called Sherriff. He refused to confirm the reprimands.

On the morning of June 22, I headed for the provincial court building on Queen Street, directly across the street from Osgoode Hall, home to the Ontario Supreme Court and the Law Society of Upper Canada. I asked a sympathetic clerk how I would go about locating a lawsuit that had been filed sometime in late 1986. She pointed me to a dented steel table piled high with thick binders dated by year. Each binder was filled with legal actions. I scanned about a dozen pages in the 1986 book before my finger landed on Pilzmaker vs Lang Michener. I took down the docket number and asked a clerk for a copy of the affidavit.

It was a simple two-page document, but I knew when I read it I had hit the jackpot. I had in my possession the names of 102 of Pilzmaker's clients — plus a puzzling series of numbered Ontario companies.

My next stop: the Ontario Provincial Ministry of Consumer and Corporate Affairs. I spent an entire day there searching the incorporation papers of the numbered companies. Those documents revealed the names of various associates and some very curious connections to people, places and business dealings.

The investigation was getting complex. There were a lot of leads and a lot of peculiar pieces to a very bizarre puzzle, but not much in the way of explanations. I returned to the *Globe* and hunkered down with Palango in his cluttered office to plot out my next move, which I figured would cost the *Globe* more than five hundred dollars. After a lively discussion, Palango decided the cash outlay would be well worth it.

The following morning, I headed for the Ontario Motor Vehicle

Bureau in downtown Toronto and ran all 102 of Pilzmaker's clients through the computer. The charge was five dollars for each search. There was a minor problem when the search snagged a dozen or more Philip Lees and Michael Wangs. But in the end, it was worth all the work and money. As I cross-referenced each name, I smiled. I had hit on a valuable cache of information.

More than two dozen of Pilzmaker's Hong Kong clients were listed as living at one of three addresses in the Toronto area. No fewer than ten Hong Kong businessmen and their families gave 6 Peterborough Avenue — a two-storey, four-bedroom brick house on a quiet street in Thornhill, just north of Toronto — as their home address. A second two-storey house at 6 Peebles Avenue in North York was listed as the residence for eight Chinese businessmen. Nearby, a third house — a luxurious bungalow at 88 Fifeshire Avenue — was listed as the residence of another half-dozen Chinese clients.

I had to figure out how these homes fit into Pilzmaker's immigration scam. But as it happened, my source phoned with another hot tip.

"I hear you've been calling Lang Michener," he began.

"Yeah. But they either won't talk or they don't return my calls."

"It's all part of the plan. One of the senior partners laughed at your story in the *Globe* on June 21. He called you a one-shot wonder."

A one-shot wonder! "Tell him I've only just begun," I said.

"Well, get your pen ready, because your next article won't have the partners laughing. Stephen Sherriff is investigating as many as fourteen lawyers at Lang Michener. He wants to have them all charged with professional misconduct because apparently they all knew what Pilzmaker was doing and did nothing about it for the longest time. They only finally reported him to the law society in early December, 1986, when they had absolutely no other choice," my source said.

"How are the boys at Lang Michener taking it?"

"They'd like to cut Sherriff's nuts off, I can tell you that. Despite a lot of pressure from a lot of powerful people with friends in high places, Sherriff isn't backing down. The chairman of discipline has Sherriff's report along with his recommendation to charge fourteen lawyers. But what's even more astounding is that the treasurer of the society has decided not to let him prosecute the case. They've hired David Scott to act as counsel if the case goes forward."

Sherriff was annoyed by my phone call, wondering how I had heard about these latest developments. His reply was terse.

"In accordance with law society practice, we do not comment with respect to any case under investigation," he said.

"I guess it's that boys' club thing, eh?" I chided.

"No, it's a basic fairness thing." Sherriff was not amused.

My next call was to Michael Eisen, my official contact at Lang Michener. He was as helpful as Sherriff.

"I think that I'm not really going to be discussing much of anything from this point on. I'm concerned that this is before the courts or other judicial bodies and it would not be appropriate for me to comment," Eisen said.

The page-one story on July 6 read: 14 Lawyers at Top Firm Investigated.

The *Globe* stories were beginning to shake the foundations of Lang Michener. That became abundantly clear when I got a call summoning me to meet with Robert Wright, former chairman of the firm. Wright was considered to be the most powerful and feared person in the place. When I arrived, I was led into his office by a secretary. Wright made a point of being rude. He didn't get up from his desk when I entered. He didn't bother to shake my outstretched hand, and throughout our brief encounter, he sat with his feet on the desk with the soles of his shoes in my face.

I'll never forget the first thing Wright said. He asked if I had noticed — as I walked through the outer offices toward his inner sanctum — that there were no *Globe and Mail* newspapers on the entire floor.

"So?"

"Well, there aren't any," he said. "We don't buy the *Globe* here anymore."

Then he got straight to the point. He wanted to know how long I was going to continue my little crusade and what the firm could expect next in the *Globe*.

"All you have to do is take the elevator to the lobby, go outside and put your quarter in the grey-and-blue box and read all about it," I replied smugly.

The silver-haired Wright was not amused. I'm sure he felt like dismissing me then and there. But there were some things he wanted me to know first: While the law society was investigating the firm, he — Robert Wright — was not a member of the firm's executive committee. Number two: He, Robert Wright, did not have any knowledge of any wrongdoing on the part of Martin Pilzmaker. He had made a personal decision in the early 1980s to cease being active in the day-to-day management of the firm. Wright admitted that he was one of the fourteen lawyers being investigated by Sherriff. He added confidently that he would be fully vindicated.

He had said his piece. I left. We didn't shake hands.

I grinned as I passed a *Globe* newspaper box. It wouldn't be long before, despite himself, Robert Wright would shove a quarter into the slot and read my latest revelation about the goings-on in his venerable firm.

Within days, a well-placed Ottawa source in Canada Customs came through with a choice chunk of information. It seemed that a number of Lang Michener's upstanding lawyers had visited Hong Kong with Pilzmaker, and on their return had smuggled substantial amounts of expensive jewelry and other items into Canada. And now (surprise!) the lawyers were suddenly overcome by pangs of guilt and decided to make a declaration to Canada Customs and pay the duty. The collective attack of conscience just happened to coincide with the RCMP investigation of Pilzmaker's activities.

For the Lang Michener smugglers, I found out, it paid to have connections in high places. In February, 1988, Paul LaBarge, a lawyer in the firm's Ottawa office, met with Milton Gallup, an assistant deputy minister in the Customs and Excise division of Revenue Canada, to discuss the problem. With a little rummaging through the *Globe* archives, I discovered an interesting tidbit: LaBarge's father, the late Raymond LaBarge, was deputy minister of Customs And Excise from 1964 until the early 1970s, and Gallup was a close family friend. Paul LaBarge apparently called him Uncle Milt.

I called Yvon Charlebois, an assistant deputy minister of Canada Customs, and asked if a meeting between Gallup and LaBarge had taken place. He confirmed that it had and also confirmed that duty on certain items had been paid by a number of Lang Michener lawyers in March. He refused to disclose the goods involved, the cost or the duty paid.

"Was a penalty assessed against the lawyers?" I asked.

"No," the bureaucrat replied.

"Why not?"

"Because they had made a voluntary declaration."

"And what would have happened had the lawyers not made a voluntary declaration?" I asked.

"They could have faced stiff fines or even criminal proceedings for smuggling," Charlebois replied. But voluntary declarations are made all the time, he stressed. "If you come forward, as long as you haven't been found out, we accept that declaration. You pay up, and that's the end of it. It happens hundreds of times a year. I can only assure you that everything was quite appropriate. I've looked into this. I've got a report, and there isn't a glitch."

"I guess it doesn't hurt to have connections, as well," I said.

"I can tell you that had nothing to do with the outcome. The duty was paid, and it's over."

I placed a call to Lang Michener to get a reaction. I had already talked to the *Globe*'s lawyers. They were nervous as hell about accusing lawyers at the prestigious firm of smuggling.

"We need more than a reply of 'no comment' before we go with the story," *Globe* lawyer Peter Jacobsen had argued, warning me about libel, slander and defamation laws. "You have to get them to confirm that this actually took place. This is just too serious an issue to go on the word of unnamed sources." After a long runaround, Eisen finally got on the line. His first comment was "no comment" when I asked about the smuggling incident.

"No comment! When are you guys going to learn?" I shouted into the telephone. Palango was standing behind me listening to my end of the conversation. "You said 'no comment' last time, and the story ended up on the front page and made you look like idiots! If you don't get back to me by four o'clock with something a little more intelligent like, 'Yeah, we did it, but we didn't do anything wrong,' I'm going to print 'no comment' and you're all going to look like idiots again."

Minutes before deadline, Eisen called back and confirmed that certain lawyers had made voluntary declarations to Canada Customs. He said, "After Pilzmaker had been required to retire from the firm, it was learned that some people travelling to Hong Kong on Lang Michener business might have imported goods for their personal use beyond the amounts declared. We indicated to those who had been to Hong Kong it would, in the firm's view, be appropriate to make a voluntary declaration and pay the appropriate duty."

"Those people travelling to Hong Kong—would one of them happen to be Albert Gnat?" I asked. Gnat was one of the senior partners and top moneymakers at the firm.

"No comment," Eisen said, his voice a nervous whisper.

When Palango and Jacobsen went over the story, they deleted the reference to Gnat.

"You know for sure that Albert Gnat was one of the smugglers?" Jacobsen asked.

"Yeah," I said.

"From where?"

"A source."

"Not good enough," Jacobsen countered.

I shot a pleading glance at Palango.

"These guys are making hundreds of thousands or millions of dollars a year and they're risking everything by getting involved in smuggling. Unbelievable!" Palango said. "But the name has to stay out until we've got a second source on it."

The *Globe* headline on July 8 read: Charges Averted After Smuggling Uncovered at Law Firm.

Next I began looking into the ownership of the homes on Peterborough, Peebles and Fifeshire avenues. I discovered that the properties on Peebles and Fifeshire were once owned by Pilzmaker. He purchased the Fifeshire house in June, 1983, for $289,000 and lived there until he sold it to his Hong Kong clients Wah Chee and Elsie Lo in October, 1985, for $365,750. But Chee and Lo didn't live there. In fact, they had never lived there. According to the crisscross directory — which lists properties by street, address, occupant and profession — the house was occupied by Gary Wiseman, one of the lawyers Pilzmaker brought to Lang Michener. And during my search of the numbered companies, I learned that Robert Lee, a Pilzmaker client, gave 88 Fifeshire as his home address for the incorporation of 640376 Ontario Ltd., also known as Persha Leathers, a leather importing firm.

In February, 1985, Pilzmaker purchased a house on Peebles Avenue for $525,000 and sold it in September, 1987, for $975,000 to George and Marilyn Morita. When I called, Mrs. Morita said mail bearing various Chinese names was delivered to the house when she and her husband first moved in, but it eventually stopped. Yet James P. Tien, forty-one, and Michael C. Yam, forty-nine, had current Ontario driver's licenses listing the Peebles home as their residence. And when Pilzmaker had owned the property, a number of his clients had listed it as their residence on applications for numbered Ontario companies. They included Kenneth and Philip Kwok Lee, with a company identified only as 629741 Ontario Ltd.; Thomas Tsui, 625572 Ontario Ltd.; William Ve-Yin Shen and Loh Chun-Yi Shen, 627050 Ontario Ltd.; Nicolas and Lorene Yeung, 635088 Ontario Ltd., which was also identified as

Baywood Forest Paper Machinery; and Cheong Wa Wong and Colin Kwok Lieng Pih, 640375 Ontario Ltd., which was also called Lindzon Fashions, manufacturers of ladies' wear.

The search on the house on Peterborough Avenue revealed an impressive list of occupants. It was purchased in August, 1985, for $200,000 by Hong Kong brothers Kenneth and Philip Kwok Lee, clients of Pilzmaker. The Lee brothers had never lived in the house. Yet telephones were listed in the white pages under their names at that address. In my computer search of Ontario driving records, I found that Jeffery K. Lam, thirty-six, Michael P. Tien, thirty-seven, Michael C. Wang, forty-four, Ronald Li, forty-one, and Philip Kwok Lee, forty-four, had given 6 Peterborough Avenue as their home address.

According to the crisscross directory, the house was occupied by Jeanne Ramsay and her husband, Everett. Mrs. Ramsay was Pilzmaker's secretary.

Pay dirt.

I phoned Ramsay at her office and identified myself. "Mr. Pilzmaker is not in at the moment," she replied quickly. "Can I take a message?"

"I'm actually calling you," I said, and waded right in. "I'm curious about what's going on at your home on Peterborough Avenue. Are you running a rooming house for wealthy Chinese businessmen?"

Mrs. Ramsay's cool office voice dissolved into a nervous quiver. "Mr. Pilzmaker has instructed me not to answer any questions." She slammed down the phone.

A few minutes later, she called my office. She was agitated. "I really see nothing wrong in what I've done," she blurted. "I do not know the intricacies of law. I'm just a secretary. I sit at my desk and when I'm told to do something I do it. I didn't go to law school, but I had this explained to me by Mr. Pilzmaker. It all seemed perfectly plausible. I saw nothing wrong in what I did — and now I'm a suspect in an RCMP investigation!"

"How many Hong Kong businessmen are using your home for whatever reason?" I asked.

"Off the top of my head, about ten. But they're not living there. It's not a home address. It's simply a mailing address. What's the difference between using my home as a mailing address and getting a post office box number? I acted strictly as a mailing address."

"So you just rent the house?"

"Yes."

"What do you pay a month?"

"It's below market value. But I maintain the place. I was so ecstatic when I got the chance to rent the house. I have nothing more to say." She hung up.

Five minutes later, she called back. She pleaded with me not to identify her or use her comments in the *Globe*. "I don't want to get into any trouble with my husband!" she said. She sounded desperate.

"Everything you told me is on the record, Mrs. Ramsay," I replied.

She slammed down the phone again.

The *Globe*'s front-page banner headline on July 15 read: Probes Seek Link Between Houses, Hong Kong Applicants. Next to the lead story was a sidebar outlining a separate story, which had been unwittingly supplied by Pilzmaker and Lang Michener. The headline read: Lawyers Put on Spot Over $342,031 in Bills.

In an affidavit prepared by Lang Michener in reply to Pilzmaker's lawsuit, the firm revealed that it had conducted an exhaustive review of the lawyer's accounts and found that $334,884 "appeared to be uncollectible as either no work had been performed or no binding agreement to do the work had been entered into. The remaining $37,147 was also dubious."

Attached to the affidavit, which I obtained from the court record, was a letter from Hong Kong businessman John L.W. Lee. In October, 1986, Lee wrote that he was very surprised to receive a reminder from the firm in September suggesting that he had an outstanding account of $20,765 dating back to May, 1985.

"I wish to advise you that I have never contacted your firm for any services and consequently I do not understand how your firm can make up such a statement of account," Lee wrote, adding, "I wish to make it clear that at no time have I ever dealt with Lang Michener or Mr. Pilzmaker and consequently I do not understand why I have a file with your firm."

Another phantom client was Steven Wong, a Hong Kong businessman with a sense of humour. He wrote Lang Michener in November, 1986, noting that it came as a surprise to receive a bill for $20,412 from the firm. "As far as my memory goes, the only person I met in your firm was a Mr. Martin Pilzmaker of which a friend has introduced me. I talked to him for less than an hour concerning immigration of which the result was inconclusive. As far as my knowledge concerns, initial business discussion may or may not cost me a legal fee and the cost of fee for one hour should not be more than $200 Canadian with the calibre of guy I have talked to. However, a one-hour discussion with no follow-up and nothing which costs that much can be listed in the *Guinness Book of World Records*. I should advise my lawyer friends in Canada to join your good firm."

Before I hit the send button on my computer to move my stories on Lang Michener to the editor's desk, I made the required attempt to contact Pilzmaker for comment. He didn't call back. But on July 20, he fired off a letter to the *Globe* on the story about the three houses. It would be his only comment, official or otherwise, on his involvement in the Lang Michener affair.

> ...The allegations which have been made against me are allegations only and have yet to be proved. Many allegations originated from a bitter personal dispute with Lang Michener...and should be viewed with some caution for that reason.
>
> Finally, you have pointedly noted that my secretary became anxious and upset under your questioning and that she reported that our clients were "petrified." Many of your readers may not find that as surprising as you do. I would venture to suggest that no one would enjoy the position we now find ourselves in, where our names are spread across the front pages of the paper with allegations and insinuations of sinister activities and with no realistic opportunity to respond.

I phoned Pilzmaker and left a message with his secretary. "Could you inform Mr. Pilzmaker that I would be more than willing to offer him and his clients a realistic opportunity to respond?"

Pilzmaker did not return my call.

My next objective was to find out what kind of business proposals Pilzmaker had put together for his clients, and what had happened to them. I contacted Kirk Bell, the director general of policy and program development for Canada Immigration, to ask if I could select at random a number of proposals to see how they had fared since setting up shop in Canada. Bell sputtered, "That is not possible." Pleading privacy legislation, he refused to let me see any business proposals. The only document he was willing to share was one boasting about the program's incredible success. It trumpeted a whopping seventy-seven percent success rate.

"How did you arrive at that figure?" I asked. To say I was skeptical is an understatement. I never believe anyone who offers me a statistic based on a percentage with no real numbers to back anything up.

Bell pointed out that the statistics were confirmed in a "very recent analysis of the program."

"Could I see the analysis?"

"It's not for public consumption," Bell said. "It's an internal document."

Much to the department's chagrin, I managed to obtain a copy from a contact in the department. After perusing it, I understood immediately why Bell didn't want the public to see it.

It was a classic bureaucratic obfuscation, and my first solid confirmation that the Entrepreneur program was in serious disarray. For the study, the department had randomly selected 1,056 entrepreneurs. But in a preliminary run-through, immigration officials could not find 395 of them. Of the 661 who were located, 308 didn't respond to the survey because they were away or refused to discuss their activities in Canada. In all, only 353 entrepreneurs across the country, or 18.8 percent of the original sample, were questioned. It was from that group that Kirk Bell and his minions arrived at the 77 percent success rating.

I set up an interview with Walter McLean, the junior minister of immigration, to discuss the program. I didn't tell him I had a copy of the confidential analysis. As I expected, McLean launched into a rehearsed monologue, proudly citing the success rate.

I asked: "How was that success rate reached, given that roughly 40 percent of the entrepreneurs could not be found in the original random sample and that 308 people from the remaining 661 did not take part in the survey?"

McLean winced and did some quick mental math. "Good question," he replied shakily. "I just got the first quasi-executive summary of the study and just had a preliminary briefing on the whole survey." Then he slickly passed the buck. "Maybe Mr. Bell could respond," he said.

Bell's hands trembled as he shuffled through his papers. "The results are statistically valid. Statistically, you can give a 77 percent success rate across the board."

I looked at Bell and shook my head. "I'm no math wizard, but even I can't buy that," I said.

Bell said that there was no reason to believe those who could not be found or did not respond were more or less successful than those who participated in the study. "They are to be considered the same. There is no reason, statistically, to believe otherwise."

Again I asked if I could select a number of entrepreneurial applications at random so I could check them out independently.

The minister refused with a flat no.

"Fine," I said, coyly waving the confidential survey in Bell's face. "I'll get them some other way."

My next stop: the Ontario government. I gave a crusty bureaucrat at the Ministry of Industry, Trade and Commerce a half-baked spiel about research I was doing for a feature story on how some of the entrepreneurial business ventures were faring. I got the distinct impression he recognized bullshit when he heard it. Maybe he had already been warned by his federal counterparts to expect my visit. But I sensed something different about this particular civil servant.

"We never had this meeting," the man said hoarsely, and ushered me into a small, square office packed from floor to ceiling with cardboard boxes. Each was full of files on business proposals that had been stamped with Canada Immigration's blue seal of approval. My heart skipped a beat.

After four hours of digging, I had located more than a dozen files of Pilzmaker's clients. Each included impressively typed proposals and glowing updates from the lawyer on how smashingly well the business was doing.

The first entrepreneurial venture I looked into involved Hong Kong businessmen Philip Kwok-Po Lee and Kenneth Kwok-Hon Lee. I was particularly interested in them because of their connection to two of Pilzmaker's housing schemes. In their application, the Lee brothers promised to make a large investment in a Toronto knitting mill. On December, 17, 1984, a detailed business proposal was forwarded to the Ontario Ministry of Industry, Trade and Commerce stating that the Lees planned to modernize and expand a Toronto-based manufacturing company known as Prestige Knitting Mills. The proposal, prepared by Pilzmaker, stated his clients would inject $500,000 into the company and in return receive a fifty percent stake in Prestige from its owners — Tony and Roza Marczak and Lenny Greenspoon. This cash infusion would create a minimum of twenty new full-time jobs.

The bureaucrats at the Commission for Canada in Hong Kong were impressed. They ushered the Lees and their families to the front of the line. Six months later, on June 23, 1985, the Lees arrived in Toronto and were granted landed immigrant status.

According to correspondence in the Ontario ministry files, officials tried to reach the Lee brothers later that year to find out how the venture was proceeding. They could not locate the two men. So in January, 1986, they sent a letter, including an entrepreneur follow-up form, to Lang Michener. Pilzmaker punctiliously filled out the form. He reported that the Lee brothers had invested $400,000 in Prestige, that they were actively participating in the management of the company and that six new jobs had been created.

The ministry officials did not question the veracity of Pilzmaker's response. On the contrary, they added the Lee brothers' venture to their tally of successful immigrant business investments.

I phoned Prestige Knitting Mills and asked to speak to Philip Lee.

"No such person by that name here," the receptionist barked.

"How about Kenneth Lee?"

"No Kenneth, either."

"Is there a Tony Marczak?" I asked.

"Yeah. He owns the place."

"Can I speak to him?"

Marczak had to comb through his memory to recall the Lee brothers. Finally he said, "Yeah, I remember meeting them a few years back. I was introduced to them by the company lawyer."

"The company lawyer?" I asked.

"Yeah. Martin Pilzmaker is our lawyer," Marczak said.

"Were the Lee brothers supposed to invest in Prestige?"

"I remember somebody mentioned something, but nothing ever happened," he said.

I phoned my new contact at the Ontario ministry and told him what I had found out. He was mildly surprised but certainly not shocked.

"Don't you guys try to check the claim?" I asked.

"We just figured the investment was made. Why should we doubt the word of a lawyer, especially when it comes on the letterhead of a firm with the reputation of Lang Michener?" he asked. "Anyway, it's a federal program. It's up to them to monitor the damn thing properly."

My next target—another brother duo, James and Michael Tien— jetted to Canada as landed immigrants on the basis of investing $100,000 each in a rattan furniture manufacturing business in Toronto called Inside Story.

I phoned Marva Mitchell, the owner of Inside Story. She vaguely recalled a brief meeting in early 1986 with her lawyer, Pilzmaker, to discuss a joint business venture. "We talked about it and then it didn't happen. It was never followed up on. It was something we discussed and I guess it just fizzled out. I never met the Tiens, and no money was ever invested by them."

I called a well-connected Canadian journalist friend working in Hong Kong for the *South China Morning Post*. Michael Bociurkiw's antennae buzzed at the mention of James Tien.

"If my hunch is right," Bociurkiw said, "this'll be big news here. I think this guy is a legislative counsellor over here. His father is one of the largest and wealthiest garment manufacturers in Hong Kong."

His hunch paid off. Cornered by Bociurkiw, James Tien confirmed his involvement in the nonexistent business venture. He said he and his brother came to Canada with their families for two weeks in the summer of 1986, expecting to obtain Canadian citizenship a year after getting the business off the ground. But, he pointed out, the idea of Canadian citizenship became less appealing when he and his brother learned they would actually have to *reside* in Canada several months a year in order to obtain it.

"We were just looking for a quick-fix way to do it with the least hassle and no problem to follow," he said.

The idea of investing in Inside Story was Pilzmaker's, Tien said, adding that neither he nor his brother ever met anyone from the company. "We couldn't care less where the money was invested. As far as I'm concerned it's just $200,000 for a passport. We couldn't care less what you do with that investment, whether it really works or not. Mr. Pilzmaker told us what we were doing was one-hundred-percent legit."

Meanwhile, James and Michael Tien still held landed immigrant status in Canada. Although they only stayed in the country a total of fourteen days, they managed to establish themselves as living in homes in the Toronto area. They also obtained Ontario drivers' licenses. James Tien's driver's license put him at 6 Peebles Avenue, which he said he used "as a correspondence address."

Michael Tien's license indicated he lived at 6 Peterborough Avenue. His explanation on the residence situation was somewhat different.

"When we first landed, we had to use a mailing address. We needed to get a driver's license. As far as I am aware, we weren't the only people to use the address. Other Hong Kong businessmen used it, I believe," he said.

I checked into a half-dozen more business ventures and found that not one had ever gotten off the ground. But all were considered up and running by Imigration Canada.

As I prepared my story on Pilzmaker's entrepreneur scam, Paul Palango insisted that we needed a photograph of Pilzmaker.

"I don't think he's going to pose for us," I joked.

"Find out where he is and we'll take one," Palango said.

That's when it struck me. I didn't have a clue what Pilzmaker looked like! I had never met the man. I called his office to find out if he was in town.

"I'd like to speak to Martin" I said, with my hand over the receiver to disguise my voice.

"He's in a meeting right now. Could I take your name and get him to call you back?" the secretary asked.

"Could you tell him to call Victor Malarek?"

She hung up abruptly, without replying.

I got hold of Jeff Wasserman, a *Globe* photographer, and together we barrelled over to the Eaton Centre.

"How are you going to know this guy if you've never seen him?" Wasserman asked.

"I've got a plan." I grinned. "I've got the license-plate numbers of all Pilzmaker's cars. We'll drive through the indoor parking lot at the Eaton Centre and see if we can find one. If we do, we'll have Pilzmaker."

Wasserman drove slowly up the corkscrew ramp as I scanned the rows of parked cars. On the fourth level, I scored.

"Over there! The Rolls-Royce Corniche."

Wasserman looked at my Ontario Motor Vehicles printout. "It says the colour of this guy's Rolls is silver. That's brown," the ever-observant photographer pointed out.

"Yeah, but the license-plate number is the same as what I have here." I jumped out of the car for a closer look. Near the fender I noticed a rock chip.

"Guess what? It's silver underneath!"

"What now?" said Wasserman.

"Wait here and get your Nikon motor drive in gear. I figure Pilzmaker will be down here in about two minutes flat. Just click away when you see a freaked-out guy in an expensive suit scurrying your way."

I darted into the Eaton Centre and dropped a quarter into a pay phone. On the second ring, Pilzmaker's secretary answered. I disguised my voice.

"Could you tell Mr. Pilzmaker that someone is poking around his vehicle?" I hung up.

Moments later, a chubby man in a gray double-breasted Armani suit scampered by me and disappeared into the parking arcade. Thirty seconds later he was back, heading toward the bank of elevators leading to the offices above. From the throbbing red vein on his forehead, I could tell he was one ticked-off solicitor.

By the time we got back to the *Globe*, Pilzmaker's lawyer, Brian Casey, was chewing off Palango's ear on the phone. Casey was threatening to slap me with a harassment complaint as well as to haul me up in front of the Ontario Press Council. He demanded the picture not be used. Palango played the diplomat. He would look into the matter, he said. But he made no promises.

On September 30, 1988, the *Globe* front-page headline read: Promised Investments Fizzle as Immigrant Status Granted. That afternoon, Pilzmaker's lawyer slapped me with a notice of intent to sue me for libel, slander and defamation.

I kept pushing my contacts in the RCMP and Immigration for more information on Pilzmaker's clients. I wanted to flush out the entire fake-residence scam and prove that these bogus entrepreneurs were using Canada to obtain citizenship and a Canadian passport as their insurance marker should the situation get red-hot when China took over Hong Kong in 1997.

On Friday, October 1, 1988, a source met me in a dark, smoky bar in the north end of Toronto. We had a beer and he slipped me a bulky brown envelope. In a taxi on the way back to the *Globe*, I ripped it open. Pilzmaker was in serious trouble.

Documents culled from Pilzmaker's files showed that Wah Chee Lo and his wife, Elsie, had applied for Canadian citizenship on November 14, 1983. The couple swore in their applications that they had lived a total of three of the four preceding years in Canada. The Los provided citizenship officials with certified true copies of their Hong Kong passports. None of the pages contained any exit or entry stamps when they were retrieved from the citizenship court records branch by the RCMP. There was also a sworn affidavit by Pilzmaker, dated February 23, 1984, that the photostats were true copies of the originals.

However, there was a second set of photocopies of the Los passports. And they told a very different story. This set was identical to the first — except for pages six through thirteen. These eight pages contained numerous entry and exit immigration stamps for Hong Kong, as well as visas to the United States and Japan. The Hong Kong entry and exit stamps indicated that the Los, who came to Canada as landed immigrants on April 8, 1976, returned to the British colony on several occasions between 1980 and 1984, and remained there for extended periods during the four years preceding their applications for citizenship.

With their citizenship papers firmly in hand, the Los applied for Canadian passports on October 22, 1984. Their trusted lawyer acted as their guarantor. The passport applications listed the Los home address as 88 Fifeshire Avenue. At the time, Pilzmaker owned and lived in the house.

Once again, Pilzmaker refused to return my calls.

The *Globe*'s headline on page five read: Passport Copies from Hong Kong Seized by RCMP.

Justice crept along at a snail's pace. No arrests, no charges, no court appearances. In late January, 1989, there was a brief flurry of activity when a pack of lawyers representing former Pilzmaker clients clamoured into the Ontario Supreme Court to ask Justice John White to quash the search warrant the RCMP obtained for its raid on Lang Michener. The lawyers argued that the files were all protected by solicitor-client privilege and could not be used as evidence against the clients.

Two weeks later, Justice White dismissed the motion. He ruled that the files "gave prima facie evidence of Pilzmaker's assisting Hong Kong residents, who were his clients, to criminally circumvent the immigration law of Canada."

In the meantime, I started digging deeper into the Lang Michener end of the Pilzmaker affair. Why, I wondered, was Stephen Sherriff so hot to nail key members of the firm's powerful executive committee? What did these lawyers do, or, more important, fail to do? How much did they know about Pilzmaker? And what was causing this once-prestigious firm to unravel?

Again I tapped into the key source I had been developing from the start of the investigation. The rules of our relationship were that we rarely spoke, and when we did, it was strictly on his terms. *I* was never to call *him*. He was very nervous about being unmasked. Most of the time, he called me from a pay phone and dropped a tidbit of information.

Until now, our tightly choreographed dance had worked well. But I needed more to keep the story alive. I had to have another inside scoop.

My patience paid off. One evening as I was about to leave the office, he called. He was in a cheerful mood fuelled by a few vodka martinis. He was ready to expand on Lang Michener's fall from grace.

"Your main protagonist in this saga is Thomas C. Douglas," he began. "He's a corporate lawyer. Been at the firm I'd guess for fifteen years." My trusty source described him as a silver-haired, chain-smoking lone wolf who walked the high moral road. A man who believed strongly in principles and professional responsibility. Douglas was the firm's conscience — whether his partners liked to admit it or not. His detractors called him an obsessive zealot. His supporters saw him as an intelligent, perceptive and determined individual with a finely honed sense of right and wrong.

The Lang Michener affair, the source continued, began in November, 1985, just ten months after Pilzmaker joined the firm. Albert Gnat, one of the firm's managing partners and the lawyer I tried to finger in my jewelry-smuggling story out of Hong Kong, asked Douglas to go with Pilzmaker to Hong Kong to check out the feasibility of opening an office there. Douglas agreed to do so. But before he and Pilzmaker left, Douglas decided to do a little background research on Pilzmaker's billings and stumbled on the outrageous billing formula Pilzmaker had worked out. Pilzmaker charged a flat fee of $20,000 up front to get landed immigrant status and $20,000 three years later when his client got Canadian citizenship. He fully guaranteed the latter. This was irregular, to say the least. But then Douglas discovered something that went beyond mere irregularity: Pilzmaker was placing the money directly into the general account *before* it had been earned. By law, it should have been placed in a trust account. Putting the money into the firm's general account gave Pilzmaker an unfair edge for a cut of the bonus pot reserved for the firm's top billers at the end of the year.

But what really troubled Douglas was the office gossip. Rumours circulated about Pilzmaker's notorious, lavish trips to Hong Kong with various senior members of the firm. Uncomfortable, Douglas approached the executive committee and voiced his concerns.

"He was told bluntly to mind his business and concern himself with the task at hand — to recommend whether or not to open a Hong Kong branch office," the source told me.

Douglas was upset and mystified by the short shrift he was given, particularly by Donald Plumley, a senior partner on the executive committee, and by Albert Gnat. Douglas angrily informed the two lawyers that he didn't need permission from *anyone* to raise or question unethical behaviour or illegal practices by a partner.

Pilzmaker was uneasy about the firm's decision to send Douglas with him to Hong Kong. He refused to allow Douglas to tag along with him to meetings with prospective clients. Unfazed, the lone wolf spent his time on the prowl for information. In conversations around town, he heard disturbing tales about Pilzmaker, particularly about improper legal advice he was dispensing to clients and unethical schemes he had devised to beat Canada's immigration rules.

Douglas confronted Pilzmaker head-on with the allegations.

"Tom, haven't you learned by now that in order to be successful in business, you have to be dishonourable?" Pilzmaker retorted with a wry smile. Then, without missing a beat, he brashly offered to smuggle an expensive dining-room set Douglas had been admiring into Canada without paying duty on it. He would simply include the furniture in the "settler's effects" of one of his clients, Pilzmaker said, making it sound like the simplest thing in the world.

Pilzmaker had misread his man. Douglas was aghast at the proposition, and flatly refused. Upon their return, Douglas immediately went to the executive committee. Once again, he reported his concerns about Pilzmaker's practice and strongly urged they investigate the lawyer further. Again, his recommendation was shot down by the nine-member committee.

Douglas pressed on with his private investigation of Pilzmaker. He hauled Lloyd Ament and Gary Wiseman into his office and turned up the heat. He demanded to know what their sidekick was up to. To his surprise, the two lawyers told him that not only was Pilzmaker involved in smuggling but that he had devised an ingenious double-passport scheme. The scam involved a client reporting the loss of his Hong Kong passport, which in fact was kept in Pilzmaker's locked filing cabinet in Canada. The client would get a replacement passport on which he would travel freely around the globe. When the time came to apply for citizenship in Canada — which requires three years' residence in the country — the client would produce the original "lost" Hong Kong passport which, of course, would show no absences from Canada.

That was all Douglas needed to hear. He stormed into Donald

Wright's office (Robert Wright's younger brother) and told the senior partner about it. A day later, on February 6, the two men confronted the lawyer. Pilzmaker slickly deflected accusations of smuggling by wondering aloud why he should be singled out as the only culprit, when other well-respected Lang Michener lawyers had done it. Then he tossed out a few choice names.

He was also asked about the passport scheme. My source said Pilzmaker threw up his hands and admitted that he had used it in, "Oh, maybe four or five cases out of a hundred."

"That's four or five cases too many," said the incorruptible Douglas. He was going to recommend that Pilzmaker be thrown out of the firm, he added.

On February 10, the executive committee held an emergency meeting to discuss the issue. Douglas was not permitted into the meeting. This was highly irregular. Douglas was, after all, a senior partner. When the meeting adjourned, Douglas was asked to submit a written report about his concerns. He did so, strongly recommending that the committee arrange Pilzmaker's departure as quickly as possible.

Strangely, the committee did not order an internal investigation. Nor did they question Pilzmaker's sidekicks, Ament and Wiseman. It seemed obvious to me that they would have been prime sources to pump for evidence about Pilzmaker's improprieties.

Instead, the committee designated senior partners Donald Wright and Donald Plumley to meet with Pilzmaker. At this meeting, my source said, Wright and Plumley "exacted a promise from Pilzmaker not to tolerate clients engaging in the double-passport scheme or any other violations of the Immigration Act."

Douglas was left in the dark. He was never informed of the committee's decision. When he asked why Pilzmaker wasn't being let go, he was told to drop it because Pilzmaker would be leaving the firm sometime in the next few months.

Meanwhile, Pilzmaker stepped into more hot water. On June 17, he approached Brian McIntomny, a young junior lawyer at the firm, and made him a "caretaker" proposition: a three-year, $150,000, interest-free mortgage. The title of the property would be in the name of a Hong Kong client for the three-year period. But McIntomny would hold a secret deed.

McIntomny made careful notes of his conversations with Pilzmaker on two separate occasions — and then reported the matter to Douglas.

Douglas, in turn, steered McIntomny to Gordon Farquharson, chairman of the powerful executive committee. Farquharson said he would look into the proposal.

This episode—which became known at the firm as the McIntomny Incident—was to be the domino that set in motion Lang Michener's downward spiral.

Mid-July. Pilzmaker was still ensconced in his plush corner office at Lang Michener. Douglas was fit to be tied. He fired off a memo urging the executive committee "to consider whether there is any obligation on the firm to report these matters to the Law Society."

The mere mention of the law society was enough to cause consternation. On July 16, Bruce McDonald, a member of the executive committee, was appointed to look into the McIntomny Incident. Two weeks later, he concluded in a report that Pilzmaker was guilty of "a serious error in judgment." Nothing more.

In the dark-panelled offices of Lang Michener, the atmosphere was suffocating. The corridors reverberated with vicious innuendo. Everyone knew Pilzmaker was bad news. But they reserved their deadliest venom for the messenger—Douglas.

By late July, with the humidex soaring, a number of partners wanted to put an end to the tension. They wanted Pilzmaker *and* Douglas booted out of the firm. They blamed Douglas for all the trouble, aggravation and acrimony. He just couldn't leave well enough alone. He wasn't a team player.

On July 28, the executive committee voted on a motion to expel Pilzmaker. The results: three against (Albert Gnat, Don Plumley, Bruce McKenna) and two for (Donald Wright and Bruce McDonald).

Douglas was allowed into the boardroom only after the vote. He blasted the members, revisiting the entire litany of his complaints against Pilzmaker. The committee found itself confronted by an unyielding force. They designated Bruce McKenna—one of the lawyers who had voted against expelling Pilzmaker—to investigate Pilzmaker's practice.

McKenna called in Ament. He got an unexpected earful. He then approached Pilzmaker and caught him in a number of bald-faced lies. McKenna was faced with a very serious dilemma. He expressed his concerns in a memo to the management committee. "I am gravely concerned that it may no longer be possible to merely end the partnership of Pilzmaker but that it may also now be necessary to advise the Law

Society and others about our concerns about Pilzmaker's professional conduct," McKenna wrote.

But instead of immediately reporting the matter to the law society, the committee retained outside counsel. On August 20, Brendan O'Brien was hired and, two days later, he advised the firm to notify the law society and to ensure that clients were informed Pilzmaker's methods were illegal.

That advice was ignored.

On September 4, O'Brien again advised Robert Wright and Bruce McDonald that they couldn't afford not to report to the law society. He warned the firm not to engage in a cover-up in an effort to avoid public embarrassment. The next day, a general meeting was hastily called and Pilzmaker's expulsion was put forward.

By September 18, the requisite number of votes needed to turf Pilzmaker — at least two-thirds of the general membership — had been obtained.

Pilzmaker was informed he had been expelled from the firm. The devastating news appeared to leave him unfazed. He didn't pack up and vacate the premises until late October. It was during that six weeks that Lang Michener decided to have a hard, long look into Pilzmaker's billing practices. There was a collective gasp in the boardroom when it was announced that a discrepancy was found that put the firm out of pocket by $342,031.

The boys at Lang Michener wanted their money. They seized Pilzmaker's files. It was a strategic mistake. Pilzmaker, naturally, wanted to get his files back. So, on November 18, he filed an affidavit in the Supreme Court of Ontario.

The Lang Michener affair had spilled into the public forum.

On December 8, 1986, Lang Michener finally got around to reporting its concerns over Pilzmaker's immigration practice to the law society.

It wasn't until late June, 1989, that I heard rumblings that the law society was finally preparing to make a move on Pilzmaker. I called Sherriff. He confirmed that Pilzmaker would be hauled before a disciplinary body in early August. I asked him about the status of his investigation into possible professional misconduct by Lang Michener lawyers. It was now a year old. Sherriff wouldn't comment. I then called Paul Lamek, the chairman of the discipline committee. He, too, refused to answer any questions.

Meanwhile, the RCMP investigation was mired in legal wrangling before the courts. I heard that Pilzmaker was winding down his law practice, that he had just sold his home on the Bridle Path for $4 million and had purchased an estate in Boca Raton, Florida, for about $2 million U.S. All of which appeared on the *Globe*'s front page on June 22, 1989.

That morning, my main source came through with a tip about the law society investigation. He told me Sherriff had handed a blistering 138-page report to the law society in January, 1989, and that on April 7, complaints of professional misconduct were sworn by the society against five senior partners of Lang Michener.

Yet nothing seemed to be happening.

I phoned Lamek. From his tone, I knew he was steamed that I had been tipped off about the charges. He bluntly refused to comment on any aspect of the investigation.

I called Lang Michener. After a lengthy runaround, I was transferred to Warren Seyffert, the latest designated spokesman. I decided to bluff and take the totally in-the-know approach.

"I've just been informed that the law society has laid complaints against five of Lang Michener's lawyers on April 7. I want the firm's reaction," I said, in as authoritative a voice as I could muster.

There was a pause. Then Seyffert confirmed that letters from the law society were received by five members of the firm's executive committee. In an officious tone, he stressed that while the firm "will continue to cooperate with the law society's investigation, we are definitely of the view that there is no valid support for the complaints. We strongly believe what we did was proper. We attempted to act properly and professionally in respect to our duty to the law society and to our clients."

"Can I have the names of the five lawyers?" I asked.

A longer pause.

"No," Seyffert finally said, flatly.

After working a few avenues, I managed to pop the names of all five. They were Donald Wright, Bruce McDonald, Albert Gnat, Donald Plumley and Bruce McKenna. In the complaint, they were accused of allegedly failing in their professional duty to report to the law society the professional misconduct of a former partner of their firm — Martin Pilzmaker. They were also charged with failing to advise clients of the firm for whom Pilzmaker was acting that he "had likely given unethical or illegal advice," and for not advising them of the need to seek independent legal advice.

On June 23, the *Globe*'s front-page headline read: Five Senior Lawyers Named in Misconduct Complaints.

I still wasn't satisfied that I really had the goods on Lang Michener. Something kept nagging me about the law society's decision. Based on what I had been told about who knew what, I figured several more lawyers should have been on the chopping block.

I started working my contacts again. However, my last story had Lang Michener and law society lawyers screaming for blood. They wanted to know who had tipped me off. The heat had driven my key connection underground.

I racked my brain for someone else to keep me on the inside track. But, as soon as I'd identify myself, the phone would go dead.

There was one person I hadn't yet called. I waited until evening and phoned Tom Douglas at home. He was having a dinner party and was annoyed that I would dare to call him at his residence. As I had expected, he hung up. I waited a minute and phoned again.

"I don't want you calling me at my home! Do you understand that?" he said.

"Well, I can't call you at your office," I said. "Look, I apologize for upsetting you. But I felt that maybe you might want to talk."

"And why would I want to talk to you?"

"Because you're interested that the truth comes out."

"I am. But I'm not interested in talking to you!"

"Well, there are a few things I've been made aware of that make me feel this whole affair at Lang Michener might be covered up by the law society," I said, speaking slowly to be sure every word made an impact.

There was a long pause. I sensed I'd piqued his curiosity.

"Look, in case you change your mind, I'll give you my phone number," I said, trying to sound offhand.

"If I change my mind, I'll find your phone number. Now good night, and please don't call me here again."

Douglas called me the next morning. His tone was very different. "You had me wondering all night about what you said. Let's say we meet at seven-thirty this evening at the Holiday Inn on Chestnut Street in Chinatown."

I knew him the minute he walked into the foyer from his trademark silver hair and his intense aura. When we met, we shook hands. His grip was firm. His piercing eyes sized me up.

"You've really upset a lot of people at Lang Michener," he said, pulling out a cigarette.

"From what I gather, so have you."

"I've given this business of talking to you some consideration and I feel strongly that the discipline panel at the law society should deal with this matter first, and if it —"

"It'll be a whitewash," I interjected.

"Now how do you know that?" Douglas took a deep drag from his cigarette.

"Let's just say I've got a strong hunch."

"Well, if your hunch proves to be correct, maybe I'll talk to you after the hearing."

"It'll be too late."

"I promise you this much, if I feel there was a cover-up by the law society in this matter, I'll tell you the whole story."

"And I'll tell you to go to hell. I'm not interested in old stories and people taking to me into their confidence after the fact. If you've got something to say, say it now."

Douglas inhaled deeply and pondered his options.

"What is it you want to know?" he asked hesitantly.

"I won't identify you," I said.

"I don't care whether I'm identified or not," he replied.

I had decided, however, that for the meantime Douglas would remain an anonymous source.

"I'm aware that Stephen Sherriff had recommended that a total of nine lawyers from Lang Michener be charged, and from what I gather David Scott supported that recommendation in his report to the law society," I began. "I know the names of the five who were charged. Who are the other four?"

Douglas lit up another cigarette.

"That stuff can kill you," I said, deadpan.

He took a deep drag. "Burke Doran, for certain. As for the other three, I'm pretty sure they are Robert Wright, Gordon Farquharson and Geoffrey Pringle."

"Do you have any idea why they weren't charged?"

"You'd have to ask the chairman of the discipline committee. From what I've heard, he alone made the decision. You go and ask Paul Lamek."

"That ought to make his day," I said. "He just loves hearing from me."

The following morning, I phoned Lamek. As I expected, he refused to discuss any details of the investigation, but he took a moment of his time to explain the process. Lamek pointed out that once an investigation has been completed, an application to lay a complaint is presented to the chairman of the discipline committee.

"I alone make the decision. Essentially it is a lonely world, a one-man decision."

Then Lamek blew a gaping hole in his defense. He told me that when he was appointed in September, 1988, he had decided to make his world a less lonely place. The decision process would no longer be a one-man show. From then on, the chairman would consult with the two vice-chairs on all decisions involving misconduct charges against lawyers. I couldn't believe what he'd just told me.

"So why didn't you do that on this case? Of all the cases on your desk, you'd think this is one where you would definitely want their input," I said.

"I have nothing more to say." With that, Lamek hung up.

I phoned Lang Michener and fired off a list of lawyers I wanted to speak to, starting with Robert Wright. Minutes before my deadline, Seyffert dutifully called back.

"We chewed it over," Seyffert said, "and we decided we can't accede to your request. We're concerned about a trial in the press and we're concerned about preempting the process."

"But these lawyers haven't been charged. They're not part of the process," I noted.

"We're dealing with smoke at the moment... unfounded allegations. It's very difficult to deal with them and I am very leery about dealing with unfounded allegations," Seyffert said.

The firm had hoped that the only news about Lang Michener that day would be an announcement by the Ontario Liberal government that Robert Wright had been appointed chairman of the Ontario Securities Commission commencing on September 1. The front-page story in the *Globe* on July 4, 1989, about the lawyers who hadn't been charged, created a stir at the firm and at the law society.

But other events were about to unfold. My RCMP sources told me to be on alert.

Late on the afternoon of July 5, the Mounties burst into the back office of the Linen Source, a boutique in the north end of Toronto, and got their man. Martin Pilzmaker was arrested, frisked, handcuffed, placed in a police cruiser and carted off to jail. A young, beaming constable was assigned the task of driving the lawyer's $180,000 Rolls-Royce Corniche to the RCMP's underground garage in downtown Toronto for safekeeping.

Pilzmaker was charged with more than a dozen counts of conspiracy, forgery and making false declarations. It was Pilzmaker's first night in jail in his life. When he was led into court the following day, he was dishevelled; his face was drawn, and he attempted a nervous smile. He looked like a scared kid trying to put up a brave front. Even I couldn't help feeling sorry for him. The judge released him on a $75,000 cash bond and ordered him to surrender his passport. Outside the courtroom, Pilzmaker bolted past reporters and jumped into a waiting Cadillac.

On August 28, the law society finally began its discipline hearing into the five Lang Michener lawyers charged with professional misconduct. Claude Thomson, the lawyer for Lang Michener, rose to complain about a scene setter I had written in the *Globe* the day before and then asked the panel to order the law society and its agents not to talk to me. I sat in the back of the room, unmoved. The three members of the panel replied that they doubted they had the power to make such an order.

David Scott laid the groundwork for the charges on behalf of the law society. He cited a chronology of events at the firm to show that serious concerns about Pilzmaker's conduct were first raised in February, 1986. He noted that subsequently there were at least two internal investigations carried out by members of the firm and that a report on one of them, written in August of that year, described Pilzmaker as "dishonest and unethical, a danger to the public [who] clearly required dismissal from the firm."

Scott maintained that by August, 1986, the firm had "clear evidence of questionable conduct." But "strangely there was no reporting to the law society" until December.

In his opening statement, Thomson defended the firm's handling of the case, arguing that Lang Michener's executive committee were concerned about "acting fairly" toward Pilzmaker, who had repeatedly denied the allegations made about him.

The tension was palpable when Tom Douglas was called to the witness box. I could almost hear the blood pressure rising in the front row when Thomson asked Douglas off the top if he had provided me with inside information about the law society investigation.

The silver-haired wolf calmly replied, "Yes." Every lawyer turned and focused icy glares on me. I inhaled sharply.

Thomson asked Douglas why he had spoken to me.

"Because vicious statements were being made about me and I feared an attempt was being mounted to discredit me and cover up the affair."

A couple of days into the hearing, I noticed the lawyers from both sides had retreated into a backroom for a huddle. Something was up. When Scott, Sherriff and Thomson reappeared, the lawyer for Lang Michener asked the panel to consider hearing the evidence of the next witness in secret.

"Hold on a second," I interjected from the back row. I scurried over to Scott and argued that if the committee was going to entertain such a motion, then I wanted to contact the *Globe* and get our lawyer in there to fight the move.

The panel broke for lunch to mull over my impromptu motion, and I placed an urgent call to the *Globe*. I explained the situation to Gwen Smith, the deputy managing editor. She said she'd send over Peter Jacobsen, our lawyer, right away.

During the break, I racked my brain trying to figure out what the in-camera hearing might be about. In a back corridor of the law society, a trusted contact shuffled by and muttered one word. At first I thought he had called me a name. In fact, he had dropped a very important clue. What he said was: "Gnat."

Peter Jacobsen, the *Globe's* no-nonsense lawyer, raced in just as the lunch break ended and requested an explanation for the closed-session move. Right behind him, I sauntered over to Scott, Sherriff and Thomson and said cockily: "I know what the in-camera hearing is all about, and if it's closed, you can bet I'll report why."

I told them the secret hearing involved Albert Gnat.

Scott pursed his lips and stared directly over his half-moon reading glasses at me.

"Who told you?" he asked.

"Come on. I'm not going to answer that question."

Sherriff jumped in. "Then tell us what the in-camera hearing will deal with."

I waited the appropriate heartbeat. "Albert Gnat and his smuggling."

The expression on Scott's face said it all. I'd hit it dead on.

He grabbed a folder and stormed off for another encounter with Thomson and the Lang Michener team.

When the hearing resumed, Scott told the panel that the request for an in-camera session was now moot because "events had overtaken the motion." An angry Thomson added that Jacobsen had informed them that a person — whom the *Globe* would not name — had spilled the beans. There was no longer any point in keeping Gnat's smuggling escapade confidential, he said in a huff.

In March, 1986, Thomson explained, Gnat spent $8,700 on watches on a trip to Hong Kong. The watches were taken through Canada Customs for him by Pilzmaker, who did not declare them or pay the required duty. However, the incident was voluntarily disclosed to Customs in early 1988 and Gnat paid $3,200 duty on the items.

Gnat was called to testify. Under questioning, the visibly shaken and contrite lawyer described the smuggling incident as "one of the biggest mistakes in my life." But he didn't dump on Pilzmaker. "He didn't force me, he didn't threaten me," Gnat said. "He just made it easy for me. The blame has to be on me." Gnat added that he had "suffered incredible pain" and embarrassment about not having declared the goods earlier.

Later in the hearing, Scott suggested that the real reason behind the decision to come clean was more of "a systematic coming forward after the firm had been advised of a police investigation into Pilzmaker." Right on, I thought. Nothing like shame and the threat of criminal charges to motivate you to do the right thing.

During the twelve days of hearings, Pilzmaker's name and reputation were dragged through the muck by his former Lang Michener colleagues. No one had a kind word for the man. He was slandered and vilified, described as unethical, devious and dishonest and called a liar, a crook and a dangerous corrupter. The final insult: Pilzmaker was labelled "absolutely stupid."

I snickered at the last characterization. Pilzmaker wasn't the one sitting in the hot seat in front of a discipline committee.

In his closing statement, Scott urged the panel to find all five lawyers guilty of failing to report promptly to the law society the illegal and unethical actions of a fellow lawyer. He argued that all five should also be found guilty of failing in their fiduciary responsibility to inform the firm's clients who had dealings with Pilzmaker that he had been expelled from Lang Michener.

Scott also noted that the five "distinguished members of a well-respected law firm," were motivated by self-interest and the financial implications to the firm. He concluded by castigating the lawyers for characterizing their colleague Thomas Douglas as a rumour-monger and troublemaker. Douglas "is a man of integrity," and the evidence clearly showed that Douglas was largely right in his original complaints about Pilzmaker.

Then it was Lang Michener's turn at the podium. Claude Thomson submitted that the five partners should not be disciplined because Pilzmaker had not yet been found guilty of any offense or misconduct. Finding the Lang Michener gang guilty would lead to a "bizarre situation" if their former colleague subsequently was acquitted of criminal charges.

On Friday, September 23, the three-member panel adjourned the hearing to study the evidence and reach a decision. But something was troubling me.

During a break in the last week of testimony, I had parked myself at a desk laden with thick folders tabled as evidence. Most of the contents were letters, memos and reports of Lang Michener's handling of the Pilzmaker situation. I riffled through them and stumbled upon a critical piece of paper: a confidential memorandum written by Donald Plumley on December 15, 1986. In it, he warned of a threat to the firm by Pilzmaker should he be disciplined by the law society. This threat was never raised at the hearing. At least, not publicly. Odd, I thought, given the potentially explosive ramifications of the memo.

I thought back over the two weeks of testimony. I recalled a peculiar, vaguely unsettling incident. On the afternoon of September 21, the panel retreated behind closed doors. Ostensibly, it was to determine whether certain undisclosed evidence would be admissible.

When the hearing resumed, I noticed that Plumley had taken the stand and began testifying without being sworn in. I figured this could only mean that the lawyer had been sworn in during the in-camera session.

When my eyes focused on Plumley's memo, I thought I had the answer. In it he wrote: "In discussing various matters...with Martin today, he mentioned that he had been contacted by the Law Society and that due to his pique over this he had mentioned certain things adverse in his view to the firm. I asked him what these might be and he mentioned the matter of the private investigator; the question of dividing income with a spouse-employee; and something else that he didn't wish to repeat because he had stated that it was based on very flimsy information."

For the next two days, I tried to make some sense of the cryptic memo. A source suggested that the memo could point to an important *political* motive for not nailing Pilzmaker much earlier.

"Does it have to do with the private investigator?" I asked.

"No."

"The thing Pilzmaker didn't want to repeat?"

"No."

"Then it's the spouse-employee thing," I said.

"Good guess," the source said dryly.

"Yeah, right. But what the heck does it mean?" I asked.

"You have a lawyer and he gets paid a lot of money," my source replied. "Let's say one hundred grand a year. He has to pay a sizeable chunk in income tax. But he also knows he can get a nice tax break if he can split that income with his wife. So the lawyer gets the firm to put his wife down as an employee, and part of his salary goes to her. Except she doesn't ever work at the firm."

"So what does this have to do with Pilzmaker?"

"Pilzmaker found out about a specific arrangement and filed it away for future considerations. That's the kind of guy Pilzmaker is. He makes sure he compromises everyone with things like smuggling, so that if ever the time comes when he's in trouble, no one will go against him because he's got them where he wants them."

"In his pocket."

"Right."

"So who was this arrangement with?" I asked impatiently.

He paused for ultimate effect. "The man that Lang Michener hopes will one day be the prime minister of Canada. The Honourable Jean Chrétien."

"Chrétien? You've got to be kidding." I could feel my pulse pounding in my temples.

How, I wondered, will I ever be able to do that? I was sure Lang Michener would tell me to eat nails at the mere mention of the memo.

The former Cabinet minister and heavily favoured Liberal Party leadership contender had been working as counsel for Lang Michener in their Ottawa office since March, 1984. In my previous dealings with him in the early 1980s when I was the *Globe*'s bureau chief in Montreal, we got along very well. The little guy from Shawinigan, Quebec, always had a funny anecdote and seemed genuine. I liked the man. In fact, he was my favourite politician and certainly my choice to lead the then-rudderless federal Liberals.

Well, the best approach in this delicate situation was to phone Chrétien himself. I left a message with his secretary. Within minutes he called back.

Chrétien immediately steered the conversation to what he referred to as the Lang Michener affair. "You know, I don't know much about that," he began disingenuously. "But the guys I know there are a good bunch of guys."

"Yeah. A bunch of Boy Scouts," I said with a tinge of sarcasm.

"No. I'm not kidding. They're a hell of a bunch." Chrétien doing his little-guy-from-Shawinigan schtick.

"Did you know Martin Pilzmaker?"

"I met him only once very briefly. I think I shook his hand at a cocktail party at the firm some time ago."

"Then could you tell me why he would threaten the firm about you?"

"I have no idea what you are talking about." Chrétien's chummy voice had taken on a slight edge.

"Pilzmaker made a threat to Donald Plumley to expose an arrangement between you and Lang Michener to split a portion of your salary with your wife," I said.

"That is the most absurd thing I have ever heard. It's just the allegation of a disgruntled lawyer to blackmail the firm. It is just revenge against the firm!" Chrétien said emphatically.

I drew in a breath and asked flat out: "Did you split your income with your wife?"

"No," he shouted into the phone. "That is absolutely crazy!"

The story behind the allegation went like this, Chrétien explained. When he resigned after twenty-three years as a member of Parliament in February, 1986, he hired his wife, Aline, to work for him at home for a few weeks. "I couldn't find a bilingual secretary so I asked Aline to do some work for me."

"You couldn't find a bilingual secretary in Ottawa?" I asked incredulously.

"I needed someone right away. It was for a very short time. She earned very little money. There is nothing to this, I tell you." He had a lot of correspondence to handle, Chrétien went on, especially after the publication of his book *Straight from the Heart*. Aline filled the gap.

Then the politician in Chrétien oozed out. He started compliment-ing me. The one thing I hated most when doing my job was having the person I was interviewing tell me how wonderful I was. I looked at it as barely a notch below, "I've got a condo in Key Biscayne, Florida, that I'm not using." And two notches below, "Can I make you out a cheque for your favourite charity?"

"You know I read your articles all the time," Chrétien began. "You are a good reporter. Objective, fair and balanced.... I tell you, Victor, there is nothing here. No story. I'm sure you agree," he continued.

"I'll let you know if there's no story, Mr. Chrétien. I've got a few things I have to check into," I said.

"But I tell you. There is nothing to this." Chrétien's tone was insistent.

"Before I do anything I promise I'll call you back."

I placed a call to Lang Michener. The firm was on red alert. Their designated hitter, Michael Eisen, was ready with a statement. He con-firmed that Aline Chrétien was paid as a secretary from March, 1984, to September, 1986 — from the day her husband joined the firm.

Well, that certainly was a lot longer than the few weeks Chrétien had claimed was the case.

Eisen noted that Aline Chrétien never worked in the office because her husband had a permanent secretary working there, then stressed that the firm viewed Pilzmaker's allegations as "a hollow threat because there was no income-splitting involved."

She was paid $15,000 a year and taken off the payroll in Septem-ber, 1986, the same month Pilzmaker was expelled from the firm.

Sounding as if he was reading a prepared text, Eisen said: "Lang Michener's position is that in return for providing legitimate secretarial and related assistance connected with firm business, Mrs. Chrétien was compensated properly. There was nothing improper with the arrange-ment in the firm's view." The lawyer added that while she did "personal work" for her husband at home, the firm regarded it as "work for Lang Michener."

When I called Chrétien back, he was fit to be tied. It was to be our last conversation.

"Why are you persisting in this? I don't see the point. Don't you have anything better to do?" he bellowed into the receiver.

"Well, for one thing, I keep getting different stories. I'm now told your wife was hired as a secretary when you joined the firm in 1984."

For a brief moment, Chrétien seemed at a total loss for words.

"Yes, if they say so! It's because when I joined Lang Michener, Aline came as a package deal. My wife was a secretary when I met her before we married. But I tell you she worked for her money. There was no 'income split,' as you put it," Chrétien stressed.

"What I find even more interesting is that your wife was taken off the Lang Michener payroll the same month Pilzmaker was expelled from the firm. And now there's this threatening memo," I said. "Is that just a coincidence?"

For someone who vaguely recalled meeting Pilzmaker on only one brief occasion, Chrétien was certainly up to speed on the discipline hearing about his Lang Michener buddies. "The panel decided not to look into the memo. You have to respect the judgement of the people who decided to look into that by means of a voire dire," he said.

"Well, what I'm curious about, Mr. Chrétien, is why the time your wife worked for Lang Michener has changed from a few weeks to a few months to a little over two years," I said.

"I already explained all that to you. Are you going to write a story?" Chrétien shot back.

"Yeah. I am."

"I think you're crazy to write it. You're just creating smoke for nothing that will cause me trouble for nothing. I always knew you were like that. This is yellow journalism, and if that is the level you want to sink to then I have no more to say." Chrétien slammed down the phone.

The *Globe* headline on Saturday, September 23, 1989, read: Lawyer's Memo Describes Income-sharing Scheme Between Chrétien, Wife

Surprisingly, the story caused barely a ripple. There was a follow-up story in the *Toronto Star* with Chrétien making the same denials he had made to me. And that was it. It seemed that the Ottawa press corps didn't see any significance in a former Cabinet heavyweight and the possible future prime minister of Canada being involved in what appeared to be a tax-avoiding scheme. The story simply died.

On October 12, 1988, I got a tip that the Lang Michener affair had claimed another victim. After eight years as the law society's chief investigator, Sherriff threw down his badge. He resigned as counsel of discipline over the society's handling of his investigation.

Sherriff refused to discuss the matter, but promised me that after the disciplinary panel had rendered its decision he'd blow the lid off the case.

On January 9, 1990, I got an urgent message to get over to the law society. The discipline panel's long-awaited decision was about to be rendered. There was going to be no fanfare. The panel quietly handed over a written ruling to the law society top brass. Only Lang Michener's Michael Eisen was present to hear it.

On the first charge of professional misconduct — failing to report allegations of impropriety and possible illegal activity by a former partner — the Lang Michener five were found guilty.

On the second, more serious charge — failing to inform clients of the firm that Pilzmaker had represented that he "had likely given unethical or illegal advice," and not advising them to seek independent legal advice — the Lang Michener boys were exonerated.

The panel's decision read more like an apology from the pulpit than a stern misconduct finding. It said: "There is ... no evidence or even suggestion that the respondents are not professionally upright and honourable." However, the panel noted, there was "a duty to report the suspected and perceived conduct of Pilzmaker," and concluded that the five lawyers "ought to have been concerned with the likelihood of serious damage to someone as a consequence of what ... were apparent breaches of certain of the Rules of Professional Conduct.... [However], the suspicions and concerns of unethical conduct on the part of Pilzmaker ... did not impose a duty on them" to inform their clients.

No obligation to inform their clients of Pilzmaker's conduct! I was shocked. If *I* had hired a lawyer from a reputable firm and paid the guy $400 an hour, I'd expect sound, legal advice. And I would also expect that if the members of the firm found out the lawyer was a sleaze bucket who was playing loose with the law, they'd have enough decency and professional integrity to warn me that just maybe I had been the victim of bad legal advice.

On behalf of Lang Michener, Eisen graciously accepted the decision. He said he was "gratified" the panel had made it "perfectly clear" that there has been no evidence or even suggestion the five lawyers "are not professionally upright and honourable."

Ten days later, the assemblage of lawyers reconvened to argue what kind of penalty should be imposed. Possibilities ranged from a reprimand to suspension or disbarment. A reprimand, akin to a rap on the knuckles, is the lightest form of punishment the law society can mete out. A suspension means losing your license to practice for up to a year—a public shaming. Disbarment means having your license removed for good—lifelong disgrace.

As I fully expected, Claude Thomson said he felt the Lang Michener five shouldn't be punished at all. Submitting a black binder, he lamented that his clients had suffered enough as a result of the news media coverage of the matter. The black binder was filled with my stories.

When David Scott rose, he sounded like a skipper who'd lost the wind in his sail. He warned that not imposing a penalty would lead to the inference that their conduct was judged too unimportant to warrant punishment. A reprimand, he suggested, would at least suggest the legal profession's collective responsibility.

Then the hearing room was cleared of the public and the media, and Donald Wright, Albert Gnat, Bruce McDonald, Bruce McKenna and Donald Plumley stood before the three-member panel for a private scolding. The tongue-lashing took all of five minutes. "Boys, that was a naughty thing you did. Now, if you all promise not to do it again, you can all go home and have a drink!" Those were not the words used, but as far as I was concerned, they might as well have been. I wasn't far wrong. Word later leaked out that the panel members began their scolding with an apology that such upstanding barristers had to be dragged before a disciplinary hearing at all.

The next day, I located Sherriff. I had a hell of a time tracking him down. Not surprisingly, he was steaming mad. But he kept his criticism focused on Lamek's decision not to charge four other Lang Michener lawyers. He added that the decision by the discipline panel "fortified" his strongly held view that the other four ought to be charged.

Sherriff noted that Lamek's decision struck at the very heart of self-government of the legal profession. "I don't believe the discipline process in this case operated fairly ... I am concerned that the process wasn't proper."

Two weeks later, on January 25, another discipline panel deliberated only a few minutes before announcing that Martin Sheldon Pilzmaker had been given the boot. He was stripped of his license to practice law. The official reason for disbarment was his refusal to cooperate with a law society investigation into his immigration practice.

The following day the benchers—the governing body of the law society—gathered for their monthly convocation. Within seconds of the meeting being called to order, the lawyers were embroiled in a heated debate on the handling of the Lang Michener affair.

Paul Lamek delivered an impassioned half-hour speech defending his actions in deciding who got charged and who didn't. "I am entitled to be wrong and to have the decision stand so long as it was made in the honest and bona fide exercise of discretion," he argued.

After Lamek's homily, the convocation voted on a motion calling for an independent inquiry to investigate the law society's handling of the Lang Michener case. When the votes were counted, the benchers were split down the middle, eighteen to eighteen. Lee Ferrier, the society's treasurer, broke the tie by voting in favour of an investigation.

The benchers then adopted a resolution to hire "an impartial person, preferably a judge or retired judge" to investigate the law society's handling of the Lang Michener matter.

They retained Archibald Dewar, a retired chief justice of the Queen's Bench. Dewar was flown into Toronto at the expense of the law society and put up in a posh suite at the downtown Hilton Hotel.

Dewar's points of reference were, in a word, laughable. He had no power to call witnesses and could only conduct private interviews. Just whom he met with in his hotel room remains a mystery. I did find out that Douglas and Sherriff spent several hours with him. After he completed his so-called interviews, he flew back to Winnipeg to write his report.

On March 28, Pilzmaker was again hauled into court. This time, on top of the fourteen charges filed against him in July, 1989, he faced forty-three charges of theft, fraud, forgery and conspiracy. They included two counts of theft of more than $100,000, and a number of charges relating to the preparation of bogus business proposals to get clients landed immigrant status in Canada.

After twenty-one months and some thirty stories about Pilzmaker and the Lang Michener affair in the *Globe* under my byline, Pilzmaker and I had never met face-to-face. We had never even spoken over the telephone. I had seen him once, for a brief moment, during the infamous Eaton Centre photo-op caper. But he had never clapped eyes on me.

Until now.

Pilzmaker shuffled into the packed courtroom. He sat down heavily in the only seat left. It was right next to me.

"Nice day," I whispered.

Pilzmaker turned, looked at me inquisitively and replied: "Not from where I sit."

"You're Martin Pilzmaker?"

"Who are you?" he asked, puzzled.

No time for small talk, I decided. "Listen," I said, "it seems you've really pissed the boys off at Lang Michener. They've said some pretty nasty things about you, and I would be only too willing to spend as much time with you as you'd like getting your side of the story."

Pilzmaker was staring at me incredulously. I stuck out my hand. "By the way, I'm Victor Malarek."

As he scrambled to propel himself out of his seat, Pilzmaker stumbled and fell into the lap of a lavishly tattooed biker. He struggled to his feet, mumbling apologies as he did so, and catapulted over Earl Levy, his lawyer, who was seated next in line.

Pilzmaker's appearance was brief. Released on his own recognizance, he promptly bolted out of the courtroom. Levy buttonholed me in the corridor. With excruciating politesse, he asked me to stay away from his client.

In May, Lee Ferrier sent a letter to all twenty-one thousand lawyers in the province urging them to read the upcoming June edition of the *Ontario Reports*. In it, the law society had inserted the full thirty-nine-page text of Dewar's report, at a cost of $7,000.

In his report, Archibald Dewar concluded: "The Law Society's handling of the Lang Michener matter was not influenced or affected by bias, partiality or oblique motive. There was no favouritism. Over all, the discipline process was properly motivated, even-handed, and met acceptable standards."

That was all Sherriff had to hear. His reaction was swift and unequivocal. He called Dewar's inquiry "a shabby whitewash."

"It was a set-up, and I walked into an ambush," he told me in an interview. "I should have sensed the outcome of this inquiry the moment I met Dewar in his hotel room. His first words to me were, 'You have got a lot of powerful people very upset with you.'"

In their "worrisome" meeting, Sherriff said, the former judge glossed over substantial concerns. "Mr. Dewar was more concerned over how information was leaking to the news media than what was leaking."

But the most disturbing aspect of Dewar's report, Sherriff said, was what was missing from it—specifically two very detailed and critical letters about the law society's handling of the case, as well as a private and confidential letter written to the treasurer of the law society. Those letters were written by Sherriff.

"He has chosen to keep secret, apparently even from the benchers, the significant information contained in my letters," Sherriff said.

I phoned Dewar in Winnipeg hoping to get some answers. He was terse, noting that he had little use for the news media, even less for me. I ignored the flattery. How had he gone about his one-man inquiry? I asked. He snapped that he used what he felt was important in the preparation of his report.

I asked why he had ignored Sherriff's letters and concerns.

"Whatever is in my report is the way I saw it. I'm not going to interpret it for you," Dewar shot back.

"Well, because of this, some people are calling your report a shabby whitewash," I said.

Dewar banged down the phone. That slamming of the phone marked the end of the Lang Michener affair.

Michael Crawford, editor of *Canadian Lawyer Magazine*, wrote in an editorial in the magazine in April 1990 that the way the law society handled the Lang Michener Affair

> ... revealed the political pettiness and cluttered logic within the country club atmosphere of our largest law society. It suggested that law firms may be ill-prepared to quickly and effectively police their own lawyers. And it confirmed for many lawyers and members of the public what they have always suspected about professional self-government.

Without a doubt, the Lang Michener affair had a profound impact on the Law Society of Upper Canada, the largest law society in the country. And it had a significant effect on Canada's legal profession. Lawyers throughout the province felt the society's handling of the case had given them a black eye, and as a result, they pushed very hard for change. When the affair finally ended, a large number of "reformers" ran for election as benchers on convocation — the society's governing body — and won. They made convocation more forthcoming and forced a shift to openness. And there was a marked improvement in the society's attitude toward the news media. The law society could have remained bitter toward journalists for a long time. But the new breed of benchers took the high road and decided to shed the cloak of secrecy that had shrouded the institution for decades.

To its credit, the law society toughened up its reporting and disciplinary process for wayward lawyers. And almost immediately, the effects were felt. In the year following the Lang Michener reprimand, three top Toronto law firms reported internal problems, and even went so far as to issue press releases.

"The *Globe and Mail* really fired them up," Michael Crawford said in an interview.

The federal government tightened its rules on business immigration. However, it didn't go after a single bogus Pilzmaker client. Kirk Bell, the program's head honcho, argued that the offending immigrants would never end up on welfare, and in the end undoubtedly would contribute to the Canadian economy.

The Michener Award is the highest journalism prize in Canada. It is given for disinterested and meritorious public service journalism. For 1988, the *Globe* submitted three entries: my series on the Lang Michener affair; a series on York regional developers by Jock Ferguson and Dawn King; and stories on the Ontario boxing commissioner by Stephen Brunt. The judges united all three into one entry and announced that the *Globe and Mail* had won the 1988 Michener Award.

At a formal dinner at the governor-general's mansion in Ottawa, Paul Palango, now the national editor, accepted the award on behalf of the newspaper. In his speech, he opined, "It's more than a little ironic that we have been recognized by the Michener Award Foundation for our work on Lang Michener." The audience laughed. Everyone, that is, except one person: Roland Michener, who was sitting in the front row with Governor-General Jeanne Sauvé. Confusion and consternation clouded his regal, lined face as he made the connection.

After the speeches, Michener approached me. "I'd just like to say that the firm has changed a lot since I left it. I don't understand what has happened there over the years. This whole matter has troubled me immensely. I recall meeting this Pilzmaker chap only once, and I found him to be a rude and brash individual."

I felt a pang of pity for the man who founded the firm that still bore his proud and honourable name.

POSTSCRIPT

At 10:00 a.m. on Friday, April 19, 1991, a maid walked into a room at a shabby hotel in Toronto's tenderloin district. Seconds later, she bolted down the hallway in a panic. On the bed was a man comfortably propped up on two pillows, wearing only silk pajama bottoms. He'd been dead for at least two days.

The hotel manager called the police. When they examined the scene, they quickly ruled out foul play. On a night table were two nearly empty pill bottles and a large, empty water glass. Although there was no suicide note, the police ruled it an open-and-shut case of suicide. They did find a wallet in the dead man's suit jacket. In it was one hundred dollars in cash, a driver's license and three dozen credit cards—all in the name of Martin Sheldon Pilzmaker.

Pilzmaker's body was sent to the coroner's lab for an autopsy. Cause of death was determined to be an overdose of barbiturates.

When I read the report in the newspaper, I phoned an RCMP contact in the immigration section. The Mounties were just weeks away from laying even more charges against the defrocked lawyer, he told me. The charges included theft, fraud and forgery involving several million dollars. The latest series of charges centred on the purchase of a large parcel of real estate in the north end of Toronto in 1986. Apparently the property was purchased by Pilzmaker, with clients' money, for about $3 million. Five years later, in February, 1989, it sold for $8 million. A month later, Pilzmaker's partners discovered that $4 million had disappeared from their bank account. They were informed by bank officials that their lawyer had withdrawn the money in four separate cheques of $1 million each. The investors were still trying to trace the money when Pilzmaker killed himself.

Criminal lawyer Earl Levy was one of the last people to see Pilzmaker alive. He had been despondent and severely depressed since his tumultuous fall from grace, Levy said.

"He'd suffered tremendous humiliation and had become a pariah to many with whom he had had dealings. I have no doubt that it was that humiliation, the fact that he was so ostracized, and his own complex personality, which led to his suicide."

CHAPTER TEN

FORGOTTEN SOULS

In the spring of 1990, I approached my editors with a proposal for an in-depth series on the world's exploding refugee crisis. I had been writing about immigration and refugee issues for about three years, and what I was finding alarmed and upset me. Every week, violence, persecution, hunger and war drove thousands of people from their homelands. There were at least fifteen million refugees worldwide, according to estimates by the United Nations High Commission for Refugees (UNHCR). That was not counting the millions who fled economic and environmental disasters. I wanted the *Globe* to examine the plight of the world's displaced people and the efforts of those who tried to help them.

Editor-in-chief William Thorsell gave the green light. *Globe* correspondents were assigned to refugee stories in Central and South America, Southeast Asia, Pakistan and Europe. The series was titled The Dispossessed.

I was sent to the Horn of Africa—a shattered piece of the world that takes in Ethiopia, Djibouti and Somalia, where millions of people were caught in the twin horrors of a devastating famine and brutal civil wars. I had read a lot about the starvation and upheaval throughout the region. The movement of humanity was of biblical proportions— millions of children, women and men forced to flee their homes and trek through hostile jungles and sunbaked deserts in search of safe haven. I pored over piles of research material. But nothing I had read or seen on television could prepare me for what I witnessed in this modern-day Heart of Darkness. And as I write this six years later, the killing and suffering in the region has not abated. The Horn of Africa remains a vast field of starvation and death.

In March, I flew to Addis Ababa, the capital of Ethiopia, where for a week I waited patiently for a listless bureaucrat to give me the necessary papers for internal travel in the country. With the nation locked in battle with rebels in the provinces of Eritrea and Tigray, the Marxist government of Mengistu Haile Mariam was leery of Western journalists and their motives for coming here. I was assigned a minder — a cross between a facilitator and a spy. Tesfaye was a wiry little weasel with shifty eyes and a cocky air. He'd landed his job through his card-carrying Marxist daddy, a mid-level bureaucrat with the Foreign Ministry. The minder's assignment was to watch my every move and diligently report everything to headquarters. He was to tell me where I could go and what was off-limits and, more important, keep army patrols and roadblocks from arresting and detaining me. In the latter capacity, he was to serve a useful function.

Before leaving the capital for the Somali border, I hurriedly packed a survival kit — two kilograms of canned meat, dried fruit and nuts, a couple of boxes of crackers and cookies, a large vial of antimalaria pills and a chemical concoction that would kill every living organism in my drinking water.

The first leg was a short hop on a 727 Ethiopian Airlines jet to Dire Dawa, the largest city in eastern Ethiopia. Upon landing, I was met by Marc Salvail, a relief worker for the UNHCR. He was gaunt, having just waged a battle with malaria. Marc, thirty-two, was from Hull, Quebec, and was responsible for the operations of three sprawling refugee camps — Kamabokar, Rabasso and Daror — holding 138,000 people.

It took eight hours by Jeep to reach Aware, a dusty oasis on the edge of the Ogaden Desert near the border of Somalia. On the way, we passed several Ethiopian military convoys dragging artillery units and tanks to the latest hot spot. The trucks were teeming with heavily armed soldiers who looked like they'd just been yanked out of high school.

The dirt roads were heavily rutted. At one point, Marc lost control of the steering wheel and we careened into a ditch, narrowly missing a stand of eucalyptus trees and a mound of boulders. We were rattled. But luckily no one was hurt.

As we entered the Ogaden Desert I was awed by the vastness of the parched, forbidding scrubland. The desert sun was unrelenting. There was no shade. And there was no water. I marvelled that anyone could live in such an inhospitable environment.

I spent the evening in Marc's prefab quarters. Tesfaye was sent into town to find a place at a local inn. Marc didn't take kindly to being spied on.

At dawn, we set out for the Rabasso refugee camp. It was a tortuous four-hour drive through the Ogaden. As we got near, small clumps of people began to materialize in the desert haze. Two women and their six children huddled together under a black umbrella in the middle of the sizzling desert in an effort to escape the intense heat. Another mother and her two children squatted in the sand, caked in layers of dust. And in the distance, ragged bands of women and children marched in silent columns with empty jerrycans on their heads, desperately searching for water.

Then the camp, baking under the sun, came into view. It was a ragtag city of wood-and-scrub huts that the refugees had constructed from whatever they could scavenge from the desert floor.

As we wove through, Marc noted that unlike the nomads and pastoralists who crisscrossed the arid plains with their camel caravans and cattle herds, these people came from an urban background.

"They were forced to leave the city lights for the mud, dust and flies," he said.

The refugees began flooding into the Ogaden in June, 1988, many wearing three-piece suits and clutching suitcases and tape decks. They were businessmen, civil servants, doctors, lawyers, teachers, merchants and engineers from the Somali towns of Hargeisa and Burao. Most were members of the affluent Issak clan, the largest tribe in northern Somalia. They were the victims of the brutal dictator Mohamed Siad Barre, whose government, in Mogadishu in the south, was locked in a vicious civil war with the rebel Somali National Movement (SNM), which was made up entirely of fighters from the Issak clan.

At the UNHCR compound, the refugee committee gathered to voice their concerns over conditions at the camp. I learned quickly that diplomacy and protocol were important, even in a refugee camp in the middle of a godforsaken desert. Camp elders were clamouring for an urgent meeting with Marc. They were upset and humiliated at what their people had been forced to suffer, and on this particular day, they were demanding that something be done about the acute shortage of water.

Marc handled the situation admirably. Calmly, respectfully and diplomatically, he explained that no money was available to have more water trucked in. But a huge, plastic-lined, earthen damn being built on the outskirts of the camp would be filled when the heavy rains arrived in the coming weeks, he assured them.

A man called Abdullahi Saeed was chairman of the refugee committee. He had a face like a well-worn road map and the demeanour of a beaten warrior. The children were being forced to wear rags and go barefoot, he complained.

"There is no money in the budget for clothes," Marc replied apologetically.

Saeed asked about blankets and tarpaulins to cover the huts.

"I'll see what I can do," Marc responded.

Next on Saeed's checklist of complaints was the lack of medical personnel. "We do not have a doctor, only a local nurse. We have equipment here that is still in boxes because no one knows how to use it. So every day people die."

Marc countered that he was hoping a doctor with Médecins Sans Frontières (Doctors Without Borders) might stop by in the near future and pitch a tent. His diplomatic air was beginning to fray, and his expression was one of exasperation.

Saeed threw his arms over his head in a gesture of frustration. He was not happy with the responses. He shouted his displeasure to the other committee members.

Next up was Mohammed Yusul Dhell, a dapper fellow in a wrinkled grey suit who bore the exalted title of educational director. He complained that the makeshift school had fallen into a sorry state of disrepair. "The children have no books or pencils and the teachers have no chalk," he noted.

"There is no money for school supplies. There is nothing I can do about that," Marc said. "As for the building, I think your people should get together and try to keep it in good shape."

Marc then took a moment to introduce me. "Mr. Malarek is a correspondent with a Canadian newspaper—"

That was as far as he got before a committee chairman jumped up and vented his anger at me. "Why has the world forgotten about us? Why should we be expected to live this way, like animals? Why will the world not help us?"

"All I can do is write about your plight," I replied lamely.

Saeed shook his head. "No one cares about us! No one cares if we live or die!"

There was a silence. Then Mr. Dhell asked if I would visit the children in his school. "I would be so honoured and the children could practice their English."

I agreed. As we passed by the gates of the UNHCR compound, I noticed hundreds of women and children standing patiently in long, straight lines under the blistering noonday sun, waiting for food and water rations. Clutching tin pots and empty plastic water cans, they stood motionless in absolute silence. The surreal quiet was ruptured by the buzz of flies swarming round their heads. In front of them in the fenced-off compound was a bloated water tanker, dripping precious water onto the sand. Behind the vehicle were two huge tents — as big as football fields — filled with bags of wheat and rice and cans of cooking oil.

All around, stretching to infinity, their meagre shelters dotted the desert floor. Made of sticks and covered with plastic sheeting, they offered little protection from the severe temperature changes from day to night. By day the temperature soared to forty degrees Celsius. At night, the thermometer plunged as low as five degrees.

Like a proud father, Dhell stuck out his chest as we approached the school. The fact that a school existed at all in this human wasteland amazed me. Here, where the bare necessities of life were at risk and despite desperate shortages of books and materials, children were learning in rickety, makeshift classrooms, with some semblance of order, discipline and even cheerfulness.

As we entered one of the rooms, about thirty beaming children, aged maybe seven to ten, leapt to their feet and with a collective giggle greeted me in English.

"Good morning. We hope you are well and we wish you a good day," they recited in unison.

"I am sorry for the small turnout," Dhell said apologetically. "Many of the children are out with their mothers in the desert looking for water."

"They're terrific!" I said, smiling broadly.

The education director explained that one day, the war in his homeland would end. "We want our children to be educated. They must know mathematics and writing. But as you can see, we have no materials with which to teach."

As he was explaining his case, a young man entered the class and passed him a message.

"You are wanted back at the UNHCR compound," Dhell said. "A meeting of women has been arranged. They want to speak to you."

As we headed back, we passed a large, open pit. A huddle of women stood before it, clutching one another and wailing. I looked in. What I saw was horrifying. It was a mass grave. The corpses, perhaps a dozen of them, were wrapped in tattered shrouds. A few feet from the wailing women, a young mother sat on the ground, cradling a small bundle swaddled in rags. It was the emaciated remains of her three-year-old daughter.

"She is the victim of malaria," Dhell said sadly. "The death toll from disease and malnutrition is very high here. Every day, we bury dozens of our people."

In a large, open tent, dozens of women had gathered for a meeting with me. They desperately wanted to tell their stories. As I sat down at a table, I steeled myself for the testimony I was about to hear. The crowd suddenly parted as a tiny woman was carried into the shelter. The woman's left thigh was shattered by shrapnel.

"I was in front of my house in Hargeisa, my hometown, when I was hit by airplane bombing," the frail woman told me through an interpreter. "The bomb hit my home, and my two sisters and my brother were killed. I blacked out. I don't know how long I lay on the ground unconscious. I remember a soldier standing over me and hitting me with his rifle butt. Then he ripped my earrings and necklace from my body. That night, the Somali National Movement came into the town and took me away. I was eventually brought to this camp. I was told by a doctor I would never walk again." The woman, whose name was Marian Ali Yusuf, was twenty-five years old.

Fadumo Abrulle Omar, a thirty-year-old mother of eight, told her story, also through an interpreter. "I was making breakfast at my home in Burao when the Somali Army fired on the town. Two of my children ran outside when the bombs began to explode around us. They were killed instantly. My husband also ran out, and since that time I do not know if he is alive or dead."

That night, during a lull in the fighting, Omar fled with her remaining six children and her mother. During their flight, her mother and two more of her children were killed. She and her remaining four children reached the camp on foot four months later.

Roda Jama Elm stared at the ground as she spoke in a hoarse whisper. She was at home when Somali soldiers forced their way into her husband's general store in Hargeisa and looted it. Her husband and two brothers were dragged to the house by a band of soldiers and taken to the bedroom.

"I heard a strange sound and looked into the room. The soldiers had slit the throats of my husband and brothers. I screamed and one of the soldiers turned and shot at me. The bullet struck my three-month-old daughter. I was holding her in my arms." The thirty-five-year-old woman fell to the ground and moaned. She couldn't continue.

All the women wept, their tears carrying the deep pain and tragedy they had endured. The stories continued until I wanted to jam my fingers into my ears. Many more women recounted horrible tales of rape, slaughter and mass executions of men, women and children. As they told their terrible stories, the wailing of the listeners grew louder, echoing over the entire camp in a haunting lament. I felt it would never end. Every single person in the tent — and there were more than two hundred — had experienced profound personal tragedy. The meeting was finally called to an end. It was time to pray to Allah.

In the early evening, I was escorted to a teahouse in the centre of the camp for a clandestine meeting with several SNM sympathizers. Most of the men were sprawled on the floor, drinking sweet green tea and chewing *quat* (pronounced *chat*), a mild, leafy, locally grown narcotic. They had a brief, simple message they wanted me to bring to the outside world.

"The dictator Siad Barre will be defeated. The SNM will win and we will create our own homeland of Somaliland," an elder vowed, his eyes cold with resolve.

I was offered a few *quat* leaves but politely declined. As we got back into the Jeep, my Ethiopian minder smirked. "They will never win," Tesfaye said. "Siad Barre is too strong. The Americans have given him a lot of weapons. These people just chew *quat* and talk."

I didn't know much about the Somali war. All I knew for certain was that it had caused untold suffering. I also knew that when you persecute a race long enough, they'll turn around and fight. And sooner or later, even if it takes centuries, they'll defeat their oppressors.

It was starting to get dark when we finally hit the road for Aware. We'd been in the camp ten hours. It had seemed like a lifetime.

Marc was extremely tense.

"Is something wrong?" I asked.

"I don't like to drive in the dark," he said. "You never know what's out there."

We barrelled across the desert. Three hours later, we approached the outskirts of Aware. Marc slowed down and flashed his lights repeatedly.

"There's an army outpost ahead," he said apprehensively. Then, rolling down his window, he shouted, "United Nations! United Nations!"

Out of the pitch black, a platoon of dark faces emerged and rushed the Jeep from all sides. They were mere kids, fresh, jittery teenaged recruits armed with Kalashnikov assault rifles. Kids who had a reputation for shooting at anything that moved in the night and checking it out in the morning. This was what had worried Marc when he'd set off on our night drive. Their weapons ready, the youthful soldiers stared suspiciously at two very nervous white faces. My minder flashed an identity card in the back window. It seemed to have no effect on the soldiers. An older conscript with a piece of brass on his collar rapped on my window. I rolled it down. He pointed to a pen in my breast pocket. I handed it to him and smiled. He waved us on. Marc and I breathed a sigh of relief.

The next day was like every day in the Ogaden Desert, hot and dry. At 6:00 a.m., we started out for another camp, called Daror. We bumped and banged through the desert for six hours. When we arrived at Daror, we were informed that a refugee had been murdered the night before. He was shot after refusing to relinquish his truck to SNM rebel insurgents. In accordance with Islamic law, the man's body was buried at dawn in an unmarked hole in the sand. Any investigation of the incident ended there.

Another refugee committee met us and we were given a tense and depressing tour. As we made our way through the camp, destitute refugees rushed up to Marc pleading for more food, water and medical supplies. But despite this, the tour began to take on a festive air as bands of giggling children followed closely behind.

Later, at the UNHCR compound, the Ethiopian relief workers invited us to join them for lunch. The concoction was a yellowy lime green, the lumpy meal spicy, chewy and oily. Hesitantly, I asked what it was, all the while dreading the answer.

"You might not want to know," Marc joked.

"Camel! You like?" a grinning relief worker asked.

I smiled wanly and feigned approval.

After lunch, we headed out for Kamaboker, a third refugee camp.

As we careened through the desert, I noticed a plume of dust approaching from the distance. Marc looked apprehensive.

"I think they're SNM," he said.

My minder shifted uneasily in his seat.

"I just hope they don't take the Jeep," Marc added. "It's a long walk from here."

I laughed nervously.

Moments later, a truck crammed with heavily armed SNM rebels pulled within striking distance. We stopped and waited. Their leader, brandishing a 9mm pistol, jumped out of the passenger side and approached Marc.

"Why are you out here?" the rebel commander asked in perfect English.

"I'm with the United Nations High Commission for Refugees. We are heading for Kamaboker," Marc answered in an authoritative voice.

"Who is this man?" he asked, pointing at me.

"He is a journalist from Canada. He is writing a story about the plight of Somali refugees."

"And that man?" he said, motioning to Tesfaye.

"An Ethiopian government employee."

He stared at me for a moment. His eyes narrowed. I was getting very uncomfortable.

"You must come with me," the SNM commander ordered.

My minder began to shake. As I got out of the Jeep, I felt my legs start to wobble.

We walked about twenty-five feet into the desert. Then the commander instructed me to sit on the ground. He yelled something to his men. Four jumped down from the back of the truck, their rifles at the ready. Visions of an execution flashed through my mind. He quickly scanned the horizon. Then he squatted beside me, his face inches from mine.

"I have a brother in Toronto and two cousins in Vancouver. They have refugee status in Canada. Your country has been very good to them," the man said.

I almost threw up with relief.

"There are a lot of Somali refugees in Canada," I replied, wondering where the conversation was heading.

"Yes, and many are from the regime of the dictator Siad Barre. They have lied to your government claiming to be Isaaks when they are not.

They do this to get refugee status in Canada so they can remain there, when in fact they are from the clan that is persecuting our people."

"I'll look into that when I get back," I said.

The commander looked at his men. He seemed lost in thought.

"Nice truck," I said after a few minutes of silence. "Where did you get it?"

I could tell from the markings that it had belonged to the Somali Army. And from the bullet holes in the windshield and the door on the driver's side, I could tell it hadn't been simply handed over to the rebels.

"One might say it was a gift from the Somali Army," the commander said.

"That's an interesting hole in the windshield. A rock?"

"No. An American M-16." He laughed.

"Where do you guys get your weapons?"

"We take them from Somali soldiers we kill in the night or we get them from Somali Army deserters who want no part of this war."

The commander yelled something to his men. They responded by holding their weapons high and cheering.

"I want you to write in your newspaper that the SNM will not lie down and let the Somali Army massacre the Isaaks!" he said. "That is what this war is all about. The brutal dictator Siad Barre will be stopped. We are putting up a powerful resistance. Today the Somali Army is very discouraged. Desertion is high. Many soldiers ask that we allow them to leave the towns we have surrounded. All they want is to go home to their families. We feel we will soon capture the whole northern region and then our people can return home and live in peace in Somaliland."

End of lecture. We walked back to our Jeep.

At my request, the rebels posed for pictures. Then we waved goodbye, jumped into our Jeep and continued our trek to Kamaboker.

After a week in the Ogaden, I bade farewell to Marc Salvail. My next adventure would take me to the other side of Ethiopia.

As I walked onto the slick, oil-stained tarmac and got a full view of the airplane, I felt queasy. It was an ancient DC-3, with Ethiopian Airlines printed in green letters on its scarred sides. It looked held together by masking tape, rust and — pushing luck — a prayer. It was scheduled to fly to Gambella on the western fringe of Ethiopia, near the Sudan border.

As I shuffled up the gangway, I felt strangely alone. I turned and caught a fleeting glimpse of my minder scuttling into the terminal building. He waved nervously as he disappeared inside.

I entered the stuffy cabin and immediately sought out the emergency exits. The seats beside them were already taken by equally grim-faced passengers. I parked myself in Seat 1-B, right behind the cockpit. I figured I could at least keep a vigilant eye on the pilots. We sat on the tarmac for an hour. The air in the cabin was stifling and rancid. Then the radios crackled and an all clear for takeoff was given. The cabin was as silent as a crypt. No one breathed. The engines sputtered and backfired, spewing out clouds of black smoke. Once, twice, three times … at last, they roared, tentatively, to life. The spectre of what was emanating from its bowels made me want to scream, "Stop the plane, stop the plane!" But my throat was as parched and mute as the Ogaden Desert.

The aging bucket of rivets charged labouriously down the runway. I whispered a frantic prayer, grabbed hold of the armrests and watched my knuckles turn white. At long last, the plane's nose greeted the mist-covered sky. I breathed a hesitant sigh of relief. Throughout the entire three-hour flight, I gripped the armrests with the force of an athlete pumped up on steroids.

Finally the pilot instructed us to fasten our seat belts in preparation for landing. Below, all I could make out was dense brush. The landing gear was lowered with an unnerving clank as we made our descent and the mud huts of Gambella came into focus. My hellish journey on wings was almost over — or so I thought.

Suddenly, without warning, the plane banked sharply to the right. The starboard wing almost clipped the ground as the engines groaned and we struggled to gain altitude once again. A few passengers who had already unbuckled their seat belts were thrown across the cabin. As the aircraft levelled out, I heard the pilot screaming wildly into his radio. I looked out the window and saw the reason he had decided to abort the landing. Several moss-coloured army tanks were crossing the runway at a leisurely pace. Fine time for a military maneuver.

A few moments later, we approached for the second time. We landed rockily, but without incident. The pilot shut off the engines, ran for the doorway and, without waiting for the gangway to be bolted on, jumped onto the tarmac. Purple with rage, he scrambled over to a group of soldiers lounging beside a Jeep and demanded to know who ordered the tanks onto the runway. Then he grabbed the man wearing the most brass in a headlock and started punching. The scuffle lasted about a minute before a gang of conscripts intervened and rescued their captain from what looked like certain strangulation. They dragged the pilot off to a nearby hangar, still kicking and cursing.

On the other side of a chain-link fence, I was met by Sunday Shorunke, a Nigerian relief worker with the United Nations High Commission for Refugees. His handshake was firm and warm, and his dark eyes were windows to the depths of a soul that had seen all there was to see.

"We are so happy you could make it. The world must know what is happening," he said, a concerned smile creasing his round face.

"I was told in Addis that the situation here is pretty grim," I said as we drove to the UNHCR compound in a white Land Rover.

"It is terrible. A monumental disaster. I have never in all my life seen anything as horrible as this," he said.

"When will I be going to the camp?" I asked.

"Tomorrow. Later today, Kingsley Amaning is arriving from Addis by Jeep. He is the regional coordinator. He will be taking you there."

"He drove here from Addis?"

"Yes. It takes about two days—a long trip, but he would *never* fly. It's much too dangerous!"

"Really? And I had such a smooth flight—in business class!"

Gambella was an impoverished town of rutted dirt roads and adobe huts roofed by cones of dried elephant grass. Naked children sat huddled outside the doorways while their mothers, bare to the waist, stood over large, blackened cauldrons steaming over hot coals. Teenaged girls gripping two-metre-long poles pounded grain into coarse flour while others washed clothes in large pots or attended to baby brothers and sisters. The men, bored-looking, squatted idly under eucalyptus trees. A group of teenaged boys kicked around a soccer ball on a mud-caked field.

It took only a few minutes to reach the UN compound. It was made up of half a dozen mobile homes and offices, fenced in and guarded round the clock. Towering radio antennas stuck out the roofs. They kept constant contact with the refugee camps and with UN headquarters in Addis.

Sunday showed me to my room and immediately left to take an urgent radio call. I sat on my cot and read up on the history of the vicious conflict raging on the other side of the border, only a dozen kilometres away. The decades-old civil war had been almost completely ignored by the Western news media. The Khartoum government was pitted against the Sudanese People's Liberation Army—the SPLA. Abbreviated reports on the conflict portrayed it as a religious dispute—Arab Muslims in the north trying to impose Islamic law on animists and Christian Africans in the south. But the grievances went much deeper than religious convictions and zealotry. They were rooted in racial bigotry, inequality and the struggle for political and economic power, which was concentrated in the Arab north.

The latest outbreak of fighting had been grinding on for six years. Caught in the middle were simple farmers and cattle herders. The war had claimed the lives of hundreds of thousands of peasants—mostly through starvation—and had triggered a mass movement of some two million refugees. The figures were almost impossible to imagine. These defenseless pastoralists were the victims of a deliberate genocide by one of the world's most repressive governments, as well as being pawns of the ruthless rebels belonging to the SPLA.

As I sifted through the reports from the UNHCR, Amnesty International and the U.S. State Department, I wondered what I would see in a desolate refugee camp several miles away near the village of Fugnido. I had heard about the horrors from UN relief workers in Addis. And Sunday had told me I would witness the depths of hell in the camp near Fugnido. I was prepared for the worst.

Kingsley Amaning arrived in time for dinner. He was from Ghana and spoke English with an impeccable British accent. His chiselled features made him appear cool, aloof and businesslike. But inside lived the soul of a man who had borne witness to Africa's Heart of Darkness.

Kingsley was one of the first relief workers to see the ordeal of the Dinka people—the largest tribe in southern Sudan. The Dinkas are a dramatic-looking people—coal-black and extraordinarily tall and thin. They are pastoralists who revere their cattle. As well as being used for food, the herds are a sign of wealth and standing in the community.

Sitting at the dining-room table, Kingsley recalled his first encounter with the Dinkas from southern Sudan. It was in mid-November, 1987, in Addis Ababa. He had received word that about forty Dinka refugees, mostly women and children, had arrived in extremely poor shape outside Fugnido.

"But when we arrived to investigate the report on November thirtieth," Kingsley recounted, "we found not forty but nine thousand refugees. Mostly boys between the ages of five and fifteen, all of them half dead. They were eating grass and leaves to survive. The children were in a state of shock, starving and suffering from diseases. It was terrible. I've never seen anything like it in my life. It was a nightmare. These Dinka boys, so tall, so lanky. To see them absolutely naked. They were living skeletons. To see their starving faces, their skin covered in diseases..."

Kingsley paused to regain his composure.

"It was a holocaust—extremely disturbing. The images of those days are branded in my mind. In the evenings after I left the camp, I would weep for hours. When I close my eyes today, I still see those boys lying under the trees dying by the hundreds—moments after they crossed the last river to reach safety."

Listening to the boys' stories, Kingsley and other relief workers quickly realized the extent of the catastrophe that was unfolding before them. After talking with scores of survivors, Kingsley estimated that for every five boys who began the harrowing trek from Sudan to Ethiopia, three died en route.

"You had better get some rest," Kingsley suggested. "Tomorrow will be a very difficult and trying day for all of us."

The next morning, Kingsley, Sunday and I set out for Fugnido. It was a gruelling three-hour drive along dirt roads carved through a jungle of thorn trees, tall grass and swamp. The only other vehicles on the road were occasional UN relief trucks carrying grain and other goods to the camp.

As our Jeep pulled into the camp, hundreds of boys swarmed round us—young, curious, faces that lit up when they saw Kingsley and Sunday. A young boy, probably about seven, gestured at me and shouted something to Sunday. Everyone laughed.

"What did he say?" I asked.

"He is wondering how anyone could be so white," Sunday said. "He wants to touch your skin. Is that okay with you?"

"Sure. It's okay," I said, reaching out to shake the boy's hand.

His wide grin exposed a mouthful of yellow teeth. He rubbed the skin on my arm, apparently mesmerized by the colour and texture.

Sunday had a lot of work to do, so Kingsley and I headed into the camp with a Dinka interpreter. The makeshift community was built

entirely by the refugees, Kingsley explained. It was a typical Dinka village of bamboo and wooden huts topped by cone-shaped roofs of long,
dried grass.

Not far into the tour, something very odd struck me about the place.
Everywhere we went we were besieged by hundreds of boys between
the ages of approximately three and eighteen. But there were no mothers washing clothes. No sisters pounding grain into flour. No women
carrying water pots or firewood on their heads. And there were very
few older men. Just flocks and flocks of boys.

I asked the obvious question. "Where are the men, the women, the
girls? Are they in the huts or somewhere else in the camp?"

"No. They were either killed or taken as slaves by the Arab militia,"
Kingsley replied. "There are more than twenty-five thousand boys here.
Seventeen thousand of them are orphans. They have no one. Most have
no idea where their families are or what has happened to them."

As I stared into the lost faces of the scores of boys gathered around
me, I suddenly realized I was in a giant, open-air orphanage. In the
oppressive afternoon heat, a cold shiver ran down my back. I thought
back to the four years I'd spent in Weredale House. There were 180 of
us in that four-storey, brick institution. We often felt alone and deserted,
as if no one cared about what happened to us. It was a sad, cruel place.
And it left its mark on my soul.

But this camp, this massive, heartbreaking orphanage without walls,
was something I could never have imagined. It overwhelmed me.

We sat down for a rest outside one of the huts. Kingsley introduced
me to Jurkuch Barach, a Dinka man who had been appointed chairman
of the refugee committee. He was thirty-eight, Kingsley told me. He
looked at least twenty years older.

"We have automatically become their fathers," Barach said through
a UN interpreter. "It is our role to see that they are looked after, cared
for. We see that they are housed and fed. That they wash and go to
work building shelters for themselves."

As we entered another compound surrounded by huts, many of the
boys dropped their poles and stared at me. They looked upset.

"They're embarrassed because you saw them pounding," Kingsley
explained. "The boys hate pounding grain into flour because their traditional role is looking after the cattle herds. Pounding is a girl's job.
But here the boys have to do it if they want to eat."

We sat down on a rickety bench. Barach invited the boys to join us.

He introduced me to seventeen-year-old Dut Ayuen Kou, a tall, muscular, healthy-looking young man. He was a prefect in the compound, maintaining discipline and making sure each of the boys did their chores, Barach told me.

Physically, Dut looked like any normal teenager. But his eyes were haunted. They told the story of his journey to hell and back.

Two years earlier, said Kingsley, Dut had crawled into the camp. He was a skeleton wrapped in a tight layer of skin.

Dut took over the telling of his story through the interpreter. In a low tone, his expressive dark brown eyes fixed on the ground, he began with the day he was tending his family's cattle herd outside his village in southern Sudan. He heard the unmistakable staccato of machine-gun and rifle fire. His heart pounding, he raced to a hilltop and watched in horror as a band of Arab militiamen rampaged through the village on horseback and in Jeeps, shooting at the terrified peasants. They set the grass and bamboo huts ablaze. Then they rounded up the girls and boys. They would be sold as slaves to Arab landowners and farmers in the north. Finally the militiamen shot the pleading fathers and mothers dead.

Then the attackers cast their eyes to the nearby fields, where several hundred cattle grazed. The cattle were the prized booty. Seeing the raiders approaching, Dut fled into the forest. There he met up with seventy-five or so terrified boys who had managed to escape from the village. So began an astonishing three-month, thousand-mile odyssey of starvation and endurance that took the boys across parched savannah, mosquito-infested swamps, rivers filled with crocodiles and rugged mountain ranges.

"We walked and we ran and we walked and we ran," Dut said. "Our feet were bruised and blistered, but we kept on going. We were afraid to stop. We moved, usually after dark, for weeks and weeks. We were afraid the militia would catch up with us and sell us as slaves. We had no food. We ate leaves, grass and twigs to stay alive."

Dut paused for a moment to gather his thoughts. "Only twenty-five of us reached Fugnido. The rest—maybe fifty boys—died on the way. Most of them died of starvation. Hyenas dragged away the boys who couldn't keep up, sometimes when they were still alive. Crocodiles attacked us as we tried to swim across rivers. Some of the boys got sick and died of typhoid and malaria."

Dut's eyes filled with tears. Remembering was too painful. He turned suddenly and ran into a nearby hut.

Barach asked another boy to tell his story. Tiop Manyiel Thon spoke in a whisper. Sitting on the ground, the fourteen-year-old recalled the attack on his village at dawn. "All the men in my village were rounded up and shot. The girls were taken. The houses were set on fire. I ran into the forest and kept running."

Thon walked for seven weeks in the scorching heat of the dry season before finding sanctuary in Ethiopia. He found rest but no peace. Since arriving, Tiop said, he had been plagued by nightmares. He didn't know what had happened to his father, mother, two brothers or two sisters.

When thirteen-year-old Nyuol Yak Akol heard the gunfire, he ran. He kept running for four months before reaching the camp. There were two hundred boys in his ragtag group when they set out. Only forty-five made it alive. "So many died on the way. So many. They died of exhaustion and hunger and disease. Animals attacked us."

Nyuol buried his face in his hands and began to weep uncontrollably. "I think about my mother all the time. I don't know if she is dead or alive. I don't know what happened to my father or my three sisters. My two brothers starved to death on the way to this camp."

The yard fell deathly still. Numbed by their harrowing experiences, the boys sat wrapped in private thoughts and nightmares. I was finding it difficult to breathe. Clearly, my body was rebelling as I searched desperately for a way to comprehend this horrific tragedy, a tragedy impossible to assimilate.

Barach led me to the edge of the camp, to the place most of the boys stumbled into, he explained, after crossing the river that separates hell from haven. A makeshift hospital—a long, narrow, open wood-frame building—stood here. Inside were the most recent arrivals. A dozen boys, rags hanging off their wretched bodies, lay on rusting army cots, a thin blanket or nothing at all covering the bedsprings. They were listless, staring blankly at the ceiling. Flies swarmed around them, attacking their emaciated bodies. Their skin was stretched over their rib cages and hipbones, their stomachs bloated, their elbows and knees jutted out like knots on a pine tree.

That night, two of the recent arrivals died.

I was horrified and spellbound. I tried to sort through my feelings. Words were inadequate: "This is so unreal, so unfair, so unjust."

"I know," Kingsley whispered.

My tour wasn't over yet. There was one more stop, one more assault on my soul. In a dreary, dusty, isolated corner of the camp, devoid of vitality, a special unit had been set up for boys suffering from severe trauma. There were thirty-six children in the ward on this day. Their young eyes were filled with terror. Many wandered around the unit in a trance, their tormented minds unable to cope. A few lay rigid on the hard mud floor; a few curled up in tight balls. All were naked.

A matronly nurse with a kind face was caring for the boys, doing the best she could with so many limits, including her finite energy and the meagre supplies. "They need plenty of caring and feeding. They have been through a terrible ordeal," she said, rubbing the head of a moaning ten-year-old.

As we talked, a boy about eight years old grabbed my hand and held on very tightly. I put my arm around him and gave him a hug. Then I reached into my knapsack and hauled out a red T-shirt. I pulled it over his head.

I had bought fifty T-shirts at the market in Addis Ababa. So here I was, feeling like an automaton in a theatre of the absurd, handing out cotton T-shirts to naked, orphaned boys. As I left the trauma unit, I turned and smiled for the first time that day as I saw all the boys out-fitted in red, yellow, blue, green, white and hot-pink T-shirts.

Then, at last, I lost it. I started to weep uncontrollably. I had tried to steel myself and shut down my emotions before entering the camp, and throughout the tour I kept forcing back the sadness that threatened to suffocate me. Now I could no longer hold back. I was utterly shattered by the overwhelming reality of these helpless boys. What could I do for these children? Nothing. Sure, I could write about their plight, inform the public in my corner of the world about the situation. But now, writing about it seemed meaningless.

I tried to make some sense of it, but nothing about this hellhole made sense. All this suffering, despair, death. For what? Power? More land? Racial superiority? An Islamic Holy War? How, I wondered, could anyone hate so profoundly that they would attack and kill helpless children? These boys had been robbed of their childhood, their innocence. They had no one to hug them, no one to love them. They were alone, staring death in the face every day. I felt angry and bitter.

Kingsley and I drove to Gambella in silence. We were both numb. When we got to the compound, I went straight to my room. I sat in the darkness, unable to move, unable even to think. I didn't know whether

I could ever write about what I had seen. It would trivialize it. I lay down on my bed and tried to sleep. It was impossible. I kept seeing the haunted faces of the Dinka boys. I kept hearing their muffled sobs. I saw them running through the jungle, terrified. And I saw them dying, hungry and in pain.

I wanted to get as far away from this place as I possibly could. I longed to go home, to hold Anna again, to hug Larissa, my four-year-old daughter. And I wanted to be held.

That morning, Kingsley received an emergency dispatch from Addis. He would have to return immediately. I begged to hitch a ride. When he said I could go along, relief engulfed me.

CHAPTER 11

SEEDS OF DECEPTION

February 20, 1989. It should have been a routine drug bust. Instead, the front pages of newspapers in Thailand and Canada announced that a Mountie had died — the first RCMP drug officer ever killed during an undercover operation anywhere in the world.

I read and reread the RCMP press release. It was terse. Suspiciously terse. Thirty-five-year-old Corporal Derek Flanagan, a father of three young children, died in Thailand in the line of duty, it said. But something about the story didn't sit right with me. What, I wondered, were the Mounties doing making a drug bust in the Golden Triangle?

Inspector Ray Singbeil, who ran the secretive Vancouver RCMP drug intelligence and field operations unit, announced in the press release that the operation in Thailand plugged a major heroin pipeline to Canada. He stated that a number of people were arrested in Thailand, including a major Canadian heroin dealer identified as Alain Olivier. And a score of drug dealers were rounded up in British Columbia and Quebec as a direct result of a wide-ranging and lengthy undercover investigation, code-named Operation Deception.

I phoned Singbeil at his Vancouver office. He elaborated on Canada's war on drugs and the significant dent Operation Deception had made in the drug trade. The streets of Canada were safer now — for the time being, at least, he said.

But I was more interested in Operation Deception and the major Canadian heroin dealer who had been busted in Chiang Mai. In our brief exchange, Singbeil's abrupt tone set off my warning bells. The undercover team was "acting in an assistance capacity" under the direction of the Thai National Police, he said; 2.4 kilograms of high-grade

China White destined for the Canadian market and worth a cool $15 million on the streets was seized in Thailand, he added.

"Who is this guy Alain Olivier?" I asked.

The inspector clammed up. "The case is before the courts," he said flatly. "I can't comment any further."

"Come on! The court is in Thailand," I said.

"Again, we cannot comment about this matter because Mr. Olivier has been charged and we do not want to jeopardize the case in any way," Singbeil said.

"With all due respect," I said, clenching my teeth, "I really don't think the judges in Bangkok, Thailand, read English, let alone the *Globe and Mail*."

"I'm sorry, but I can't comment," Singbeil said, his voice strained.

"Look, it can take years before this guy goes to trial. All I want to know is who he is and how this bust went down." I wasn't going to let the cop off the hook that easily.

"No comment," he replied and hung up.

Now I knew something was fishy. In other major drug operations I had covered as a reporter, the RCMP were always champing at the bit to boast about their busts. They staged dog and pony shows for the news media, hauling out bales of the dope, flipping open attaché cases filled with hundred-dollar bills and heaping praise on the undercover team. This time there was none of the usual bravado and hype.

I smelled a cover-up.

I had recently completed a book about Canada's illegal drug trade called *Merchants of Misery*. In Montreal, Toronto and Vancouver, the RCMP had been tremendously helpful. Drug cops described numerous undercover operations from coast to coast involving tons of marijuana and hashish and scores of kilograms of cocaine and heroin. They took me along on raids of heroin shooting galleries and crack houses. I got an understanding of the kinds of pressures and dangers they faced almost daily in their work, and the lowlifes they had to deal with to get information. And I met a handful of sleazy informants who acted like cops. On the surface, these snitches were always treated like one of the boys, but the cops loathed the ground they sullied. They saw these people as gutter rats whose only driving force was money.

For my research, I had travelled to the Golden Triangle to follow the trail of China White from its source to its final destination: the seedy alleyways and flophouses of Vancouver, Montreal and Toronto. I learned that the U.S. Drug Enforcement Administration (DEA) estimates that the Golden Triangle, which is made up of Burma, Thailand and Laos, produces upward of two thousand tonnes of opium a year. After chemical processing, that would translate into two hundred tonnes of ninety-nine percent pure high-grade heroin. I was told the key players in the international heroin trade were the leaders of powerful and dangerous Chinese Triads based in Hong Kong. These highly secretive criminal organizations had tentacles stretching around the world with strong links in Vancouver, San Francisco, Toronto and New York. DEA intelligence shows that the Triads, or Black Societies, with names like Sun Yee On, Kung Lok and 14-K, control the flow of heroin at every step of the process, moving large shipments from remote jungle laboratories in the Golden Triangle to distribution networks throughout North America, Western Europe and southeast Asia, and ultimately into the thirsty veins of hundreds of thousands of heroin addicts. It's a multi-billion-dollar-a-year business.

So why would an RCMP undercover drug team wing it to Thailand and set up shop in Chiang Mai for a paltry 2.4 kilograms of heroin? I wondered. In the Golden Triangle that was dust in the wind. Singbeil's $15 million price tag interested me, too. An amazing sum for three, eight-hundred-gram packets of refined powder!

The Mounties' numbers had been dutifully reported in the news stories unchallenged. Hey, the police never engage in hyperbole, do they? I pondered the extravagant figure and decided not to report it. I figured that the undercover cops probably had paid about $20,000 for the dope. If they spent more, they got royally ripped off. So how could the heroin suddenly end up being worth 750 times more than the cops had paid for it?

I knew the going rates from my research for *Merchants of Misery*. The Mounties had provided me with their official price breakdown for heroin, from the peasant grower, to the addict on the streets of North America. It sounded like a quick course in creative accounting. It went like this: the farmer sells ten kilograms of raw opium for $1,000 to $1,600. It is then treated with chemicals at a jungle laboratory along the border of Burma and Thailand to make one kilogram of ninety-nine percent pure heroin, which sells for $4,400 to $5,000. The distribution centre in Bangkok or Chiang Mai sells it to organized crime syndicates for $6,000 to $8,000 a kilo. If the smuggler successfully imports the illicit shipment into North America, it sells for between $120,000 and

$200,000 a kilo. Then the drug is carved up by mid-level dealers in the distribution network. An ounce (twenty-eight grams) would go for $6,000 to $15,000. A gram would sell for $650 to $1,000.

At this point, the pure heroin is cut or diluted with powdered laxative and sold at twenty-five to sixty percent purity to the addict for $75 to $100 a point (one-tenth of a gram).

The RCMP and DEA use this rock-bottom accounting method—the injection of the final product into the veins of junkies—to arrive at the astronomical price tag of $15 million for 2.4 kilograms of white powder!

At the *Globe*, I sat down with Gwen Smith, the associate managing editor, and Paul Palango, the national editor, to persuade them to let me loose on the story. Smith was tough, assertive, and wasn't going to hand out airline tickets for a foreign assignment without knowing the payoff. The rumpled, stout Palango was less skeptical. His first instinct always was to send his reporters out to kick butt.

"What do you think is really going on?" Smith asked me.

"Hard to say. But the RCMP have slammed the lid on this one. Something is definitely uncool about this operation. I can smell it."

"You just want a trip to Thailand," Palango needled me.

"Yeah, yeah," I replied impatiently. "Look, I *know* there's more to this undercover operation but I just can't put my finger on exactly what it is. I called a couple of solid RCMP contacts, and all they would tell me is that there's a black cloud hovering over the heads of the cops involved in it."

"What do you expect to get in Thailand?" Smith asked.

"At the very least, I'll get a picture of what really went down. I'm going to speak to a couple of Thai generals who head the drug enforcement units in Bangkok and Chiang Mai. I met them last year when I was working on the drug book. And I'm going to try to speak to this guy Alain Olivier and get his version of events."

"You have anything on this Olivier character?" Palango asked.

"Well, I contacted a Montreal cop I know in the organized-crime squad and asked if he could run the name. It came up zip, no criminal record. But he's known to the cops as a junkie and nickel-and-dime pusher. And that certainly does *not* jive with how the Mounties are describing him."

"What do you mean?" Smith was starting to get interested.

"The Mounties described Olivier as a major heroin dealer. My contact says the guy is nothing more than a wart on the ass of the drug scene."

Palango chuckled at my description.

Smith grimaced. "I hope you don't describe him that way in your story."

"Well, he certainly isn't someone who would be considered a major dealer. Major user, yeah! Major dealer, no way," I said.

"You're right. Something about this doesn't jive," Palango said.

"And I really wonder about this bust," I went on.

"What about it?" Smith asked. She was sitting on the edge of her chair, looking at me intently.

"It came down to 2.4 kilograms of heroin. I'm not boasting, but I think even I could make that kind of a deal in Thailand without too much hassle. Look, if you've got the money and the dealers don't smell cops, they'll sell to just about anyone. But the one key thing to keep in mind about Thailand is the Thai government has never been inclined to slam down the heroin trade. Sure, the Thai cops make busts here and there, but they're little busts, just for show. They arrest foreigners at the airport, force them to swallow laxatives and make them sit on a plastic garbage pail until nature calls. If condoms filled with heroin show up in the crap, they're busted."

Palango grinned. Smith winced.

I continued. "Anyone caught with more than a hundred grams in their possession is carted off to jail. That's the cutoff point. Below it is considered personal use. Above it, you're trafficking. But the thing to keep in mind about Thailand is there are no conspiracy laws. That means that a big-time seller could set up a deal, send out couriers with the dope and not face a single charge if the dupes making the delivery get caught. Only the people with their hands on the drugs get charged. I bet the person who sold the drugs to the Mounties in Chiang Mai never got arrested. And I'll bet a thousand bucks the so-called pipeline the RCMP are saying was plugged is still wide open for business."

Smith leaned forward. "That's all very interesting. So why do you think the RCMP went over there in the first place?"

"That's what I want to find out. I've got a hunch and I don't like what I'm thinking," I replied.

"What is it?" Smith asked.

"I think these guys are cowboys. I think they went over there for the thrill of doing a bust in the infamous Golden Triangle and things got out of control. A Mountie died."

"How long will the trip take?" Palango asked

"About ten days."

I had a story.

March 27, 1989. Bangkok is a congested city trapped in a twenty-four-hour traffic gridlock. Black diesel fumes choke the air. Toxic smog hovers over the office towers and golden Buddhist shrines as cars, trucks, buses and *tuk-tuks* inch their way through the meandering streets. The noise is constant and nerve-jangling. On every other vehicle, the muffler is a straight pipe. The city sounds like a place under siege with the rat-a-tat backfiring of cars and motorcycles and louder backfiring of trucks and buses.

It took me three hours by taxi to get to Thai police headquarters from my hotel. I could have walked there in forty-five minutes. I had set up a meeting with General Bamroong Kheo-Urai, the head of the narcotics division of the Bangkok Metropolitan Police Force.

His office was not what I had expected a general's office would be like. It was Spartan: a teak desk, a few hard-backed wooden chairs and a cheap book stand. On the wall behind the desk was a framed portrait of the king of Thailand. On the opposite wall was a bronze plaque emblazoned with the RCMP coat of arms. The general pointed it out proudly. "It was presented to me by the RCMP," he said.

Bamroong impressed me as a gentleman. He was pleasant, helpful and forthcoming. He began by recounting his visit to Vancouver at the invitation of the RCMP drug unit. He was in love with the majestic beauty of British Columbia, and his praise for the men in red tunics was fulsome. As for Operation Deception, Bamroong was forthright. He was first approached about Operation Deception by Staff-Sergeant Ken Kelly, the RCMP liaison officer at the Canadian Embassy in Bangkok, in early February, 1989. "Sergeant Kelly made a request to carry out an investigation in Thailand on this man Alain Olivier. We agreed to help them in whatever way we could."

"I was led to believe that the RCMP were here in an assistance capacity to help your guys out on a drug operation," I said.

"No, that is not correct. *We* were in the role of assistance," Bamroong replied. "We never asked them to come. They asked us, and we agreed to help them in their investigation."

The general called in an officer who had assisted the undercover team in Chiang Mai. They chatted in Thai for a few minutes, then Bamroong introduced us.

"The captain will accompany you to Chiang Mai and show you where the accident happened. He will answer whatever questions he can. All I ask of you is to consider that we have a special relationship with the RCMP in Vancouver and we do not want to place that in jeopardy," Bamroong said.

"All *I'm* interested in is finding out what really happened here," I said. "I'd also like to ask if you could arrange for me to meet with Alain Olivier."

"I will try. But he may not want to speak to you," Bamroong said.

"As long as you try."

As the captain and I left the general's office, I thought how accommodating he was — a welcome relief from the strangely obstinate and antagonistic attitude of the RCMP.

The captain had dark, intense eyes and the solid frame of a martial arts expert. We sat down in his office, starkly furnished with a wooden desk, a battered swivel chair, two steel chairs and a bank of banged-up filing cabinets. He ordered tea. He had one request — that I not identify him by name. "If I have this agreement, I will talk candidly," he said.

I agreed.

"Flanagan was a great man, a good police officer. I feel deep sorrow for his tragedy and for his family. The officers who accompanied him, Barry Bennett, Jack Dop and Jim Girdlestone, are also very good policemen," the officer began.

Boy, I thought, lay on the tributes and adulation.

"They conducted themselves very professionally. They were all very eager to make the bust," he continued.

"Eager?" I asked.

"Yes. They wanted to make this bust. It was important to them."

"Was it important here in Thailand?"

"Small time. Very small time. We have known the source the drugs were purchased from for a couple of years. But we could not arrest her because she was never in possession of heroin. We did not charge her in this case because she did not have possession of the drugs."

"No conspiracy laws here in Thailand," I interjected.

"That is correct."

"What about Alain Olivier?"

"We know he has been to Thailand on two separate occasions and we suspect that both times he smuggled heroin back to Canada," he said.

"How do you know that?" I asked.

"We have been informed that this is the case by the RCMP."

"I gather that when Olivier arrived in Thailand, you put a tail on him," I said.

"Yes. We knew where he was every minute of the day," the captain said, pulling a file folder out of his desk. He began to read aloud. "We followed him from the airport to a guest house in an area of Bangkok where many foreigners go to inject heroin. He arrived on February 12. Then on the fourteenth at seven o'clock, he took a bus to Chiang Mai and arrived the next morning. There he tried to make contact with someone who would sell him drugs in quantity. He talked to many people and finally appeared to make a connection on the seventeenth. But the drug dealers would not deal for the ten kilograms that had been requested. They agreed on five and the deal was to take place at six o'clock on the eighteenth. But it did not happen because the undercover team did not like the way it was arranged. Another transaction for that day was made, but that, too, fell through. On the nineteenth, the supplier was supposed to make a delivery to the hotel room at ten but it did not take place. Then a deal was set up for 2.4 kilos that would take place in a parking lot at night. Unfortunately, there was a struggle and Flanagan fell off the back of the truck when the driver drove off in a panic. We stopped the truck several kilometres away and arrested the couriers."

"Couriers. They weren't the dealers," I said.

"No, they were not at the level of dealers. They were the delivery people. We did not arrest or charge any dealers."

"And where does Olivier fit in?"

"He was charged with possession of heroin," the captain said.

"But he didn't have his hands on the dope. The worst he could get is conspiracy, and you don't have conspiracy laws," I said.

"No. He was charged correctly." The captain's eyes remained fixed on the report. It was obvious he did not want to be drawn into an uncomfortable situation. "He had a packet of heroin in his wallet," he added, without any conviction in his voice.

"And what does Olivier face?"

"The death sentence by firing squad. But it no doubt will be automatically commuted to life in prison."

Chiang Mai was once the walled capital of a thirteenth-century kingdom. Today, it is a colourful tourist town whose state flower is the crimson poppy. It is also the principal centre for consummating heroin deals in southeast Asia. At the end of each opium harvest in the Golden Triangle, narcotics dealers in the upper echelons of Chinese Triads send in their buyers. In swank hotel suites, guarded by heavily armed local thugs, deals involving tons of China White are sealed with a handshake and a trip to a local bank where millions of dollars are transferred with a simple phone call. A lot of that money is channelled into the numbered accounts of a score of opium warlords holed up in mountain fortresses in the Golden Triangle. Under their control are more than forty thousand heavily armed, loyal rebels.

The captain drove me to the area where the bust took place. It was a quiet, tree-lined dirt road.

"It happened very fast," the officer recalled. "Flanagan had a one-way transmitter and a gun. When the transmitter was pressed we were supposed to go into action. But it failed to work. So we didn't know for a while what was happening. We were told Flanagan jumped on the back of the pickup and tried to take the drugs away from one of the couriers. The driver got scared when she realized what was happening and she hit the gas pedal. Flanagan was thrown from the truck and his head hit the road. It was all very tragic."

"Why is it that nobody in the RCMP wants to talk about this operation?" I asked.

"I have no idea. You would have to ask them. But there's one thing for sure — it wasn't needed," he said.

"What wasn't needed?"

"This operation. It accomplished nothing. The people who were arrested were not high-level. Many of us wonder why the Mounties came here."

I looked at the captain and realized my hunch was dead on. But I was still a long way from proving it.

March 30. I was back in Bangkok. At the Canadian Embassy, I met briefly with Staff-Sergeant Ken Kelly. He wasn't talking "because the case is before the courts."

Why in the world was I wasting my time on a sleaze like Olivier? he asked me. "Flanagan was a good police officer."

"I'm not here for Olivier. I'm here to find what your guys were doing in Chiang Mai. And since your guys aren't talking, I figured

I'd try to talk to Olivier. Maybe he might shed some light on what happened."

Kelly gave me an icy stare.

Bam Bat is a sprawling, grossly overcrowded prison on the outskirts of Bangkok. As we drove up, I thought of the chilling TV commercials back home warning Canadians about the grim and frightening consequences of being arrested for drug smuggling in a foreign land. As I got out of the police car, I was blindsided by a smothering blanket of diesel exhaust and sewage. An odd droning sound punctured the dense wall of humid air. I stood by the cruiser for a moment trying to figure out what I was hearing. Then I saw what was making the sound: millions of green flies swollen from feasting on human feces.

The visiting area at Bam Bat was in an enclosed courtyard that reeked of human excrement. A fly-infested moat clogged with feces and urine leaked from the inner prison, cutting a swath through the yard before dribbling under a thick, rusted steel-grilled hole in the wall. Overhead, fans whirred labouriously, trying to move the stalled wall of putrid air. Scores of men, women and children, crowded on wooden benches, shouted at inmates. They were separated from the prisoners by a wall of steel mesh and grates, a two-metre gap and more steel bars.

I thought I might be given special treatment, perhaps permitted to interview Olivier in a private area reserved for lawyers. I got Thai visiting privileges, no more.

Olivier was wearing jeans and a yellow T-shirt. He was thin, wiry and tanned. He looked at me with intense suspicion in his eyes.

"I guess you're here to write a story about the piece of shit who got a good cop killed," he began. "Well, you can forget it. You can fuck right off."

"I'm here to find out what happened," I shouted above the din.

"Yeah, sure. You fuckin' reporters say one thing and write another. I don't trust any of you."

"All I can say is tell me your story. I've got an open mind."

"Until you leave this place!" he sneered. "Then it's poor cop and fuck Alain Olivier." He sat ramrod straight on his bench.

"What happened?" I asked.

Olivier stared directly into my face. I stared back. It was a standoff. Olivier blinked.

"I was set up," he yelled. "The RCMP set me up. They paid my airfare to get me over here. They paid for my hotel room and they even gave me spending money. They led me into a trap."

"You came here of your own accord. No one put a gun to your head."

"That's what you think because that's what they told you. But you're wrong. They made me believe they were big-time drug dealers and killers and that they were washing drug money."

"Who?" I asked

"Derek Flanagan and Barry Bennett. Bennett came with another guy to the fishing charter company I was working for in B.C. and left in a boat. Only Bennett came back. The guy I was working for said Bennett killed the other guy and dumped his body in the ocean. I found gun shells on the boat and blood. I was scared that I'd be the next body." Olivier paused and looked at the ground. Then he sighed and added bitterly, "Now I know it was all an act."

"I find that a little difficult to believe," I said

"It happened!" Olivier yelled.

"But in the end, you went along with the proposal," I said.

Olivier glared at me. "I was shit scared of them. I thought they were killers. They conned me. They entrapped me. I was *never* a big heroin dealer. I don't even have a criminal record. You can check that out if you want. You'll see I'm not lying."

"Yet you came here to help them set up a drug buy."

"They were after me to do it. They asked me if I knew anyone who could sell them heroin and if I could take them and set up a deal. I said I probably could. Then before I knew it, they brought in this other guy Jack, who organized the whole trip. They even paid for my airline ticket on Northwest Airlines. Bennett bought the ticket and I flew out on February eleventh. He paid for my room and gave me three hundred and fifty dollars for expenses. Shit, man, if I was so big, why couldn't I even afford to pay for my own airline ticket, and why would I stay in a cheap guest house instead of a hotel? Ask them if they didn't pay my way over. *Ask them!*" Olivier shouted.

"What was in it for the RCMP?" I asked.

"What was in it for *them?* Those guys were trying to make a name for themselves. They wanted to have something to brag about back home. Man, they were going to make a bust in the Golden Triangle! And now one of them is dead. I hope they're proud of what they did. It wasn't like I was part of a big international drug ring or anything like that. And they know it! They were looking for somebody who is big, big, big. That's not me. I'm small. I wasn't worth the effort."

After several grinding days of trying to put together a deal, it was looking as though they would go home empty-handed, Olivier continued. The people he'd approached couldn't get hold of the quantity of drugs demanded by the undercover cops.

"One day, we were waiting in this restaurant and Bennett said they had a plane and pilot ready to take off with the stuff. They threatened me. They said if they went back without the drugs I was going to have problems. They said they would kill me."

The next day, at the eleventh hour, Olivier's *tuk-tuk* driver nailed down a buy for 2.4 kilos. "But the thing that really gets me is why the RCMP went so far with me to convince me they were drug dealers and talk me into coming here to buy heroin. They led me into this. It wasn't as if I was bringing this stuff in with a gang. They wanted the drugs. They asked me to set this whole thing in motion, and for what? What was the purpose?" Olivier asked angrily.

"I don't know. I'm still trying to piece this thing together. I don't know what to believe, but if what you're telling me is right, something is very wrong here."

"You don't believe me, do you?"

"Let's just say your story is a little far-fetched. But I'll check it out."

"You're just like everybody else. You're going to, dump on me because I'm a ready-made target!"

"I said I'm going to check it out."

A guard tapped Olivier on the shoulder. The visit was over.

I left the prison with more questions than answers. But I knew one thing for sure: if Olivier's story panned out, the Mounties had a lot of explaining to do. Especially if his claim that the RCMP had paid his way over was true.

But the boys in red weren't about to open up. When I got back to Canada, I was referred to a designated spokesman for the force. I asked who had targeted Olivier as a major heroin importer. No comment. I asked about the fake murder scenario. No comment. I asked if the RCMP had paid for Olivier's trip to Thailand. No comment. I asked what the Mounties were doing in Thailand. No comment.

April 10, 1989. My story was on the front page of the *Globe.* The headline read: Lured into Mounties' Trap, Says Canadian Held by Thais.

The article triggered several vile and angry phone calls. Most came from nameless, pissed-off Mounties who called me bastard, prick, son of a bitch and much worse. They felt I had defamed the memory of a fallen comrade by talking to "a piece of shit" like Olivier. Flanagan's widow, who worked as a civilian radio dispatcher for the RCMP, left a nasty message on my answering machine. She wondered how I could sleep at night defending garbage like Olivier.

The calls bothered me. It wasn't the insults. I was used to that kind of attack. What rattled me was the depth of the bitterness, and the fact that as far as the callers were concerned, I had taken sides. It didn't matter to them that, as I had pointed out in the article, the RCMP were stonewalling and ducking behind the veil of "no comment." What rankled them was that I had dared to question the RCMP's reason for the Thai bust.

Several undercover officers who had taken me out on drug buys, stakeouts and busts when I was researching *Merchants of Misery* accused me of crossing the line of decency.

Mid-April, 1989. I got a phone call from Paul McEwen, the chief investigator for the RCMP Public Complaints Commission — an independent watchdog body that had recently been set up by Parliament to investigate complaints from the public against the Mounties. McEwen, a criminal lawyer by profession, said Richard Gosse, the chairman of the commission, had read the *Globe* story and was troubled by it.

"Then maybe he should do something about it," I said unsympathetically.

I didn't trust watchdog agencies. They always ended up climbing in bed with the very people they were supposed to be investigating.

July, 1989. The RCMP Public Complaints Commission announced in its annual report that it had launched a full-scale investigation into the ill-fated drug bust in Thailand. Gosse said he wanted to find out what went wrong with the operation, whether it was properly authorized by senior officers and whether it was, as some had claimed, a cowboy escapade.

In his report, Gosse noted he was particularly "troubled over certain allegations and statements" in the *Globe* story and wanted answers to the following questions:

- Was Olivier set up over a two-year period by undercover RCMP officers posing as big-time drug dealers who wanted him to find a heroin seller in Thailand?

- Did the RCMP pay for Olivier's ticket to Thailand?
- Were officers engaged in an operation in Thailand in which there was proper authorization?
- Was the operation carried out according to RCMP policies and procedures?

The *Globe* wasn't really interested in chasing the story any further. The editors felt Olivier was not a sympathetic character. He went to Thailand to buy heroin. He went with his eyes wide open. So why push it? He got what he deserved.

But for me, Operation Deception was an unfinished story. I had Olivier's version and I had the Thai side. The Mounties had shut me out. I was certain the story was much bigger than Olivier. For me, the real issue was how the undercover team managed to convince the RCMP brass that Olivier was a major heroin dealer, then somehow lure him to Thailand to seal a deal the likes of which, on his own, Olivier could only have dreamed of.

March and April, 1990. Two Vancouver men charged separately in Operation Deception went on trial. I knew the *Globe* would never spring me to cover a low-level drug trial in British Columbia, but I had a strong hunch that vital information would come out in the trial. The trials were ignored by the local news media. But through an insider, I managed to keep abreast of what was transpiring in the courtrooms. My hunch proved right: the trials afforded a dramatic glimpse into the RCMP undercover operation.

The first trial involved a man named Michael Wheelihan, arrested and charged with selling four ounces of marijuana to an undercover cop. Boy, now there was big-time drug bust, I thought.

The second trial involved Michael Cahill, a construction supervisor charged with selling fifty-nine grams of cocaine to undercover cops. Another big-time bust.

Both of the accused claimed they were lured into the drug deals by Glen Howard Barry, a charter-boat owner in Gibsons. Barry, it turned out, was a highly paid police agent and the pivotal player in Operation Deception.

Wheelihan was found guilty of unlawfully trafficking in marijuana. But the guilty verdict was undermined by a stinging judgement from the judge, who ruled that Wheelihan had been entrapped by Glen Barry. Judge Stuart Leggatt observed that he was "unimpressed with [Barry's] veracity. In the course of his cross-examination, he made a clumsy attempt to cover up a previous criminal record. He denied being a drug user himself, although substantial evidence contradicted this, and I accept the evidence of those contradicting witnesses. I am satisfied that he has misled the court in several areas and therefore certainly had the capacity to mislead his RCMP handler."

Judge Leggatt cited a 1989 decision by Supreme Court of Canada Justice Antonio Lamer on entrapment: The police must not, and it is entrapment to do so, offer people opportunity to commit crimes, unless they had a reasonable suspicion that such people are already engaged in criminal activity."

The judge pointed out that "it was only through Barry's pressing and importuning of his friend to help him get into the drug business that this transaction took place at all. [Barry's] conduct is clearly unacceptable," the judge added. "It violates our notions of fair play and decency."

In the Cahill trial, Barry's behaviour once again was completely disparaged, this time by a long list of witnesses. At times, it seemed it was Barry who was on trial, not Cahill. And the evidence during the two-week court case painted a very disturbing picture of the RCMP's elite Vancouver undercover drug unit.

The court heard that between January, 1988 and March, 1989, the drug squad was involved in an extensive drug investigation known as Operation Deception. This operation began in Gibsons, British Columbia, and spread to other parts of the province, as well as Quebec, before becoming an international operation when it jetted off to Thailand.

The seeds of deception were sewn by Glen Barry. In early 1987, he called Corporal Barry Bennett asking if he could work undercover as a paid civilian police agent — an informer. Barry, whose real name was Jean Marie Leblanc, was a wannabe cop who knew he could never get a badge because he had a criminal record. In 1980, he was convicted on three separate occasions, for fraud, possession of stolen property and possession of drugs.

An upstanding citizen!

Barry did not turn informer out of any sense of duty to his country. He was motivated by money, and he knew how to get it. He offered Bennett what he craved — a drug kingpin. He somehow convinced the Mountie that Alain Olivier was a big-time heroin smuggler. Bennett bit, and Barry reeled him in.

Bennett was the first witness to testify at the Cahill trial. He sat with his arm on the edge of the witness box and was matter-of-fact in his responses. He said he was a member of the RCMP, had been working with the Vancouver Drug Enforcement Unit for thirteen and a half years and had been attached to the undercover unit for six and a half years. He had worked undercover and he'd handled agents.

The Mountie explained that Operation Deception started unofficially in July, 1987. He was working undercover when he got a call from Barry, who was eager to get back to work as an informer.

He had first met Barry in 1982, Bennett testified. Barry had worked as an informant in Ottawa, Toronto and Lethbridge, Alberta. He had become a paid informant in Vancouver for the RCMP in a cocaine undercover operation.

Barry said he already had a couple of targets in Gibsons the RCMP might be interested in. One of them was Alain Olivier.

The first time he met Olivier, they talked about Thailand, Bennett recounted. Later, he confirmed that Olivier had been to Thailand with, "we suspect, the purpose of bringing heroin back."

Under cross-examination by Cahill's defense counsel, Douglas Jevning, a tough Vancouver criminal lawyer, Bennett admitted that while he was Barry's handler, he let his agent operate without supervision a large part of the time. But even though he saw Barry rarely, Bennett was sure his man was not dealing in narcotics while he was working for the RCMP.

Jevning asked Bennett if it would be fair to depict Deception as a planned operation in which the police hoped to attract people to sell drugs to undercover agents.

Bennett replied; the police were looking for people who already were in the business of buying and selling drugs. The RCMP did not encourage people to do something they hadn't done before.

Jevning asked about a little play he had enacted for Olivier's benefit involving Barry's boat. Bennett denied staging a fake murder. But he confirmed that he had used Barry's boat at one time; that he had left spent bullet casings on the boat, which he surmised were later found by Olivier; that there may have been fish blood on the deck; and that Barry may have planted an impression in Olivier's mind that the missing person had been murdered.

But the Mountie hotly denied having anything to do *himself* with planting that impression. Barry seemed to think it was rather funny that Olivier believed a murder had taken place, he added.

Bennett admitted he was aware Barry had a criminal record on some "minor matter." Were fraud, possession of stolen property and possession of narcotics the minor matters? Jevning asked. Yes, Corporal Bennett replied. But the undercover cop defended his agent, saying he believed Barry would not do anything that would cast the RCMP in an embarrassing situation.

What did the RCMP pay their trusted agent for his dedication and hard work? About $500 a week, Bennett said. And a reward of $80,000 at the close of Deception. All of it tax-free!

Glen Barry, comfortable and cocky and basking in his reputation as police agent extraordinaire, was next in the box. With a large notebook in front of him, he looked like a cop hard at work.

In an officious tone, Barry told the court he had been doing undercover work for the Mounties on and off for twelve years. He did it because he was "against drugs," he said. He was trying to help his country the best way that he could as a Canadian citizen.

His mission as an agent for the RCMP, while he was living in Gibsons working as a charter-boat operator, was to seek out people who were dealing in drugs and pass that information on to his handler. He met Olivier in Gibsons and fingered him as a major importer of heroin from Thailand.

Based on Barry's assessment of the situation, Operation Deception was hatched.

When asked by the Crown prosecutor whether he had used drugs during Deception, Barry replied he had not. When asked whether he had sold narcotics during the course of the operation, he testified he had not.

However, under an intense cross-examination by Jevning, Barry reluctantly admitted he had a criminal record. The lawyer asked him about the time he had thrown a man into the water from the dock over an unpaid cocaine debt. Barry said the misunderstanding was over a lady. He couldn't remember the lady's name.

Jevning suggested that he was dealing cocaine out of a local bar. Barry denied that, and also denied he had ever given cocaine to other people to sell for him. The lawyer asked if he had threatened to blow up a boat belonging to another charter operator. Barry denied that ever happened. He also denied beating up a sixty-eight-year-old wood carver.

Barry denied ever leaning on Alain Olivier to put together a drug deal or using scare tactics against him. The two-bit junkie was so money-hungry he would do anything, the agent said.

What about the fake murder scenario? Jevning asked. Barry recalled the incident but denied telling Olivier that Bennett was an enforcer in the organization. The agent did admit that Bennett had borrowed his boat. He also said he thought it funny that *somehow* Olivier got the impression somebody had been murdered. But when Olivier asked what had happened to the missing man who had gone out on the boat with Bennett, Barry told him he didn't know and suggested that Olivier should ask Bennett.

Barry was lying, and Jevning had evidence from Cahill's preliminary hearing that proved it. Jevning challenged every statement the agent made and caught him in a string of bare-faced lies. Then he smeared icing on the cake by calling a string of witnesses from Gibsons who had firsthand experience with Barry when he was not being supervised by his RCMP handler. They delivered a devastating mass of evidence detailing Barry's involvement with drugs, as well as his personal violence and bullying tactics. For example:

- A construction worker who'd worked on the CBC television series *The Beachcombers* testified that Barry was known in Gibsons as both a drug user and a dealer who sold drugs out of his charter-boat office on the wharf. He'd personally seen cocaine and marijuana in Barry's possession numerous times and he'd seen him sell drugs both at the marina and at Alphie's Cabaret in Gibsons.

- A commercial diver testified that Barry had tried to get him to go into business with him selling drugs and once had thrown him into the bay for not paying for a gram packet of cocaine. For good measure, Barry kicked him several times when he tried to pull himself onto the dock.

- A woman who had dated Barry said that he openly used coke and marijuana. Once, at a birthday party at her house, Barry put cocaine on the table and asked the eight people at the party whether they wanted some, she said. When she broke off with him, Barry threatened to kill her. "He said he was going to get his gun and his boat and come back and blow my head off." When asked by the Crown what she thought the trial was about, the woman said it was about a guy called Glen Barry who threatened and scared people in Gibsons and pushed people into dealing drugs because he had money and power.

- A pub owner testified that Barry was a frequent customer at his bar and described him as "a liar and a cheat." He finally barred Barry from the pub because he caused too much trouble. He fought with patrons and on one occasion hit an elderly man. He also refused to pay for drinks and tried to entice the better-looking waitresses into working for him on his boat as prostitutes.

- A weather-beaten old salt who had lived in Gibsons for twenty years and ran a boat-charter service out of the local marina testified that Barry had threatened to "blow my boat out of the water" after he had accused Barry of overfishing. The man reported both Barry's overfishing and his threat to the RCMP—and got no response from the Mounties. Barry continued to threaten him with remarks such as: "I'm going to get you before the summer is out. You won't be around at the end of the summer." The man was so afraid Barry might tamper with his boat that he "put in additional alarm equipment and marked all the...diesel caps and water-tank caps on the boat."

Several of the witnesses at Cahill's trial seemed sympathetic toward Alain Olivier. The construction worker from *The Beachcombers* gave Olivier a ringing character reference, describing him as "a wonderful guy" and "an excellent piano player" with "a dynamic personality." He said he "admired [Olivier] for the qualities that he had" and that if there was anything he could do to help him, he would. A masonry contractor testified that Olivier told him he was "scared to death of these guys who were giving him problems" because these "real heavy guys had knocked off somebody in Gibsons Landing."

Cahill was convicted and sentenced to twenty months in jail. However, Barry was fingered as the moving force behind drug dealing in Gibsons. In a written ruling, the judge concluded that the "evidence establishes beyond any doubt that Barry seriously abused his position as a police agent in the small community of Gibsons and virtually terrorized the community."

Even after the Cahill and Wheelihan trials, the RCMP refused to talk about Operation Deception because, they said, Olivier's case was still before the Thai courts, and the RCMP Public Complaints Commission investigation was ongoing.

Some time after the trial, I phoned Jevning for his take on Operation Deception. He didn't mince words: "The thing about this case," he said, "is why on earth the Canadian government has any interest in going and busting dealers in Thailand. It's beyond me. Alain Olivier was a small-time labourer who was always looking for the big break. He was a penny-ante junkie and dealer of drugs who was wooed into grandiose delusions about his abilities by this police agent Glen Barry. Why the police believed this pathetic little person could make such a humongous contribution to their operation is absolutely beyond my ken."

"At the trial you really went after the RCMP agent," I said. "Why?"

"I have never met a more despicable character than Glen Barry," Jevning replied, disgust in his voice. "This guy sucked money for lies and for garbage. He was sapping the taxpayers' money, living the good life, lying to the police, telling them what they wanted to hear and then providing them with a couple of minnows. He built Olivier up. He told the police that Olivier was a major trafficker in heroin and cocaine, and they took it all at face value. Looking at Olivier would have convinced anybody that he was a pathetic hustler who couldn't have been a major anything. The guy owed money everywhere!"

"Surely the Mounties must have seen Barry for what he was," I said.

"I know sometimes in that job you have to play with the devil," Jevning replied, "but I have no idea why they trusted Barry. There's their agent out there making five hundred a week tax free — and later gets an eighty-thousand-dollar reward — and he's in this little burg where people buy and sell quarter ounces of pot. There is no major drug dealing going on over on the Sunshine Coast. There's only small-time selling between friends. This guy had a wonderful gig. He had a boat. He was lounging on it selling dope and snorting coke and kicking back and reeling in the small fish."

"So how did the undercover cops get hooked by this guy?" I asked.

"I think Barry was a good salesman. And the police want to believe they can do things. They have no real intelligence about what goes on in large areas of the province in terms of drugs. They've got their informers. They've got some idea of the Chinese gangs and the Hell's Angels and their involvement, but that's about it."

July 1990. I left the *Globe* for a career in television. I joined the CBC's *the fifth estate* as a co-host. It was a whole new medium, with new demands. I was busy. But I couldn't get Operation Deception out of my mind.

August 15, 1990. Alain Olivier was led into a sweltering courtroom in Bangkok. Before a Thai judicial tribunal, he admitted his guilt. He was sentenced to death. Then, following local custom — because he pleaded guilty — the sentence was commuted to one hundred years in prison.

The verdict was welcome news to Jim Girdlestone. "Personally, I think he should have hanged," the Mountie told the *Vancouver Sun*. "There's a prisoner exchange program between Canada and Thailand but I certainly hope he isn't repatriated. I don't feel the Canadian taxpayers should have to foot the bill for his custody. He committed his crime in Thailand and that's where he should stay."

Barry Bennett, who had been Flanagan's best friend, told reporters a day hardly went by that he didn't think about his dead comrade. He felt bitter that the operation was under investigation. What's more, he would not cooperate with the Public Complaints Commission (PCC), he said defiantly. The decision by the PCC to investigate the undercover operation, Bennett said, was based on "the flimsiest of grounds." He refused to speak to me and blamed me directly for triggering the investigation.

July, 1991. After announcing its investigation two years earlier, the PCC chairman, Dr. Richard Gosse, accused the RCMP of stone-walling.

Gosse wrote that he had been frustrated by the lack of cooperation from the Mounties involved in the Thai drug bust. "It has been a major disappointment to the chairman that this investigation has not been concluded. It remains incomplete because the members involved have refused to give interviews and the force has failed to give them the direction to do so."

March 18, 1992. The PCC finally published its report on Operation Deception. There was no press release. No press conference. No fanfare. As a result, there was scant news coverage.

I read through the 144-page document slowly. It was a carefully crafted report and, reading between the lines, it was a clear, albeit backhanded, indictment of Operation Deception. But there was something disquieting about the way it was written. I had the distinct impression the wording had been sanitized.

For example, the report's comment on Glen Barry. Citing the Wheelihan and Cahill trials, the commission concluded, "The conduct of Mr. Barry ... leaves much to be desired." And, the report noted, Barry's conduct as a police agent "has been the subject of unfavourable judicial comment." An interesting choice of words, I thought.

Oddly, the commission ignored the role of the agent's handler, Corporal Bennett. I figured that since Barry was accused by two judges of being a liar, a cheat and an all-round nasty bit of business, the PCC might have offered something on the informant's leash holder.

The commission also cited secretly taped conversations between various undercover cops and Olivier while in Chiang Mai, and concluded that nothing in the transcripts indicated that "Mr. Olivier was acting under any threat made by members of the undercover team. The discussions are on the whole entirely amicable," said the report.

Yet on February 19, 1989, the transcript cites Corporal Bennett telling Olivier there will be some "pretty fuckin' unhappy people at home if it doesn't fuckin' work out."

I think if someone spoke to me like that, I'd get the message.

The commission report also touched on the "incident" on Barry's boat, noting that it was carried out in order for the Mounties "to prove their 'bona fides.'"

The Mounties had submitted a written report to the PCC, giving their side of the story. The PCC report quoted the RCMP lawyer:

> I am instructed that Bennett did on occasion use a boat of Glen Barry's but there was certainly no murder scenario staged by Bennett or any member of the force. It did come to the attention of Bennett at one stage that Barry may have, either for his own purposes or as a joke, told Olivier that Bennett was a dangerous character and that he had committed a murder. There may have been shell casings on the boat because Bennett can recollect using a weapon for target practice and there may have been blood from fish on the boat (which is not uncommon). Apparently Barry was thought to have mentioned something to Olivier along the lines of suggesting that Bennett was a dangerous character, but when Bennett found out about this he cautioned Barry not to spread these sorts of rumours around.

Target practice. What was he shooting at? Seagulls? And why leave the shell casings on the deck? Did Bennett report to the RCMP that he had discharged his weapon outside an approved firing range? And what happened to the man who failed to return to the dock?

The commission report didn't deal with these questions.

On the issue of entrapment, the commission concluded that "it is most unlikely that Mr. Olivier was entrapped." But, the report added, "this is a matter that *only* a Canadian court of criminal jurisdiction should decide." Then why make the conclusion?

In its written submission, quoted in the commission report, the RCMP stated that there was

...a delay or hiatus in the progress of the operation when Olivier did get sick, apparently from using an infected needle in injecting himself with a drug...At one point...it appeared to the members that he might not be capable of proceeding but he then later contacted the members and advised them that he had made a trip over, had brought back some heroin and in fact wanted to sell them the heroin. It was at this point that they decided that...he was able to do what he claimed and the operation proceeded.

The RCMP also admitted that the force paid for the airline ticket to Thailand and gave Olivier some money. "But that arises out of his supplying a certain amount of heroin to the members to show that he was in fact able to deal in heroin and once again, it was he who was... eager to get on with the transaction and [he was in no way] coerced into doing what he was eager to do."

April, 1992. I did a little digging. Several Mounties told me privately that no one had ever believed Olivier could deliver on his promises. One undercover drug cop called Olivier a nickel-and-dime street dealer. Others described him as "greedy" and "a con artist who was always bumming off everybody." "The problem with him was you didn't know when he was lying to you or telling the truth," said another.

But based on Barry's adamant insistence that this guy was big-time, and backed up by Bennett's professional assessment, Operation Deception was born. For a year, Bennett kept tabs on Olivier with a view to getting the operation airborne by early 1988.

RCMP documents submitted to the PCC and referred to in its report stated that in late May, 1988, the Thai leg of Deception was officially set in motion. A briefing note prepared by the Vancouver drug unit indicated that Olivier had approached the undercover team with an "offer" to sell ten kilograms of heroin to them in Thailand.

A red-tagged request was sent to Ottawa to okay the "buy and bust" operation. It galloped up the chain of command at RCMP headquarters. Before giving it final approval, the Mounties "carefully reviewed" to what degree, if any, "adverse attention" would be placed on Operation Deception and their agent, Glen Barry. They concluded that the arrest of the "target" (Olivier) in Thailand would not have any negative impact. In other words, they didn't anticipate any bad publicity in Canada about Olivier being arrested in Thailand. They were right. Nobody, including me, would have taken any notice if the drug bust had not gone awry.

RCMP headquarters was informed by the Vancouver drug squad that the Bangkok Metropolitan Narcotics Unit "would welcome the Force's presence in efforts to dissolve an international heroin importing and trafficking organization."

The plan was approved by the commissioner of the RCMP, whose main concern, according to documents, seemed to be ensuring the security of the RCMP's $70,000.

But the operation was postponed, the RCMP reports indicated, because Olivier had contracted hepatitis from using a dirty needle and was sick.

A later RCMP file quoted in the PCC report indicated that Olivier wouldn't be able to pull off the buy because he required the "sanction of an associate" before a sale could be made. The associate was a man from Quebec whom the RCMP had initially identified as the major importer of heroin into Canada. He was the key link—the dealer with the drug connection in Thailand—and he had used Olivier as a mule on two occasions to smuggle condoms filled with China White into the country. According to RCMP intelligence, this person had travelled to Thailand on four separate occasions to import heroin into Canada, and on one of his sojourns he got Olivier to swallow a half-dozen condoms filled with a hundred grams of China White.

The commission report identified him only as "Mr. A."

With Olivier incapacitated by hepatitis, Bennett and Flanagan approached Mr. A. with a view to a deal. In conversations, the importer admitted he had used Olivier "as a runner." But he also told the Mounties that his heroin-addicted associate would never be able to orchestrate a drug buy in Thailand without his assistance, since only he had the contacts and the credibility to pull off a deal for a large quantity of heroin.

According to notes in the RCMP operational files, Mr. A. warned the Mounties that Olivier was untrustworthy, in desperate need of money and under pressure to pay outstanding debts.

In his dealings with the undercover team, Mr. A. adamantly refused to be involved with Olivier in a Thai drug deal because Olivier had a big mouth and posed a serious security risk.

By the summer of 1988, the RCMP files indicated that the undercover team was "positive" that Mr. A. was the main Bangkok heroin source and that Olivier was his "junior partner."

The undercover cops pursued Mr. A. but soon realized even this big fish had no cash to make a major buy. The Mounties considered financing the entire operation, including paying for travel and accommodation for Mr. A., but decided to drop the idea after assessing the implications "should all these circumstances be presented in court."

By the fall of 1988, RCMP reports show, the force was clearly aware of the need to avoid "negative reflection" on the RCMP. A handwritten note outlining the proposed bust cautioned that sufficient evidence must be generated during the investigation to preclude "an entrapment defense."

RCMP reports note that in early October, 1988, the undercover team met with Mr. A. and Olivier in Magog, Quebec, and that a rift between the two seemed to have healed. Mr. A. confided that he was going to send Olivier to Bangkok in November to purchase and smuggle back a hundred grams of heroin.

RCMP intelligence was unable to trace Olivier's flights to and from Thailand. They learned only after his return that he had left on December 6, 1988, and come back to Canada on December 30. Mr. A. told the undercover cops he had put up the money. Olivier was strictly a mule.

A subsequent RCMP report indicated that Olivier phoned Bennett in early January from Magog and chatted about his successful trip to Thailand. He told the undercover operator he could easily put together a four-kilogram deal, at $15,000 a kilo.

A meeting was arranged for a face-to-face talk with Olivier to work out the details. But the report stressed that if the Thailand deal was stalled one more time, the plan would call for the immediate arrest of Olivier and Mr. A. in Montreal. The duo had already sold small quantities of drugs to undercover agents and could have been charged at any point in the operation.

Then Olivier and Mr. A. had another falling-out. The two were no longer on speaking terms, and Mr. A. swore he would never deal with Olivier again. The rift was over Olivier's theft of twenty of the eighty-five grams of heroin he had smuggled into Canada on his December jaunt.

In late January, 1989, at a high-level meeting at RCMP headquarters in Ottawa, it was decided that the undercover team would continue its efforts to get Olivier to arrange a heroin buy in Thailand. In a meeting with the undercover cops in Quebec on January 19, 1989, Olivier boasted he could pull off the buy without Mr. A. He bragged he had been in a room in Bangkok containing a hundred kilograms of heroin.

According to RCMP files quoted in the commission report, negotiations were concluded when Olivier promised to make a five-kilogram buy and the undercover cops agreed to give him a ten percent cut of the shipment. The details were set out in a report penned by the Vancouver drug unit, which again identified Olivier as "a major drug importer into Canada" and pointed out that the Bangkok Metropolitan Narcotics Unit would welcome the RCMP operation "in efforts to dissolve an international heroin importing and trafficking organization." Operation Deception, the document stressed, would curb this importation route into Canada.

In late January, 1989, there was a curious communiqué from Staff-Sergeant Ken Kelly, the RCMP liaison officer in Bangkok. He reminded the undercover Mounties in Vancouver that Thailand does not have conspiracy laws and that the drugs must be in hand to secure an arrest, charge and conviction. He also informed them that the going price for one kilogram of heroin was $5,000.

When Operation Deception was planned, a Ministerial Directive on Police Assistance to Foreign Nations issued by the Department of the Solicitor General was in effect. The directive set out detailed procedures to be followed in foreign operations. The directive states that the RCMP may provide police assistance only where *the request is initiated by the foreign authority.*"

The RCMP report approving the trip said clearly that it was doing so in response to a request by the Thai police to provide "investigative assistance."

Yet General Bamroong, the head of the Bangkok drug squad, was unequivocal when he told me the RCMP made the request. There was no conceivable reason for Bamroong to lie. It was a Mountie-inspired operation.

In a wishy-washy sort of way, the PCC report didn't buy the RCMP version. It concluded that although the Mounties insisted they were acting to assist the Thai police, "this was not the assistance contemplated by the Ministerial Directive."

The PCC also wrestled with what it described as "a fundamental ethical question" — the acceptability of a police operation resulting in the arrest and conviction of a Canadian citizen in a foreign country in accordance with foreign, rather than Canadian, law. "The issue before the Commission does not turn on whether or not anyone should feel sorry for Mr. Olivier," the chairman wrote in the report. "The issue is larger than Mr. Olivier. The issue relates to the fundamental principles of Canadian criminal law and the social values which support that law."

The operational plan for Deception clearly indicated that Olivier would be arrested in Thailand, the PCC report pointed out.

> Beyond that, there is no discussion about the ethical question which that immediately raises: namely, the appropriateness of an operation which will deprive a Canadian of the benefit of a trial in accordance with Canadian law.

The commission chairman recommended that "efforts be made to transfer Mr. Olivier back to Canada" to serve his sentence in a Canadian prison. The commissioner of the RCMP should "request that these efforts be made."

In a letter to the PCC dated February 7, 1992, RCMP Commissioner Norman Inkster bluntly refused to contact "relevant Canadian authorities" to have Olivier returned to Canada.

September, 1992. I called the PCC for an interview on the report. I sensed something about it was not quite right. Something was missing. I felt it should have been more forthcoming and much tougher.

J.B. (Bert) Giroux, the executive director, called back and said the PCC didn't want to pursue the matter. He said the report "speaks for itself. It's the way the PCC saw it and when the final report is submitted, that's the end of the process."

There seemed to be nothing more I could do.

September 16, 1995. Three years had passed. I hadn't thought about Operation Deception for some time. And then I received a letter at *the fifth estate* from Alain Olivier. The return address was Bang Kwang Central Prison, Building 16.

"Here's Alain. It's been an awful long time," he began. It was a ten-page wandering epistle written in very neat longhand.

Olivier was infuriated and upset with the PCC investigation. He called the final report a "whitewash" and a "cover-up." He rehashed the operation and argued that all he wanted was to get his day before a Canadian court "to get justice which has been denied me all these years."

Olivier ended his letter: "I believe you're the only one back there with enough guts to carry on with the task of exposing the truth and the facts."

I always knew he had been set up. I knew I had accomplished nothing in the stories I had written. Worst of all, I had given up.

I wrote Olivier, telling him that I was going to reopen my stalled investigation.

With a renewed sense of purpose, I called RCMP headquarters. I felt right at home: they immediately gave me the runaround. Eventually I was referred to the Vancouver detachment. Sergeant Peter Montague was assigned to handle my inquiries.

Montague was new to the story. I filled him in on the background. "When the operation went down in Thailand, I was told no one could comment because Olivier was up on charges in Thailand. Well, he's been long convicted. So I'm back. Five years and two months later."

I told the sergeant I wanted to speak to someone who could answer questions about Deception. Questions like how and why the operation got off the ground and what the fallout had been inside the RCMP. Montague promised to pass along my request. Three weeks went by. No word. I called back.

The officer apologized for not getting back to me. "I've done some scouting around on this trying to get some answers. I haven't had a chance to get to the bottom of this. It did happen a long time ago, and a lot of the people who were in charge then aren't here anymore. Give me another week or so, and I'll see what I can get."

To make a long story short: Nothing happened with any of my requests to the RCMP. They continued to stonewall me.

October, 1995. As so often happens with long investigative stories, I got a break when I least expected it. Only three weeks after Olivier's unexpected letter landed on my desk, someone with inside knowledge of the PCC investigation called me.

The anonymous caller told me that Paul McEwen had quit the PCC. He wouldn't sign the report.

The investigation team was originally McEwen and Henry Kostuck, my caller told me. Kostuck was a former chief superintendent with the Ontario Provincial Police. He was also an investigator for the MacDonald Royal Commission into RCMP wrongdoing. He's a top-notch investigator. But Kostuck was replaced by Bert Giroux.

I ran Giroux's name through newspaper databases and learned that he was a former Mountie. And not just any Mountie. He'd been a deputy commissioner of the RCMP. I phoned him.

"You were one of the investigators on the Olivier case?" I asked.

"Yes," Giroux replied.

"The job of executive director, does it include doing investigations?"

Giroux hesitated. "I haven't looked at my job description for some time, but I don't think there is any reference to investigations."

"How did you get on the investigation team?"

"This was determined by the chairman, and for whatever reason, he asked me to participate in it," Giroux said.

"I gather Paul McEwen and Henry Kostuck were the original team?" I asked.

"Paul McEwen was part of it. I don't think Henry Kostuck was. He may have assisted in the investigation. He was not assigned to the investigation. Not that I recall. But this was 1989."

"I gather at one time you were a deputy commissioner of the RCMP?"

"Yes. This is a long time ago."

"Did you not feel that because you had been a deputy commissioner of the RCMP, you might be in a conflict of interest investigating the RCMP?"

"I think there is a conflict of interest every turn you make. It's the way you handle it."

"You must have known some of the top officers when you were looking into this case?"

"Well, yes."

"And you didn't feel there was a conflict of interest?"

"I didn't know any of the investigators. I didn't think there was a conflict that I could not handle properly."

"So you never said at any time, 'For the sake of public perception, I should beg off? Maybe I should let someone else handle it?'" I asked.

"Well, I'll let other people judge my conduct."

October, 1995. Another break. I received an unexpected package in the mail that contained the original, unsanitized report on the RCMP Public Complaints Commission investigation into Operation Deception. I read all 177 pages and compared it to the public version. I understood why Paul McEwen, the chief investigator for the commission and author of the original version, quit his job.

The original version was nothing short of a searing indictment of the RCMP's involvement in Deception from start to finish. It forcefully and unequivocally concluded that Operation Deception "was a sting conceived by the agent, Glen Barry, approved by his immediate handler, Corporal Barry Bennett, and participated in by many members of the Force all the way up to the Commissioner."

Operation Deception, it said, "was conceived by a man who was highly motivated to make big money. It would appear that it was begun on a whim. There was little, if any, reason to believe, initially, that Alain Olivier was involved in the drug business. Glen Barry, the RCMP agent and the person Corporal Bennett relied on when he approved the operation, did not have a reasonable suspicion that Alain Olivier was already engaged in drug trafficking when he called Bennett and told him that he knew somebody in Gibsons who was a major importer of heroin who had contacts in Thailand."

The unexpurgated version stressed that once the wheels of Deception had been put in motion and plans had been drawn up and approvals given, the operation took on a life of its own.

"The major players decided that Alain Olivier was expendable. He was induced to go to Thailand and once he had done what he was supposed to do, make the introductions, he was arrested by the RCMP, handed over to the Thai police and left to face a justice system which has little concern for human rights and imposes the death penalty for trafficking in narcotics, the very crime created by the members of the RCMP who approved Operation Deception."

On the fake murder scenario: "It is beyond question that the incident occurred, that it was staged for Olivier's benefit, that it was meant to be taken as a threat by Olivier and that it had the intended effect on him. Thereafter, he was convinced that Barry Bennett and the others were killers as well as drug dealers and Olivier, not without reason, was afraid of them. The message was clear: Barry Bennett and the others 'took care' of people who gave them problems. If Olivier became a problem or didn't co-operate, they would 'take care' of him."

On the issue of entrapment: "Assuming Olivier . . . was tried and convicted of a drug offense he would then have been able to argue before the trial judge that the conduct of the state was an abuse of process because of entrapment. If he had been convicted, he would likely have succeeded on an entrapment argument."

On the issue of RCMP conduct: "The conduct of the RCMP agent Glen Barry, his handler Corporal Barry Bennett and the other members of the Operation Deception undercover team regarding Alain Olivier is conduct which, barring an explanation, violated all notions of fair play and decency and demonstrated blatant disregard for the qualities and humanness which all of us share. Even if the implied threat in the fake murder scenario, directed at Alain Olivier, was the only conduct of the police and its agent being scrutinized, it would surely meet the test of unacceptability. But it didn't end there. Olivier was a drug user. He was addicted to heroin. He was broke most of the time. He owed people money. He was often sick when going through withdrawal. Yet all the while, Glen Barry and the undercover members persistently requested that he accompany them to Thailand and introduce them to a heroin source there. Indeed they went beyond being persistent and importuning in their efforts to get him to go to Thailand. They gave him money in Magog and in Chiang Mai. They told him that if he went, he would have all the drugs he could wish for. They offered to bring back into Canada for him 10 per cent of any drug transaction that he could put together for them in Thailand. This was certainly a powerful inducement to a drug addict."

On the operation itself:

It seems, on a balance of probabilities, at least, that Glen Barry, Corporal Barry Bennett and the other agents of the state involved in Operation Deception, created the crime and then directed their efforts at ensuring that Olivier would be convicted of the crime they created.

This conduct of the agents of the Canadian state is not only unacceptable, it is shocking and outrageous. Alain Olivier was the victim. After reviewing heavily edited (censored) materials relating to Operation Deception secret tape recordings, court transcripts and various interviews and statements with police and witnesses one is left with a sense of unreality.

The sense of unreality comes from realizing that the only person who has not had an opportunity to tell his story fully and without fear of facing serious consequences is the victim, Alain Olivier. Perhaps that's the way members of the undercover team wanted it to be. Olivier is in jail in Thailand for life. He can't tell his story. He couldn't have a trial. He had to plead guilty or risk being sentenced to death. He pled guilty to a crime that was brought about not by him but by members of the RCMP undercover team. He was threatened by them. They persisted in their efforts to get him to go to Thailand with them for well over a year before he agreed to go. They played upon his drug addiction. They promised him money and they promised him drugs. They bought him a plane ticket so that he could go to Thailand. They visited him in Magog, Quebec when he was sick and going through withdrawal. They gave him money. He bought heroin with it to ease his symptoms. When they returned to Vancouver and he phoned them from Magog, they told him "to get himself organized."

They directed their efforts to ensure that he would be arrested and jailed in Thailand because they didn't have any evidence against him in Canada. One can understand why the RCMP would not want Alain Olivier to be able to give evidence in a Canadian courtroom. The story of his treatment by the RCMP would, if believed, bring the administration of justice into disrepute.

The original version of the PCC report also concluded that information provided by the RCMP has been extensively selected and edited by the people whose conduct is the subject of this investigation. "One must ask what weight can be given to it. Indeed, the only information available to the Commission in this case, which can have any significant weight, is contained in the transcripts of the evidence of the witnesses in the Cahill and Wheelihan trials."

The report recommended that the PCC chairman seriously consider calling a full public inquiry "where the witnesses will appear and give evidence and be cross-examined; where the focus will be on the conduct of the RCMP members and their agent who were responsible for Operation Deception and where every effort will be made to secure the attendance of Alain Olivier even if that attendance must be secured through the intervention of the Government of Canada."

POSTSCRIPT

For the RCMP undercover team that trotted off to Thailand, there were no commendations from the top brass for a job well done. This in itself is a telling statement. In fact, there was an internal investigation carried out by the RCMP but it is being kept secret.

The most significant player in Deception, Corporal Barry Bennett, flatly refused to talk to me. He blamed my one story in the *Globe* back in 1989 for making his life miserable.

But Bennett did tell a *Globe* reporter that he had refused to cooperate with PCC investigators. He described their efforts as a "bare-faced attempt to justify a free road trip to Thailand."

As far as Bennett was concerned, the PCC investigation was set up on the "flimsiest of grounds. To hell with them. I think they owe me an apology personally," the Mountie said.

In the spring of 1996, I had a brief and somewhat testy conversation with Jim Girdlestone. At that time, he told me he has the "only file that hasn't been shredded" on Operation Deception and added caustically, "I'll be damned if I'm going to give you the sweat off my ass."

As for the infamous RCMP civilian agent, Glen Barry, well, he's out there somewhere. I was told he might just talk to me, for a price. Money is still his prime motivator.

Paul McEwen, the chief investigator for the PCC, resigned when he realized that his report was being whitewashed.

"I did not agree with the final report," he told me in a brief interview. "That whole case and the outcome was the reason I left the PCC. By the time I left, the PCC had become a paper tiger."

While not wanting to get into detail, McEwen added, "the RCMP were completely and totally uncooperative, despite the fact that the official version of the PCC report says they were cooperative and provided information. They didn't. We had a hell of a time dealing with them."

Also during my investigation, I learned the real identity of Mr. A. He was the "prominent target" in Operation Deception and had used Olivier as a "mule" on at least two occasions to smuggle small quantities of the heroin from Thailand into Canada. He is Michel Beaulieu, a resident of Ste. Julienne, Quebec. After Flanigan was killed, Beaulieu was arrested and charged in Montreal with conspiracy to traffic and trafficking in heroin. On October 23, 1989, he was found guilty of importation of heroin and sentenced to thirteen years, eight months in prison. He also received two concurrent six-year sentences for trafficking in heroin. But on May 13, 1994, after serving less than five years, Beaulieu was granted parole.

Meanwhile, Alain Olivier languishes in a Thai prison wondering if he'll ever get out alive — or ever get a chance to tell his story in a Canadian court or before a full-scale inquiry.

As I began research for this book, Olivier made an ominous request in a letter to me. "I'd like to ask you not to do anything that will prompt the people I'm up against into trying silly things against me through the prison system. And please, Victor, don't think I'm acting out of paranoia or something like that, because I'm not. Considering all I've seen done in here behind these walls over all those years, I'm in fact being quite conservative when I say that the people I'm up against can have access to me. Anyway, if ever something happens to me, whatever this might be, I want you to know that it sure won't be of my own making."

In total, Operation Deception cost the Canadian taxpayers in excess of a million dollars. The question is: For what? A good cop was killed. A few small-time drug dealers got a few months in prison. Only one dealer, Beaulieu, got hard time in Canada. And Olivier, a nickel-and-dime junkie, rots in a Thai jail. The only person who made a good buck out of all this was Glen Barry. And when you look closely at the facts, you can't escape the conclusion that all this wasn't worth the effort.

Operation Deception was the first major investigation by the Public Complaints Commission — its first real test as an independent watchdog of the RCMP. It could have sent out a strong message that it meant business. Instead, its roar was ineffectual.

With what the PCC found out during its investigation, the chairman could have called for a full public inquiry into the RCMP's handling of Operation Deception. The chairman decided it wasn't necessary, even though the unsanitized report strongly recommended one.

But the very fact that the original report on Deception was suppressed and replaced by a heavily censored, whitewashed version, now puts the role of the PCC in question. More than ever, this first report cries out for a public inquiry into the Public Complaints Commissions's own investigation.